Neglected Policies

NEGLECTED POLICIES

Constitutional Law and Legal Commentary

as Civic Education

Ira L. Strauber

Duke University Press Durham and London 2002

Typeset in Scala by Keystone Typesetting, Inc.
Library of Congress Cataloging-in-Publication data appear
on the last printed page of this book.

In blessed memory of
Abe Strauber

CONTENTS

ACKNOWLEDGMENTS

All things considered, it has taken a rather long time for this book to come to print. There are three main causes for that, the second and third of which I would not change even if I had the power to do so.

First, I wrote this book almost as much to convince myself of the merits of its arguments as to persuade others to take those arguments seriously. And, in keeping with the spirit of the main theme of this book, I was as persistently skeptical of my own arguments as I could possibly be. Consequently, and for better or worse, this skepticism compelled me to confront my limitations in answering the questions I posed to myself about constitutional commentary as civic education. Perhaps those with fewer limitations, or those better at surmounting them, might have completed this book much sooner.

Second, this book took its own time because I was fortunate to benefit from the hard work of a number of people who were careful, sometimes (if not often) severe, and always especially constructive skeptics of what I was trying to do. Leif H. Carter read a number of earlier, rather different drafts of the manuscript, and his astute and sympathetic analysis of it compelled me to reconsider just how much more work I needed to do to make it a publishable work. Susan Strauber brought to the final version of this manuscript the same scrupulous attention to linguistic detail that she brings to her own work in art history. However frustrating that scrutiny was to endure, it compelled me to make the internal logic of the arguments as harmonious as possible.

The anonymous reviewers for Duke University Press were incisive readers who motivated me to meet their criticisms as best as I could. Writers cannot ask more of their reviewers. One anonymous reader in particular

("Reader 5") provided specific advice about changes in the structure and content of the near finished manuscript to make it the best possible publishable work. Even though I know I did not satisfy this reader completely, I am grateful for the opportunity to make the effort.

But it is Mathilda Liberman, my friend and editor, who got inside the soul of this book. Sometimes she understood what I was trying to say better than I did. Sometimes she even persuaded me to say something else and better. It was Mathilda Liberman who persuaded me to rewrite every sentence, over and over again, to engage a challenging process of revisions that would, if one were successful, meet the most exacting standards of intelligent writing. Unfortunately, I did not meet those standards but, to paraphrase a comment of Reader 5, the process itself made this book as good as it could be.

Along these lines, I would also like to thank a number of people who supported me through the process of turning a manuscript into a book. Since the day that Stanley Fish agreed to consider the manuscript for publication, Miriam Angress has been a source of support, confidence building, and advocacy for this book. Six student research assistants—Erinn Gilson, Margaret Hainline, Michele Host, Kendra Kopel, Camarin Madigan, and Ellen Salecheerfully did all the small, but not minor things that go into making a book. (I would like to thank the Grinnell College Grant Board for funding the work of these students.) Then, at the very end, when I was at my lowest ebb emotionally, Bev Garcia took administrative control of the manuscript with craft, care, and exceptional sympathy to make a final product ready for the press. In fact, if it were not for Bev Garcia, I might still be working on the copyedited version of the manuscript. I would also like to thank Maura High and Pam Morrison for their diligent copy editing. Naturally, whatever infelicities, errors, and omissions remain in this work are my responsibility.

Last, this book would have been finished much sooner, aside from my own limitations and revisions, if it were not for Susan Elizabeth Strauber and Alison Rebecca Whitesell Strauber. They are, for whatever complex and ineffable reasons, the paramount objects of my emotional and intellectual energies. So the third reason that this book has taken so long to come into print is the blessings of my life.

Sadly, as this book finally made its turn into proofs, a peak of sorrow imposed itself on me with the unexpected death of my younger brother, Richard Bruce Strauber. This book thus comes into being situated between the blessings and sorrows of my life.

Neglected Policies

INTRODUCTION

The death of democracy is not likely to be an assassination from ambush. It will be a slow extinction from apathy, indifference, and undernourishment.—Robert Maynard Hutchins (1954)

Inconsistencies of opinion arising from changing circumstances are often justifiable. —Daniel Webster (1846)

The premise of this book is that teachers and critics (primarily journalists and academics outside law school) are unreflectively and mistakenly devoted to a complex group of intellectual and political ideas about constitutional and legal commentary that needs to be challenged. I refer specifically to their self-image as civic educators in an interpretive community and their ideas about the law's formalisms (i.e., the law's argumentative rules and structures, principles, concepts, and doctrines), the Constitution as a text, the reasoning and arguments of litigators and adjudicators, philosophical theories, and the role of courts in liberal-democratic politics. Unreflective devotion to their current self-image and their ideas, which I refer to as "the ideology of involvement" and "intellectual jurisprudence" respectively, is a mistake because it exacts too high a cost in constitutional and legal commentary.

Specifically, the ideology of involvement leads teachers and critics to presume that they are more efficacious as civic educators than they actually are or can be. It therefore assists in repressing their awareness of how difficult it is to make a more democratic contribution to commentary about law and policies that breaks with intellectual jurisprudence. Intellectual jurisprudence leads teachers and critics, and therefore their audiences as well, to neglect too much that is important about law, politics, and especially policies in a liberal-democratic polity. Most especially I am concerned with pursuing the implications of giving more attention to the context-specific, circumstantial, and consequentialist social fact considerations that are at the core of colliding political perspectives and controversies in a pluralist polity.

Yet, despite the cost, I believe that it is not practical—nor is it intellectually or politically prudent—to replace altogether either the ideology of involvement or intellectual jurisprudence. Rather, for a more politically sufficient commentary, I recommend a set of tenets that fosters an alternative habit of mind to the one fostered by the ideology of involvement. This habit of mind is oriented toward recovering what I am terming "neglected policies" and shaping a more prudent and, it is to be hoped, efficacious approach to civic education. I call this habit of mind "agnostic skepticism." The tenets of agnostic skepticism have their provenance in sociological jurisprudence, legal realism, and, ultimately, critical legal studies. What differentiates agnosticism as a habit of mind from its sources is that it is more resolutely skeptical about liberal-democratic law and commentary than are sociological jurisprudence and legal realism, and less resolutely skeptical—to say nothing of being less cynical and ideological—than critical legal studies.

The sine qua non of agnostic skepticism is its mandate to resist an unreflective devotion to lawyerly methods and legal, political, and moral abstractions as they are ordinarily deployed in doctrinal analysis, jurisprudence, and legal philosophy. In a most unlawyerly way, an agnostic mandate calls for commentary that mixes and merges these methods and abstractions with commonplace contingent and/or circumstantial social-fact, social-scientific, and consequentialist considerations. This approach requires a willingness to be situated "on the outside looking in" on the law, its advocates, its judges, and its commentators. It requires a habit of mind that is, ultimately, at home with a relativism that is based on the premise that constitutional and legal commentary should always be understood in terms of various shades of gray.

As I have characterized it in this book, agnostic skepticism gives narrative shape to commentary in three major ways. First, agnostic skepticism provides descriptions and analyses of conditions and relationships that challenge unmerited solace in the political credibility of legal, political, and moral abstractions. Second, these descriptions and analyses provide strong reasons to resist the allure of predetermined conclusions, on both the left and the right, about the strengths and weaknesses of liberal-democratic law and facets of political power, as well as about when law and policies ought to be conserved or criticized. Third, these descriptions and analyses provide strong reasons to oppose the compulsion to read constitutional and legal opinions in terms of whether they are rightly decided or not, and to oppose fixed or totalistic conceptions of the role of courts in major controversies.

The narratives of agnostic skeptical commentary are meant to incline teachers and critics and those who learn from them to take a more experimental and venturesome approach than usual to the materials of legal and political commentary. I cannot predict what is yet to take place, but I think that these experiments, if they come to pass, could well have substantive results quite different from my own. So the case studies I present—which I eventually refer to as commentary to "a law and policies of a middle course" (as described below)—should be read in the light of that possibility. As for my experiments, they build out from Justice Benjamin Cardozo's "ordered liberty" conception of rights, powers, and interests related to maintaining the common good, political stability, and popular rule (what I will refer to as *sovereignty* interests). From this base point I relativize the implications of ordered liberty beyond what Cardozo and case law have done. To do so I draw on often heavily qualified, hypothetical ("if-then") social fact claims and accounts of the "underdeterminacy" of legal formalisms and political and moral abstractions.

By "underdeterminacy" I mean the tendency of legal formalisms and abstractions to justify a multiplicity of competing and equally credible results. These results are very often logically inconsistent with one another (i.e., they may have different policy implications from case to case, instance to instance). They also often have an incongruous fit with conditions and relationships in the polity; that is, they may be at odds with more practical social, economic, political, and historical considerations. But, or so I argue, legal formalisms and political and moral abstractions are not necessarily fatally flawed by virtue of their inconsistency or incongruity with social fact considerations. As the second epigraph, from Daniel Webster, is meant to point up, contingent and circumstantial fact considerations often make inconsistency (and incongruity) justifiable.

Three major civic education lessons arise out of agnostic commentary's experiments with hypotheticals and underdeterminacy. The first lesson is that hypotheticals and underdeterminacy might well take agnostics to conclusions at odds with their political or moral preferences. The second is that commentary to a middle course leads one to shuttle back and forth between arguments that justify both conservation and criticism of the law's formalisms and facets of political power. In the wake of these first two lessons, the third lesson is that there is less certainty and more doubt to be had about the widespread conviction that courts are always a politically prudent venue for articulating the uppermost political and moral aspirations of the polity.

These lessons bear directly on the place of teachers and critics as civic educators in an interpretive community. In contrast to commentary in the grip of intellectual jurisprudence and the ideology of involvement, I do not follow up these lessons with counsel to change or to improve what litigators, adjudicators, public policy-makers, or courts do. I hold back because common social facts about knowledge, power, law, and policies lead me to recommend that skeptical commentators abjure the pleasure of giving any such counsel because it is more than likely going to be inefficacious. Instead, I recommend that teachers and critics, and those who learn from them, concentrate their energies on a potentially more efficacious but no less hard to accomplish goal: civic education to what I will refer to as a more "Jeffersonian civic culture." A Jeffersonian civic culture is one in which an elite of properly educated citizens is increasingly predisposed to learn about law, politics, and policies so that they can tolerate legal and political ambiguities and contradictions inherent in a pluralistic polity. This predisposition would make them suspicious and tentative about *all* claims having to do with the Constitution, law, and policies, be they the claims of lawyers, scholars, journalists, or themselves. When persons are predisposed in this way they exhibit a kind of pragmatic judiciousness that has traditionally been identified with the American mind and with citizens' relations. By "pragmatic judiciousness" I mean the kind of enlightened self-interest that Thomas Jefferson (and Benjamin Franklin) believed was unique to Americans. They had in mind their fellow citizens' inclination to channel their political conflicts away from abstractions, and other impediments to their relationships, into ways of thinking that offered them greater promise for concessions about what could constitute their general welfare (Ketcham 1965: 76).

Agnostic commentary is an attempt to pragmatic judiciousness by fulfilling the following four commitments:

1. Agnosticism does not try to evade the inevitable complexity, ambiguity, inconsistency, and incongruity of things. Therefore, arguments—one's own or those of others—which appear to be certain or beyond rejoinder ought to be appreciated for their rhetorical robustness and then treated suspiciously as insufficient.
2. If nothing is certain or beyond rejoinder, then it is judicious to differentiate not only between weaker and stronger reasoning and justification but

also to discover what is weak in the stronger and vice versa. The primary benefit of this kind of judiciousness is that it acts as a check against premature judgments and an unjustifiable confidence that judgments are rightly decided. The costs of this kind of judiciousness are that one may lose one's certainty of argumentative touch, or wander off into pitfalls and fallacies of thought.[1]

3. The costs may seem high compared to the benefits, but they are worth paying if they help to purchase civility and tolerance, which themselves entail a self-critical and empathetic (if not compassionate) regard for the unpredictability of the course of political events.
4. The goods of civility and tolerance are worth purchasing if they are as useful, if not more so, for private relations as they are for legal and political relations.

The first three of these claims will be developed in various ways throughout this book. But the fourth claim may not even be recognizable as tacit in my case studies. So now it is time to be somewhat more explicit about it. This fourth claim is crucial. It blurs distinctions between lessons about public and private relations. It is meant to teach that commentary is worth doing, politics and law aside, because it helps develop attitudes and skills that might prove useful in the conduct of the personal and intimate dimensions of life.

Here is my thinking behind the fourth claim. Most persons are much more likely to be attentive to lessons about private relations than public ones. The obvious and important reason for this is the extent to which for most persons daily private relations are more conspicuous and important than public ones. What I recommend then is that teachers and critics exploit this fact by inventing stories about mundane incidents that are "closer to home" in order to enhance skeptical commentary about less familiar public ones. However, it will take enough words to articulate the first three claims that the fourth one, as crucial as it is, will have to remain an unelaborated allusion until the final chapter.

It is also the case that my remarks about civic education and citizens are as hypothetical as the case study scenarios that precede them. But I trust that will make them no less provocative as I argue my way to the conclusion that it is possible for skeptics to be hopeful about nurturing Jeffersonian civic sensibilities. Still, it is necessary to say up front that my hopefulness in this regard is tempered by two caveats about obstacles to an effective civic education.

Both of these caveats are foreshadowed in the sentence above wherein the term "citizens" is modified by the phrase "properly educated." The first concerns the ever present possibility that civic education will go awry for one reason or another: its lessons could be misinterpreted or interpreted in an unanticipated way or have unwelcome unintended results. Wherever the fault may lie, candor and prudence dictate that teachers and critics acknowledge the problem of improperly educated citizens and unintended results when they are apparent. It is a cliché, but no less true for being so, that diagnosing a problem is one thing and deciding what to do about it is another. What I do here is to anticipate a set of charges that skepticism and commentary to a middle course will trigger unintended results, and then I offer as candid and prudent a rejoinder to those charges as I can muster.

The second caveat concerns the recognition that ours is a nation at educational and civic risk. It is a commonplace that primary and secondary school education and basic civic sensibilities and capacities have been degraded. To be sure, the presumed (initial) audience for skeptical commentary—an educational elite of college- and university-trained persons—is not generally thought of as intellectually undernourished or as apathetic about policies as less-educated citizens are. But neither is it exempt from the effects of degraded education, as these effects have spilled over into higher education and hindered the cultivation of more sophisticated civic sensibilities and capacities. This means that the educated elite is less accomplished than it could be in both intellectual and political spheres.

None of this (as I say) is news. Laments about the degradation of education in this country go back to colonial times. The familiarity of these laments does not of course make it any less imperative to address the effects of an education so compromised, though we might suppose there is no imperative, given the apparent indifference to these effects shown in commentary as we know it. Still, as the epigraph from Hutchins points up, the demise of democracy is hastened by neglect, so promoting Jeffersonian civic sensibilities becomes one way to make some contribution to slowing down the demise of civic education to democracy.

With that end in mind, one way I try to manage these effects of compromised education is to invest my case studies with "thick," sometimes intricate details. The strategy behind this detail is to create a common ground between less tutored readers and myself. These detailed studies will require some patience on the part of readers. Readers who have less patience than other readers may find the level of detail in these studies an undesirable distraction. As the book progresses and more common ground is laid down, my case studies become less thick and the prose style varies to depict the several ways that politically sufficient commentary can manifest itself, from the rather abstract to the more concrete expressions of it. I hope that readers will nevertheless appreciate the importance of creating common ground and the strategy for securing it. My trust is that by this strategy readers who do have the patience to read carefully will find that they are engaged in a process of challenging the ways in which they think about law and policies. Another way I try to manage the effects of degraded education is by anticipating cognitive dissonance attendant on civic education to skepticism. Cognitive dissonance is that disconcerting tension that we all experience, at one time or another, when we are aware that we have knowledge, attitudes, values, and the like that do not fit together. For some (unspecifiable) number of persons, even degraded education is sufficient to lay down attitudes, beliefs, and norms that will trigger resistance to the counterconventional lessons of skepticism. This reaction creates complications and causes skeptics considerable difficulties. But it presents them with opportunities as well: even as a skeptical agenda pulls teachers and critics into accounts of law and policies that threaten to intensify the effects of cognitive dissonance, it also pushes them to make concessions to cognitive dissonance in order to be persuasive about their accounts.

In this bind (for so it may be seen), the move I make is to incorporate a few major (always explained) and a greater number of minor (often left unexplained) argumentative concessions. I hope by these means to mitigate the effects of cognitive dissonance without doing any great injustice to skepticism. My readers will determine whether these concessions work. But at this juncture I can say that they at least have the virtue of signaling my commitment not to be naive about the tasks that await those who teach and criticize, whether it be to encourage commentary as usual or to encourage more Jeffersonian sensibilities.

Another problem arises from the interface between two predicaments, neither of which is unique to skeptical civic education: (1) what makes for a good fit in the academy too often differs considerably from what matters outside it, and (2) even for those who are otherwise best prepared to assimilate it, higher civic education is rendered more problematic, both intellectually and psychologically, by the diminished quality of prerequisite primary and secondary civic education.[2] My gambit for attacking these two predicaments is not played out in the body of this book but is characterized at its very end (for reasons best left for last). The thrust of this gambit, which I proffer with some trepidation, is that lessons about public law and policies are more likely to stick if they are merged with lessons about private relations.

From the perspective of the forest rather than of the trees, the significance of these caveats about civic education and my efforts to manage the effects of degraded education is that they encapsulate a major sentiment of this book: teachers, critics, and those who learn from them will be better situated to recover neglected policies, and to promote a more Jeffersonian civic education and *sensibilities,* if we adopt a habit of mind that is more keenly self-aware and tolerant of the ambiguities, underdeterminacies, and contradictions that arise in the law, policies, and civic education in a pluralistic polity. Toward that end I recognize that I must say some difficult things about commentary that others have not said, and to say other things that build on what others have said but to say them in unexpected, provocative, even threatening ways.

It has been my experience with teaching to agnostic skepticism's middle course that even individuals who have very strong convictions and feelings about law and politics come to see at least some personal and political merit in its habit of mind. If nothing else, agnosticism can teach one to be more self-critical about the strengths and weaknesses of one's own commentary. To the extent that that may prove true for my current readers as well makes me cautiously optimistic about the prospects for doing something constructive about commentary in the grip of ideological jurisprudence and the ideology of involvement.

Plan

Part I of this book consists of three chapters. The first chapter introduces my arguments about the ideology of involvement and intellectual jurisprudence. It also identifies my concerns for a more politically sufficient commentary. The second chapter explains why the law's formalisms are an enemy of politically sufficient commentary, and it introduces the tenets for more politically sufficient commentary and agnostic skepticism as an alternative habit of mind. The second chapter also presents the first case study, a criticism of conventional commentary on the First Amendment flag-burning case, *Texas v. Johnson*. The main purpose of this case study is to illustrate how the tenets of political sufficiency direct one to keep a critical eye on the way commentary that tries to answer the rightly decided question leads to neglected policies. The third chapter revisits *Texas v. Johnson,* this time to illustrate how the tenets play out in an analysis of whether solace in the central formalism of an opinion, in this instance, the marketplace formalism, is merited or not.

Part II consists of six chapters. They share a central aim, which is to define agnostic skepticism's exact place in jurisprudence and to explain how the tenets of political sufficiency lead to a deeper appreciation of the way in which the law's formalisms and facets of liberal-democratic political power obscure important political conditions and relationships. The fourth chapter introduces the issue of the complicated differences and similarities between skepticism and a principal source of its inspiration, critical legal studies (CLS). Here a case study of the marketplace formalism and facets of regulatory power in another First Amendment case, *FCC v. League of Women Voters,* is compared with a treatment of the marketplace formalism, governmental power, and sovereignty interests derived from a version of CLS I call "radical revisionism" (constructed from the jurisprudence of Roberto Unger). The purpose of this comparison is to show why, despite the extent to which solace in legal formalisms and facets of regulatory power may be unmerited, agnosticism does not buy into a revisionist agenda that liberal-democratic law and politics is necessarily fatally flawed or harken to its call for a radical transformation of it. Then, in the fifth chapter, via a brief analysis of the controversy over sexually explicit materials on the Internet, I commit myself to the idea of "underdeterminacy" as central to politically sufficient commentary that shuttles back and forth between arguments for the conservation and criticism of the law.

The sixth chapter refines and enlarges this commitment and completes the comparison with CLS, with an in-depth analysis of the formalism of federalism and sovereignty interests in *McCulloch v. Maryland.* The results of this analysis are put in the context of a case study of federalism derived from a version of CLS I call "radical rejectionism" (constructed from the jurisprudence of Mark Tushnet). Radical rejectionism is driven by the belief that the rule of law is a myth, that liberal-democratic law and politics are simply incapable of doing anything but obscuring the severity of societal dysfunctions, and that federalism is a sham as a rule-of-law limit on federal power. Taking these convictions at face value, I argue that although the law may be inconsistent and incongruent with political conditions and relationships, that is insufficient grounds for concluding that the rule of law is a myth and that liberal-democratic politics is incorrigibly dishonest.

The seventh and eighth chapters cover the question of whether federalism is a sham. I argue that there is some merit to this rejectionist critique, but that a selection of more recent federalism cases, and public law considerations, indicate that some considerable degree of solace in the ideas and practices of federalism is still merited (including a prudential form of originalism in constitutional interpretation related to environmental politics and policies).

The ninth chapter finalizes the definition of agnostic skepticism's place in jurisprudence by explaining its problematic relationship to legal philosophy. On the one hand, legal philosophy is an enemy of skepticism because it is so deeply implicated in teaching lessons about the rightly decided question and about the centrality of moral abstractions to legal and political commentary. On the other hand, legal philosophy does make important contributions to our understanding of the relationship between moral and legal concepts. Thus, there must be a space for legal philosophy and moral abstractions, but one wherein they are used skeptically: their lessons cannot be independent of, logically superior to, or more weighty than those learned from circumstantial and context-specific fact considerations. To illustrate what this skeptical use of philosophy and moral abstractions amounts to, I compare Ronald Dworkin's treatment of precedent in *Planned Parenthood v. Casey* (the decision that sustained and revised *Roe v. Wade*) with an agnostic treatment of it. By virtue of this comparison I show how agnosticism and moral convictions can coexist.

Part III consists of three chapters. The aim of two of them is to illustrate the different ways that commentary addressing ordered liberty recovers neglected policies and counsels a middle course by shuttling back and forth between the conservation and criticism of the law for two different kinds of constitutional and public law controversies. Each chapter concludes with a different take on the role of courts in liberal-democratic politics, especially as they might be seen to provide guidance to higher political and moral values for the polity.

The tenth chapter focuses on pornography. It raises what I hope readers will find to be acute questions about solace in the role of abstract, mutually exclusive freedom-of-expression and equality principles and the role of courts (the Supreme Court in particular); all are commonly understood to be pivotal for understanding what is at stake in the controversy over regulating pornography for its role in subordinating women and producing harms to the cultural environment (*American Booksellers Association v. Hudnut*).

The penultimate, eleventh chapter closes out the case studies with a brief analysis of the controversy over what constitutes a "family" and "family relations" as it manifests itself in the public law of adoption custody battles.

This is not common fare for mainstream legal and political commentary. Nevertheless, and not coincidentally, this controversy suits my purposes especially well because it provides a very clear, even poignant, example of the practical need for and successful accomplishment of adjudication to a middle course. The eleventh chapter also provides a bridge, via my discussion of the problems that judges confront in adjudicating "family" and "family relations," to my discussion of some problems that skeptical teachers and critics should expect to experience in reaction to their commentary and their efforts on behalf of civic education. The chapter concludes with a discussion of a cross fire of charges against agnostic skepticism that serve to indicate its strengths and weaknesses. In the process of constructing rejoinders to these charges I confront the problems of civic education gone awry and the cognitive dissonance attendant on agnostic skepticism as civic education. Finally, in the twelfth chapter I address my recommendation for coping with cognitive dissonance and the degraded state of education by merging private and public lessons to increase the efficaciousness of civic education that is suspicious and tentative even of itself.

PART ·I·

· 1 ·
The Purposes of an Interpretive Community

> [To] argue in a lawyerly fashion today is not to argue the way a lawyer would have done fifty years ago, although both the lawyer of today and the lawyer of fifty years ago would, if competent, fit comfortably within . . . an interpretive community.
>
> The community consists of advocates, who undertake through the interpretation of legal materials (texts) to advance their client's cause; the judges, who pick and choose among arguments and engage in disinterested interpretation (disinterested at least in the sense that it is not oriented toward one's client); and the teachers and critics, who evaluate outcomes and seek to shape tomorrow's results.—Harry H. Wellington (1991)

With these words, Harry Wellington, former dean of both the Yale Law School and the New York Law School, matter-of-factly posits the existence of a collective discursive enterprise constituted by three separate, yet interdependent conventional activities—advocacy, judgment, and scholarly analysis—all of which are shaped and animated by the intellectual authority of legal reasoning and arguments about legal texts.

This book challenges readers to question, very deeply, the intellectual and political implications of the enterprise Wellington characterizes for us. In particular, I argue that a gulf exists between the reasons and arguments made in the course of the first two activities (advocacy and judgment) and practical and quite common social, economic, and political conditions and relationships. This gulf is perpetuated largely because these conditions and relationships are neglected by teachers and critics and their audiences, who, intentionally or unintentionally, too closely mimic the reasoning and argument mode of litigators and adjudicators. Admittedly, there are some adjudicators, litigators, and teachers and critics (inside and outside law school) who are alive to the existence of this gulf. But by and large their descriptions and evaluations of it are framed in such defiantly ideological or partisan terms that the gulf is merely reproduced in ideological or partisan forms. (Much more of this later.) Some others, of course, do see more deeply into the gulf than their more ideological or partisan colleagues. Consider for instance those in the interpretive community who commented on the misleading way oral arguments before the U.S. Supreme Court framed issues in the assisted suicide cases of *Vacco v. Quill* and *Washington v. Glucksberg* (1997).[1] But such recognition of the gulf between legal commentary and neglected policies is not only relatively rare but also is not perceived as fundamental to commentary as civic education.[2] Making it fundamental is what I want to do in this book.

This first chapter defines and elaborates on the concepts of the ideology of involvement, intellectual jurisprudence, political sufficiency, and agnostic skepticism. These terms establish the context for the analytic points I make throughout the rest of this book about the gulf between legal reasoning and politics, why it is costly to constitutional and legal commentary, and how commentators might go about reducing those costs and recovering neglected policies. Let me begin then with a full description of all four terms.

The term "ideology of involvement" refers to the current self-image of teachers and critics in relation to litigators and adjudicators. "Intellectual jurisprudence" refers to the scholarly habit of mind that accompanies this self-image, specifically in regard to legal reasons and arguments and the intellectual authority of the Supreme Court as the pinnacle of the judicial system. The term "political sufficiency" refers to alternative reasons and arguments for commentary that put a brake on intellectual jurisprudence. And "agnostic skepticism" refers to an alternative self-image that reorients teachers and critics both to the ideology of involvement and the significance of more common relationships and conditions. The specific roles these four terms play in promoting a politically more constructive constitutional, legal, and political discourse will become apparent in a closer examination of Wellington's words about the purposes of constitutional commentary.

The Ideology of Involvement and Commentary as Civic Education

You will note that Wellington's matter-of-factness about the interpretive community is so deep-rooted that he does not think it necessary to provide either a historical or a theoretical defense for its existence. Apparently, both its history and its theory are sufficiently established by reference to the activities of its three constituencies and by the allusion—in those words about lawyers being members of the same craft even though legal methods may change—to the community's stability over time. There are, as it happens, some very good reasons to treat the interpretive community in this matter-of-fact way. First, as John Brigham has so aptly (if not approvingly) put it, legal "professionalism has come to characterize the interpretive community" (Brigham 1987: 73–74), so much so in fact that few would challenge the conviction that the intellectual skills of lawyers make the interpretive community what it ought to be.

Second, Wellington's implication that each of the three constituencies is a full partner in the community resonates with participatory democratic values deeply embedded in the civic culture. In fact, I suspect that commentators outside law school, as well as journalists, undergraduates, and perhaps even politically active citizens, readily and comfortably read themselves into Wellington's little portrait of a community wherein they play the role of the judiciary's watchdogs and agents of social change.[3]

Third, and most important for the concerns of this book, Wellington's words bespeak an ideological self-image (Bourdieu 1977)[4] that shapes and motivates the academic enterprise of commentary. This self-image, which I refer to as "the ideology of involvement," is structured by a set of beliefs and values implicit in the idea that constitutional interpretation is a form of civic education.

By "civic education" I mean the lessons that litigation, adjudication, and commentary are *supposed* to teach about the conservation or, alternatively, the transformation of law, policies, and culture in a liberal-democratic polity.[5] The idea, both within and—equally important—outside law school, is that all those who engage in constitutional and legal commentary thereby help to articulate competing visions of lawmaking that are essential to building a vibrantly free political community. They believe also that a partnership in commentary is indispensable for maintaining a connection between the creed of democracy and the rule of law. Most especially, they have the deeply held belief, as Wellington's portrait implies, that the text of the Constitution alone, by virtue of its being an object of legal adjudication and commentary, is sufficient to constitute participation in the interpretive community for all those who engage it.

There is no denying one commendable consequence of this ideology: it elevates the academic and journalistic enterprises of commentary so that all those who purposefully engage in them may see themselves as contributors to the intellectual, moral, and even spiritual understanding of law and policies. It could be argued that this assessment of commentary and those who practice it owes much, historically and theoretically, to the Protestant ethic, whereby education—especially civic education—is encouraged as essential to preserving democracy and intellectual vitality in a free polity (Madsen 1994). But finally it is more to the point to locate the roots of the idea of commentary as civic education in a relatively recent conception of scholarship and the political role of the Supreme Court. Pursuing this inquiry will permit us to gauge just how far commentary's view of itself is to be commended.

The Ideology of Involvement and the Supreme Court

It was Eugene Rostow, arguing that the "democratic character of judicial review" would advance the cause of individual rights, who most prominently fostered the academic belief that civic education was one of the Supreme Court's main functions. Rostow portrayed the Court as *the* institution in American politics responsible for developing comprehensive moral principles in the face of the politics of expediency practiced by the legislative and executive branches of government. Thus the Court was to be seen as an "educational body," and the education it offered concerning the nation's fundamental "moral code" had the potential to constitute a "community experience" that would revitalize and motivate democratic forces in the polity to move toward social change (Rostow 1952).

In portraying the Court as an agent of civic education and social change, Rostow was inspired by hope and a felt necessity to build a bridge from the Court to the populace and thereby offset objections that judicial review was hierarchical and antidemocratic. This hope of casting the Court as an agent of community opinion is no less powerful today among contemporary teachers and critics than it was for Rostow half a century ago. It is true, of course, that over the intervening years both political events and social science should have made us more skeptical about civic education. For example, the Warren Court did teach us about how Supreme Court litigation and adjudication may encourage social change and inspire a polity and its citizens to higher political and moral aspirations. But juxtaposed to those lessons are others learned from experience: that Court intervention may inflame public prejudices as much as it may educate to egalitarian civic values, and that judicial intervention may just as easily supersede or immobilize as encourage broad-based political action. There is, in addition, considerable social science evidence that courts and law are in many instances rather feeble instruments of social change (Rosenberg 1991).

Moreover, despite the role that legal rights and the consciousness of them have played in mobilizing political constituencies to action at all social and economic levels (Minow 1987, 1990; Cain and Harrington 1994; McCann 1994), too many citizens are too ignorant of the Court as an institution and usually too oblivious to its opinions to participate in Court-conducted civic education in any meaningful way. And as if this weren't enough, there is evidence that many citizens are increasingly cynical about participation and less willing than in the past to take part in associational activities that help build citizenship (Fukuyama 1995; Putnam 2000).

Yet even in the face of such sobering considerations, there is ample evidence, on both the left and the right, that Rostow's image of the Court as an agent of civic education remains a central tenet among teachers and critics, who eagerly accept leadership from the law school community. Consider five of our most prominent scholars, all of whom clearly have had an impact on commentary inside and outside law school. Each of them invents an encompassing phrase—like Wellington's "interpretive community"—to convey two convictions: that there is, and ought to be, an educational relationship between the Court and the populace, and that academics (if not necessarily journalists) have a role, if not the crucial role, via legal and political commentary, in this Court-centered process of civic education.

Ronald Dworkin, one of our most prominent legal philosophers, views the Court as a "forum of principle" that is supposed to check and balance the interest-based orientation of politics as usual. Academic constitutional commentary, for its part, is supposed to watch over "modern constitutional jurisprudence" by evaluating how well constitutional opinions protect the rights of minorities from the politics of mere political prejudice (Dworkin 1984:31). In other words (to quote Dworkin's extended metaphor), although the courts may be the "capitals of law's empire, and judges . . . its princes," they are not "its seers and prophets." Rather, it "falls to philosophers, if they are willing, to work out the law's ambitions for itself . . . within and beyond the law we have" (Dworkin 1986: 407). This ambition for the philosophically inclined echoes Rostow's conviction that the Court has the responsibility to teach egalitarian political and moral lessons; it also amplifies it by assigning academics a central role in overseeing the work of the Court.

On the opposite side of the political spectrum is Robert Bork, who, as judge and scholar, shares with Rostow and Dworkin the conviction that the Court is responsible for sustaining a "community of ideas" for the polity at large (Bork 1990: 249). Dworkin and Bork differ, of course, on the legitimacy of majority power and the extent to which the text of the Constitution protects minority rights. Bork has been one of the most vocal advocates of the position that it is the task of academics to criticize a Court that fails to protect legislative majorities from those who use judicial power to advance the merely private and transitory prejudices of intellectual elites at the expense of the many (Bork 1990: 249). The point is that, despite their disagreements, on substance, they do agree that academics should watch over constitutional and legal ideas to ascertain whether the polity is headed in the correct direction.

Laurence Tribe, one of the more visible constitutional scholars and Supreme Court litigators, writes in much the same vein as Rostow, Dworkin, and Bork about commentary as civic education. He and coauthor Michael C. Dorf use the term "conversation" to characterize the activity that connects the Supreme Court and its academic commentators. For them, the Court instigates public debate, and commentary's contribution is to help the polity discover how judicial opinions indicate the "nation we are becoming" (1991: 31, 110). James Boyd White, who seeks to bring the insights and criteria of literary analysis and poetics to bear on commentary, expresses the same thought when he writes that the Court and commentary constitute a "community of discourse" that conserves, critiques, and transforms fundamental constitutional, legal, and political values of the polity (White 1990: 267).

The similarity of terms is not a coincidence. Each of these scholars shares the conviction that commentary is politically indispensable. They, and those who read them, bear witness to the ease with which teachers and critics accept Wellington's characterization and betray their and their readers' susceptibility to the ideology of involvement. But to the extent that there is social truth to this ideology of involvement, in the sense that it conveys important beliefs and values operative in academic practices, it also represses—as ideologies frequently do—other aspects of the social truth it would constitute.[6] To understand what I mean by this reference to repression, we need to reflect further on the significance of Rostow's attempt to defend judicial review as a democratic institution.

Intellectual Jurisprudence and Other Academic Realities

In conceiving of the Court as an educational body, Rostow assumed that Court activism in defense of individual rights both reflected and encouraged a political consensus for civil liberties and social change (Smith 1985: 89). Whatever the validity of that image of judicial activism, the social truth it repressed was that, even then, the defenders of activism had seen but could not resolve the contradiction between their approval of post–New Deal judicial review in the name of civil liberties and their disapproval of pre–New Deal judicial review in defense of fundamental economic rights (Wolfe 1986: 25). The attempt to resolve that contradiction has helped produce a mass of commentary about such now familiar issues as neutral and general principles, the paradox of due process, traditionalist versus adaptationist conceptions of the competence of courts, Framers' originalism, Coase's theorem for an economic analysis of rights, the nature of legal rules and principles, textualism, interpretivist and non-noninterpretivist theories of the Constitution, and the influences of race, gender, and class on legal reasoning. Yet, despite its failure to resolve these issues, this literature is still dominated by the conviction that the Court and its commentators are the *ultimate* civic educators about judicial review, constitutional democracy, and fundamental rights.

Wellington's words about the interpretive community, and those of the other scholars, show the degree to which they take this conviction for granted. Which is all well and good, perhaps, except that we know as a matter of brute social fact that only the first two constituents of this community—litigators and adjudicators—are directly engaged in the practices of interpretation. Thus, by not ranking the three constituencies, Wellington and others invite commentators to see themselves not only as full partners with the others but also as capable of resolving the contradictions attendant on judicial review. Absorbed in this task, and caught up in this self-image, teachers and critics neglect some rather obvious (but no less important for that) common social facts about knowledge, power, law, policies, and the Constitution, even as they conveniently forget the undemocratic conditions of their participation in the interpretive community.

There is more. The ideology of involvement also allows teachers and critics to forget that it is the values, skills, and conclusions of litigators and adjudicators, not their own, that constitute such civic education as there is about the Constitution. That is to say, advocates and adjudicators control the production, consumption, distribution, and exchange of knowledge about the law in general and the Constitution specifically. Thus it may be said that legal commentary, as a first-order activity, is a monopoly of the politically powerful and well educated; it is written and taught by Justices, judges, and lawyers, and its lessons are learned directly by the few.

As a second-order activity, legal commentary is something done by persons politically less efficacious: professors, in law school and out, a few journalists and law students, a small percentage of undergraduates, and those members of the mass public who follow or who engage in constitutional politics and legal conflicts. So the lessons taught by legal commentary as a first-order activity are diffused largely among a professional elite. Then they are dispersed to other constituencies: to the teachers and critics in Wellington's interpretive community and even beyond them all the way down through the polity toward the persons who are far less sophisticated about law, policies, and the Constitution (and even more ignorant of the commentary that follows in the wake of legal opinions). This means that commentators, inside and outside the academy, participate primarily, if not exclusively, as consumers of what the other two groups produce. This means as well that intellectual jurisprudence—the questioning, clarifying, formulating, categorizing, and analyzing of legal materials and issues the way lawyers do (even if one is not engaged in legal practice)—is the true core of commentary as civic education.

With lawyerly ways of reasoning predominant, the ideology of involvement goes hand in hand with intellectual jurisprudence, each reinforcing the other but also, we should see, in tension with each other. That is, in principle, democratic civic education is supposed to be nonhierarchical, in the sense that ruler and ruled educate each other through the interplay of elite decision-making and mass political participation. But, in practice, every democratic polity is at odds with this principle because intellectual and political power inevitably is unequally distributed, and that maldistribution can be a virtue only to the extent that the rulers' knowledge and experience are turned to the benefit of all. So, if civic education occurs at all, it is mainly although by no means exclusively hierarchical, and therefore something rulers do for the ruled. This is no less true of the kind of civic education under examination here.

By way of summary then, it is both remarkable from the perspective of social facts, and perfectly understandable from the perspective of the ideology of involvement, that teachers and critics are so deferential to the Court as the institution that they insist ought to have the last say about the Constitution as *the law*.[7] It is also perfectly understandable that they are so deferential to the intellectual jurisprudence of Justices and lawyers as advocates of what the Constitution and law require (Brigham 1987). Indeed, although commentary's decidedly undemocratic character as a first-order activity is well appreciated when it comes to thinking about judicial review, commentators tend to their second-order activity as if they have a central intellectual and political role in civic education even though, as a matter of social fact, not even the text, the Constitution, "belongs" to them.

It belongs, in practice, to advocates and judges: it is an instrument of political power and social control and a scarce resource over which the practitioners fight battles to settle conflicts over other scarce resources. It would seem too obvious for anyone to deny, except for those so tightly in its grip that they cannot see it, that the ideology of involvement encourages teachers and critics (and those who learn from them) to forget that intellectual and political authority is unevenly distributed among themselves and practitioners, to forget the undeniable social facts of their isolation, to forget that "by and large [they] *are* marginal" (Carter 1985: 67), and even to forget the smallness of their audiences.

The point is that while this forgetfulness helps to maintain the image of an interpretive community and a fruitful civic education (Nagel 1989: 124), it exacts a lamentable cost when it comes to the breadth and scope of commentary. By imitating the form and substance of advocacy and judgment and by partaking in commentary as if the text of the Constitution alone, by virtue of its being a shared object of interpretation, were sufficient to constitute their participation in the interpretive community, teachers and critics might too often fail to address the implications, for themselves and a democratic polity, of their commentary as a second-order activity.

For one thing, they fail to see that the intellectual and political role they seek for themselves in the interpretive community does not necessarily fit with the needs of a democratic and constitutional polity. In other words, they maintain the mistaken impression that worrying about *the things* lawyers do is necessarily the same thing as worrying about the common and practical difficulties of policies. It is this mistaken impression that makes it too easy to overlook the gulf between legal and political realities. This book is about putting a brake on the ideology of involvement and the unreflective devotion to lawyerly methods and the things attached to them, in order to recover neglected policies and recall teachers and critics to a richer and more complicated sense of what it means to make a truly democratic contribution to civic education about law and policies.

The Political Need for an Ideology of Involvement

The burden of my argument so far is that the ideology of involvement encourages teachers and critics to think of themselves as part of a great conversation with litigators and adjudicators, even though they should know that in these "conversations" the real "teachers" (lawyers, judges, and Justices) ignore whatever the "students" (teachers, critics, and their audiences) have to say. They do so, if not with impunity, then at least with the supreme confidence that litigators and adjudicators are ultimately accountable to no one but themselves, political events, and history. If this analysis is correct, then the question is, "Why persist in commentary at all, even to recover neglected policies?"

The answer is that even within this illusory world of an interpretive community there is something positive about the ideology of involvement. If it makes teachers and critics forgetful and neglectful, it also encourages them to be hopeful. Let us go back to law school for a moment. Wellington is not altogether oblivious to the maldistribution of power in the interpretive community. He admits that litigators and adjudicators are often insensitive to the interests of others. But, he says, over time, conflict within the polity eventually compels those in power to respond to advocates inside and outside the legal community for legal, social, and political changes (Wellington 1991: 16).

This is a pluralist gloss on politics, and I admit I share to a considerable extent the pluralist's hopefulness about the potential for and the consequences of group conflict. I also know that such hopefulness is easily brought into question by what is now, at least for academics, a familiar line of troubles: for example, the extent to which a relative lack of intellectual and political resources makes it more difficult for those out of power to mobilize; the extent to which the unequal distribution of such resources shapes the political agenda and public policies in the interest of those who benefit from that maldistribution; and the paradox that the costs of engaging in political conflict over that agenda and those policies is highest for those who have the least means to absorb those costs and that, therefore, the most politically disadvantaged are the most discouraged from engaging in collective action. These and other inequalities are as resistant to amelioration as they ever were, yet the full awareness of them is impeded by the ideology of involvement.

All of this leads me to recommend that teachers and critics would be better served by resisting an unmerited solace in pluralist conflict and instead make more present in their minds the work that needs to be done. We can acknowledge that teachers and critics may only rarely find themselves somehow at the vanguard of intellectual or political forces that are usually beyond their immediate control, that their audiences are small, and that they are estranged from legal and political practices—we can acknowledge all that and still not abandon the belief that there is always some potential for civic education to take root and to blossom.

Given what has been said so far, even such a qualified hope would make us appear somehow guilty of wishful thinking, for in a fully rational universe the ideology of involvement would be abandoned altogether. But to understand convictions as ideological is also to recognize that they are not so easily dismissed.[8] Nor ought they necessarily be dismissed, for the ideology of involvement has some political significance, notably if it encourages an ethos of detachment from the day-to-day realities of litigation, adjudication, and the legal profession.[9] In other words, it has the potential to oppose, as difficult as this may be to do, the law's tendency to close itself in. Thus it would be arrogant to dismiss any ideology, the ideology of involvement included, as merely a mistake (Eagleton 1991: 26–31).

To put it another way, no one committed to a democratic political ethos should be willing to let either logic or social facts undermine totally the conviction that the Constitution is a shared cultural object and a fundamental element of all civic education. However much this conviction reflects the same ideology that represses social facts about hierarchy in the interpretive community, it is still a virtue simply because it is an expression of democratic optimism.

Recently, from the left wing of the legal academy, Mark Tushnet has given voice to an optimism verging on the edge of the conviction that I want to endorse. Tushnet is a sometime public commentator on legal issues and a coauthor of one of the most widely used law school casebooks in the country. He is also the author of (radical) commentary that is taken very seriously by academics who share his concern about how legal doctrines should be understood as inseparable from politics and power. At this stage in his scholarship, Tushnet has mounted what he regards as a frontal assault on the Court's elitism, judicial review (specifically, the authority of the Court to declare federal and state action unconstitutional), and lawyerly ways of thinking about the text of the Constitution.

In *Taking the Constitution Away from Courts* (1999), Tushnet, in effect at odds with his own law school casebook, now advocates a break with what he calls the "thick Constitution," which is the familiar one now dominated by the lawyerly thinking of judges, lawyers, and their intellectual collaborators. Tushnet's idea is to replace it with a "thin Constitution": one that would consist solely of those parts of the Preamble and the Declaration of Independence that bear witness to general principles of universal human rights (e.g., freedom, equality, and the public good) and self-governance. This "thin Constitution" would inspire the people to be the source of a "populist constitutional law" through everyday political debates of their elected representatives and other public officials.

By this commitment to a populist constitutional law, Tushnet intends to arrest any direct political and educative role for the Supreme Court. However, Tushnet's Supreme Court does retain some adjudicative functions, such as those associated with statutory interpretation. Tushnet also credits the Supreme Court's readings of the "thick Constitution's" Equal Protection Clause as effective toward helping shape public debates about the principles of a "thin Constitution" and public policies. And although he does keep the door open to reject a populist politics that produces a pattern of "disagreeable" policies, or at times "truly vile ones" (1999: 31), Tushnet would commit us to trust the unpredictable politics of the polity as the basis for constitutional law (1999: 187).

Tushnet's "thin Constitution" and populist constitutional law are a provocative attack on judicial review, "its" Constitution, and the lawyers and scholars behind it. At one level, Tushnet's attack can be read as a challenge to the ideology of involvement and intellectual jurisprudence. Specifically, Tushnet's ideas about populist constitutional law are a break with commentary in the grip of the Court, judicial review, and the text of the Constitution as lawyers read it. Furthermore, Tushnet maintains a hopeful democratic optimism in *a* constitution as a shared cultural object for resolving political conflict.

That said, some readers of Tushnet's book (myself included) would find that his optimism elides a number of troublesome questions. For example: Are voters competent to determine what their views are about policies and a "thin Constitution" or to match them with the positions of candidates? Do the structure and the inequalities in the political process make it any less elitist than judicial processes? If not, what needs to be done about political and electoral processes to make them more genuinely democratic? Even if these processes were more democratic, granted worries about unmerited solace in pluralist political conflict, does rejecting a "thick Constitution" and judicial review neglect too much of what we know about the virtues of judicial checks and balances against popular politics?

Some measure of repression is inevitable in commentary (and agnostic commentary is no exception). So the fact that questions like these can be raised is not necessarily an implied criticism of the relative merit of Tushnet's ideas. In fact, Tushnet or his audience may indeed have interesting answers to them. That Tushnet does not address the issues to which these questions relate leads me to suggest that his ideas, at another level, are not really an assault on the ideology of involvement and intellectual jurisprudence. It seems highly questionable that commentary that is truly concerned with contributing to citizens' education about law and policies would not make these issues central to its project, for answers to them may well lead citizens to question Tushnet's optimism about a populist constitutional law. Therefore, their neglect is sufficient for me to suggest that Tushnet should be interpreted as essentially involved in the ongoing debate, inside and outside law school, about the Court and judicial review and that his ideas are ultimately part and parcel of the ideology of involvement.

This is not to say that Tushnet's ideas are irrelevant to agnostic commentary. To the contrary: as we shall see later, they are a main inspiration for, and challenge to, what agnostic commentary tries to achieve by way of civic education. Nevertheless, my version of pragmatism summons me to put some distance between Tushnet's version of a break with the ideology of involvement and intellectual jurisprudence and the break I want to encourage here. That summons is answered by this book's commentary, which seeks to give outsiders—teachers, critics, and their (intellectually elite) audience outside of law school—more of what they need to know about for their civic education in law and policies, quite apart from lawyerly debates about what is or is not important about understanding the courts and law. This is what I characterize as politically sufficient commentary. And this is the basis on which this book argues that teachers and critics should maintain the ideology of involvement—they should teach and write hopefully—but, as said before, they should at the same time remember to keep social facts about the lack of their intellectual or political power ever present in their minds by putting themselves at odds with intellectual jurisprudence.

Politically Sufficient Commentary

Writing hopefully in this way requires ideological self-discipline. The next chapter will introduce some tenets that might guide and promote it. But as a first step in this process of learning ideological self-discipline, it is important to understand what I have in mind in urging a brake on the intellectual authority of advocacy and judgment—that is, a brake on an unreflective devotion to commentary conducted in a lawyerly fashion. My suggestions build upon already well-established, familiar academic efforts to reshape both the form and the substance of commentary about the meaning and purposes of legal relationships and political arrangements. But if we are truly concerned about restoring neglected policies, we need to acknowledge that even these academic efforts, in and out of law school, do not go far enough. What to endorse and what to reject need to be clearly set forth.

To be specific, from the new republicanism[10] comes the hope, which I endorse, that scholarship and public discourse can be revitalized by encouraging a wider range of reasons and arguments that better encompasses the diverse views that citizens and groups in a pluralisic society might bring to debates about law, policies, and intellectual authority. These reasons and arguments challenge those of advocacy and judgment by identifying indeterminacy as the concomitant of plurality: legal materials are understood as always susceptible to a multiplicity of competing and contrasting interpretive ideas and policies and therefore of competing visions of the past, present, and future (Michelman 1988: 1504, 1518, 1529; Brest 1988: 1624).

From the "new constitutionalism" comes the hope, also endorsed here, that commentary as civic education can be remade by polemics that oppose both the confined conceptions of legalisms arising from litigation and adjudication, and the notion that commentary should focus exclusively on "the protection of individual liberties by limiting the scope and power of government" (Elkin and Soltan 1993: 5).[11] These polemics are also antagonistic to using moral and political philosophy as the source of prescriptive standards, at least to the extent that it mistakenly carries with it a presumption of its own practical relevance (Soltan 1993: 14) or disparages the pursuit of commentary as a form of practical reasoning. This practical reasoning has as its starting point the fact that "there just *are* conflicting values in the world, and no amount of ratiocination will shape them into some coherent whole" (Elkin 1993: 127).

There is also some hope for remaking commentary as civic education from the recent scholarship devoted to various feminisms, as well as that arising from critical race theories, sexual differences, and critical legal studies generally. These too have tried to expand traditional legal and political analysis by resisting the monopolistic authority of legal abstractions with emotive responses and with reasons and arguments that depend on pragmatic, contextual, historical, and even anecdotal considerations not customarily reflected in conventional legal doctrine and politics.

The best of this scholarship has already delivered upon its promise of greater heterogeneity in conceptions of law and politics than is the case in commentary that slavishly mimics litigators and adjudicators. However, the heterogeneity that I am calling for is not defined exclusively in terms of persons, groups, and values that are discriminated against or repressed, as those are conventionally understood. Rather, it is based on the presumption that in a pluralistic polity "our actual experiences of political, economic, and social life are too messy, too mixed, and too ambiguous to support . . . categorical, wholesale answers" (Michelman 1989: 313). In this book I will carry that presumption so far as to recommend that commentary should be skeptical enough to resist rigid partisan agendas, from the left or the right, in analyzing the troubling questions before the polity.

This recommendation is compatible with a social scientific spirit. Here I do not mean to imply any specific methodological orientation or analysis but rather a habit of mind that seeks tenets of description and evaluation that make one relentlessly skeptical of the political sufficiency of legal and abstract ideological claims. The academic efforts characterized above that I read as a challenge to intellectual jurisprudence (the new constitutionalism, etc.), while insightful, nevertheless do not go far enough because they do not test their own abstractions against circumstantial consequentialist considerations. That is, they tend not to provide the pertinent details or consider the unintended repercussions of their guiding abstractions, and so they tend not to set forth as balanced an account as desirable of relevant social, economic, and/or political exigencies.

To put it still another way, commentary on the left is skeptical enough of conventional uses of the law and its fit with politics "properly" conceived. But this skepticism arises largely from a tendency to interpret the law in terms of domination and hierarchy, if not to dismiss its legitimacy altogether. Moreover, commentary on the left privileges itself as uncovering unreflective assumptions about social fragmentation in the polity that others are either too corrupt or too dazed by ideological blinders to see, and it revels in emphasizing the costs of unmerited solace in shared values and institutions. Such gambits deserve skepticism in their turn because they too often give emotional safe harbor to educated classes, sustaining the conceit that they are estranged from the polity and that everyone else who thinks "rightly" ought to be similarly estranged. This conceit excuses them from the self-discipline necessary to grapple with the fact that in actuality many ordinary persons (inside as well as outside the United States) hold to the ideology and the reality of the "American dream."[12]

Commentary on the right, to the extent it exists in academe and gets a hearing, tends to dismiss the law as having been captured by special interests at odds with fundamental and traditional political and legal values, to privilege itself as the guardian of the polity, and to revel in unreflective assumptions about social unity in the polity and the benefits of solace in shared values and institutions. These gambits deserve skepticism because they too often give emotional safe harbor to educated classes, sustaining their conceit that they are estranged from the polity, and that everyone else who thinks rightly ought to be similarly estranged. This conceit excuses them from grappling with the fact that in actuality many ordinary persons are deeply troubled about the ideology and reality of the "American dream."

In contrast, the politically sufficient commentary I recommend promotes a bolder approach to analysis—if it may be so characterized—by first requiring a relentless scrutiny that makes commentary skeptical, as much as that is ever possible, of even its own engagement with law and policies. In short, politically sufficient commentary attentively seeks to avoid blanket ideological or partisan approval or condemnation of the law from either the left or the right.

This self-critical attentiveness will not be easy to accomplish. However, it is abetted significantly by an approach to law and politics that political scientists refer to as the "new institutionalism." The new institutionalism is critical of conventional scholarship in law school and its impact on undergraduate education. In that criticism the new institutionalism analyzes courts and therefore legal reasoning and legal actors as part of a manifold process, structured by the background institutional, political, cultural, historical, and ideological forces of the polity. From this perspective, constitutional law is shaped by these social forces and in turn shapes them. This perspective is at odds with intellectual jurisprudence of the legal model, which comes to terms with courts and the law by analyzing them from the perspective of rules and principles, independent of context considerations. On the other side, it is also at odds with the attitudinal model, which comes to terms with the law by analyzing it solely from the perspective of ideological attitudes and values.

Thus, for new institutionalism, the law's materials, organizations, and personnel are understood in terms of a constantly evolving process where citizens and institutions (and, granted the ideology of involvement, scholars!) construct political conflicts, policies, and thereby relations among individuals, groups, and institutions. Although scholars who share the new institutionalist approach to courts and law understand them within this broad, even diffuse, context of social forces, rational choices, and historical conditions, they do not deny that courts and the law can and do constrain individuals, groups, and institutions. What new institutionalists insist upon, though, is that, granted the complex web of diverse social forces that constitute the law, there is no *formulaic* way to characterize or analyze how courts and the law do constrain. It would seem to follow logically from this contextualism that there are a multiplicity of nonformulaic ways to specify how and why social forces impact courts and the law. If so, then it also would seem to follow that new institutionalists are especially well situated not to fall prey to single-minded ideological or partisan approval (or condemnation) of legal reasoning and courts.

But intellectual jurisprudence intercedes and proves to be stronger than this logic. The evidence for intellectual jurisprudence's strength is to be found in the introduction to Howard Gillman and Cornell W. Clayton's superb survey of the new institutionalism's present and future research approaches and agendas. In their *The Supreme Court in American Politics: New Institutionalist Interpretations* (1999),[13] the editors assert that new institutionalist scholarship "parallel(s) the direction of much of the work in normative jurisprudence by faculty in law schools, work that increasingly conceptualizes legal doctrines either as a form of normative political philosophy or in a critical fashion as political ideology that rationalizes unequal power relations" (1999: 5). What this similarity to law school scholarship means in practice is that new institutionalist scholarship has a strong tendency to locate legal and political processes in the context of race, gender, and class (1999: 4), and it does this almost formulaically from left-wing ideological perspectives.

From the perspective of the goals of politically sufficient commentary, new institutionalism's stated commitment to normative jurisprudence cannot but place it at odds with its own commitment to analyze the law from the contextual perspective (that is, of the web of diverse forces that constitute the law). By this logic, contextualism should orient commentary toward emphasizing the extent to which social fact considerations about social forces in a pluralistic polity coincide with a multiplicity of plausible specifications about how those forces impact law and courts (Kahn 1995: 13).[14] But, in practice, the new institutionalism's tendency to parallel the direction of normative jurisprudence orients it toward employing (selectively, while shrewdly) "those versions of the facts that are most sympathetic to the plight of the disadvantaged and oppressed groups and classes . . ." (Gillman 1995: 8).

Therefore, if politically sufficient commentary, abetted as it is by the new institutionalism, is to achieve its goal of avoiding blanket ideological or partisan judgments of the law (condemnation or approval), then those who undertake that commentary must be wary of falling prey to new institutionalism's intellectual jurisprudence. The key to achieving this wariness lies in the aforementioned social scientific spirit. If that spirit is maintained, it should lead commentators and their audience to a more provisional view (less ideological or partisan) of the relationships among norms, social forces, politics, and the law, a view that tends to reinforce "nonideological, non-doctrinaire, and pragmatic tendencies among those who study [them]" (Huntington 1988: 4).[15] In turn, these tendencies should help create a habit of mind that undertakes analysis of relations between law and policies by treating them as more complex, ambiguous, and unpredictable than the prescriptions of normative tendencies or philosophy are inclined to acknowledge.[16]

For me, to adopt this scholarly habit of mind is to concede (for reasons that will be set forth later) that normative philosophy is essential to politically sufficient commentary. That said, adopting this habit of mind should make the insights of normative philosophy conform to a nondogmatic and pragmatic approach to law and policies. One way to do that is to superimpose on normative philosophy and critical authorities the weight of social fact and consequentialist considerations, which is to say, make the latter the standard for evaluating the utility of the former.

It is tempting to adopt federal judge-cum-scholar Richard Posner's expression "pragmatic moral skepticism" (1999) to designate this superimposition. It would be an appropriate designation, but only to the extent that Posner's term conveys two ideas: (1) social fact and consequentialist considerations must be the standard by which to evaluate the significance of normative philosophical claims; and (2) there are a multiplicity of normative philosophical claims about law and policies but no shared normative or social fact criteria for saying which claims are "better" or "worse."[17] But Posner's term also carries with it connotations not inherent to politically sufficient commentary—namely, specific metaethical convictions about moral values (of no concern here), an outright antagonism to political and moral philosophy, commitments to an economic analysis of rights, and an interest in making legal practice and judging "better." Hence, my neologism "agnostic skepticism" will be used here to indicate a nondogmatic and pragmatic habit of mind. This habit of mind recognizes the diverse ways in which the same or competing social facts can be employed to defend (just about equally well) competing normative claims.

Politically Sufficient Commentary and Agnostic Skepticism

Agnostic skepticism is characterized by its efforts to encourage the eclecticism of politically sufficient commentary.[18] The neologism "agnostic skepticism" in and of itself represents this image of eclecticism. For one thing, as we have learned, agnostic skepticism is not quite the same thing as Posner's pragmatism. Agnostic skepticism does bear a resemblance to that pragmatism in the sense that both dissent from normative theory, but otherwise they are quite different from one another. For another, the terms "agnosticism" and "skepticism" in "agnostic skepticism" connote different things there than they do separately and as conventionally understood. Conventionally understood, skepticism is the position that there are no criteria for knowing or justifying a belief in the "objectivity" of things. But "skepticism" in "agnostic skepticism" refers more specifically to the position that doubt is justified because there are a multiplicity of plausible criteria for knowing or justifying beliefs about the "objectivity" of relations between law and policies. As for agnosticism, in its weaker and more defensible formulation, it is the position that it is impossible to know anything for certain. But "agnostic" in "agnostic skepticism" refers to the specific position that, granted the diversity of ways in which social facts can be employed to defend competing normative claims, there results a multiplicity of equally well-justified ways to be certain about relations between law and policies.

Accordingly, my neologism refers to that eclectic habit of mind that chooses, as much as possible, to be tentative and suspicious about all claims about relations between law and policies. This suspicion and tentativeness are justified, even though there are sometimes rather good reasons (either normative or empirical) for certainty, for being "sure" that claims are well founded. What justifies this suspicion and tentativeness is the understanding that the relations between law and the "facts" of politics and policies are so complex that all claims about them are necessarily inadequate, and that knowing more about them will likely make one more suspicious and tentative rather than less so.

In some respects, agnosticism's suspicious approach to law, politics, and policies is to be identified with the path-breaking work of political scientist H. N. Hirsch. In his book *A Theory of Liberty* (1992), Hirsch took what was then the remarkably bold move of counseling fellow scholars against the then (and now) dominant view in the discipline that legal formalisms are to be taken at face value in evaluating constitutional arguments. Hirsch appealed to scholars to depend upon scientific and social fact considerations to evaluate critically how well legal formalisms in specific cases actually fit with the politics and policies that those formalisms seemingly addressed. This appeal was based on the implicit premise that social and political fact considerations are unavoidably embedded in the formalisms, conceptions of rights, and claims about the meaning of the Constitution that Court arguments depend upon. This premise lay behind Hirsch's challenge to scholarly commentary to attend to the "arbitrariness" of legal and constitutional arguments: that is, to evaluate the extent to which "the law ignores social reality" and therefore suppresses the normative power of legal formalisms, conceptions of rights, and the text of the Constitution.

At one level, the tenets of agnosticism and politically sufficient commentary (to be considered later) can be understood as one way to orient oneself to Hirsch's task of evaluating the potential "arbitrariness" of legal and constitutional arguments. However, for Hirsch, to evaluate the law's arbitrariness means to determine the extent to which legal formalisms and social fact considerations can be used to justify left-liberal policy goals and a theory of liberty oriented toward protecting minority rights. At this level, the tenets of politically sufficient commentary and agnosticism's suspiciousness are at odds with Hirsch's understanding of what it means to evaluate the "arbitrariness" of the law. For reasons that will be specified, evaluating the law's "arbitrariness" from an agnostic perspective requires an appreciation of the extent to which competing conceptions of legal formalisms, conceptions of rights, and claims about the meaning of the Constitution are associated with competing, and often incommensurate, conceptions of the relevant social facts in a case. There are, it should be said, some (a few) political scientists and even some (fewer) law scholars who share this point of view. But even they do not insist on the point that will be central to this book: these connections between social facts and the law should encourage commentary's break with intellectual jurisprudence and, perhaps most especially, with all those efforts in commentary to provide supposedly conclusive reasons why constitutional and legal arguments are rightly or wrongly decided.

Thus agnostic skepticism is a habit of mind open to integrating the analysis of the law with both commonplace political observations and social scientific results (if they are available). And it hopes by this means to make contingent social fact considerations worthy competitors to the more abstract and philosophical considerations that characterize commentary in the grip of intellectual jurisprudence. Its commitment to political sufficiency allows it consistently to bring into question the political privilege accorded the intellectual authority of legal elites, the cultural privilege accorded the law's reasons and arguments, and the cultural privilege accorded both hierarchical judicial politics (i.e., the judicial system and Supreme Court discretion) and the abstractions of academe. The ultimate goal of this skepticism and its commentary is to be as pragmatic as possible in the face of the lure of legal and political abstractions.

This is a daunting challenge, and that is exactly why the ideology of involvement, despite its problems, makes legal commentary an exhilarating intellectual and political pursuit, in fact a hopeful one. And, to the extent that it is successful, the skeptical and politically sufficient commentary recommended here should encourage teaching of the kind implied by Paul Brest's reference to "discursive participation—participation that induces us to listen to other people's positions and justify our own" (Brest 1988: 1624) in the most careful and precise ways possible. This book is thus written in the hope of contributing to more Jeffersonian sensibilities that make teachers, critics, and their audience as free as possible from intellectual jurisprudence, and therefore tentative and suspicious about what they think they know about relations between law and policies.

It is true that to a considerable extent this predisposition to agnostic skepticism sometimes, and perhaps often, will be at odds with what advocates and adjudicators who educate each other almost exclusively through practice find to be persuasive and would prefer. This is a problem, if that is the right term for it, for efficacious civic education in general and for politically sufficient and skeptical commentary specifically. It is moreover a problem complicated by the fact that "what counts as a good academic fit often turns out to differ considerably from what counts as a good fit in the legal and political communities themselves" (Carter 1985: 16).

But this is not the appropriate place to confront this problem: the issue of efficacious civic education, that is, teaching and scholarship, is postponed until the very end of this book. There we will return to it, as promised, after having dealt at length with a number of intellectually, politically, and perhaps even emotionally complicated issues relating to different ways of reasoning between skeptical teachers and critics, on the one hand, and litigators, adjudicators, and the commentators who follow them, on the other. What we should attend to more immediately are some substantive analytic points about how the law makes it so very difficult to bridge that gulf between it and neglected policies.

· 2 ·

Formalisms: An Efficacious Enemy of Politically Sufficient Commentary

If teachers, critics, and their audiences adopt agnostic skepticism, then they need to learn how to challenge, at every turn, unmerited solace in the law's formalisms. By invoking the law's formalisms I mean to draw attention to its argumentative rules and structures, its principles, concepts, and doctrines, and the habit of mind that ensues from them. The law's formalisms are the natural place to begin because they are at the heart of intellectual jurisprudence and constitute, as we shall see, an intrinsic limit on efforts to democratize the intellectual authority of the law.

Stanley Fish, a legal and literary scholar, has nicely sketched the effect of legal formalisms on such efforts in "The Law Wishes to Have a Formal Existence" (in Fish 1994). There Fish argues that the law's formalisms are bound to vitiate academic arguments for change because their use fosters a habit of mind that makes the intellectual authority of the law independent of other methods of reasoning. This autonomy, to be precise, arises out of the belief that the law's argumentative rules, principles, and language in general are, and ought to be, "self-executing" (Fish 1994: 142), that is, altogether independent of the differences between persons who might put them to use. The law, then, channels arguments by means of its formalisms and rejects the intellectual authority of any criteria but its own. Formalism as a habit of mind makes the law, qua law, intrinsically resistant to discovering or fundamentally revising its own values.[1]

However, unlike classical jurists of the late nineteenth and early twentieth century, Fish does not claim that the law's formalisms objectively and formally determine legal results. In fact, he concedes, as many others do, that formalisms cannot determine results because they must always be interpreted within the context of competing choices about facts and precedents on a case-by-case basis. This indeterminacy, he says, has two implications. At a theoretical level indeterminacy provides scholars with opportunities for unrelenting criticism and proposals for social transformation, based on the principle that the law allows for different interpretations from those litigators and adjudicators give. At a practical level indeterminacy means—even though lawyers and judges may deny it—that legal arguments, coming down on one side or another of a legal question, inevitably will be embedded with the very nonlegal criteria that formalism as a habit of mind denies are appropriately part of legal reasoning.[2]

Even so, Fish contends, those commentators who rely on theoretical or practical indeterminacy as a weapon of intellectual and political change underestimate the difficulties they confront. The law, as Fish sees it, always succeeds in defending its own argumentative boundaries, either by providing reasons for rejecting outside arguments as arbitrary, subjective, or political and therefore not properly part of legal reasoning or by absorbing those into mainstream law and thus watering them down. From Fish's point of view, the only advantage is that the law's indeterminacy accrues to itself. It permits the law to shape "its identity out of the stuff it disdains" (Fish 1994: 156), and this process of "efficacious formalism" (152), as Fish calls it, tolerates only those multiple interpretations of law that are compatible with deciding the case at hand. The law, Fish warns, is not philosophy or literary analysis. It is a results-oriented activity, and as such it necessarily closes out any transformations of itself that are broader or deeper than those required by the material facts of legal conflict and the need to win and to settle cases. The law, in short, attends to its own conservation and change.

It is important to know that this lesson about the law's efficaciousness in attending to its own conservation and change is not unique to Fish's notoriously strong views about the contingency of legal judgments, or to his correspondingly dim view of abstract legal and political theory and principles (Fish 1999). Consider, for example, what is, in the final analysis, a rather similar general view of the law's formalisms and constraint by Frederick Schauer. Schauer, is, in contrast to Fish, a mainstream scholar. Indeed, he is one of law school's very most distinguished First Amendment scholars, as well as unabashed enthusiast of the importance of the philosophy of law and analytic jurisprudence. Yet, in *Playing by the Rules* (1991), Schauer agrees, in effect, that conflicts between legal rules and principles are inevitable, and that the application of a rule always involves the allocation of power. The law's formalisms thus open themselves up to judges (and, for that matter, litigators) to permit them to characterize complex events in a multiplicity of ways. Schauer also agrees—and I do more than slight his refined philosophical arguments about how various kinds of rules do and do not constrain in saying this—that there is not much more to say theoretically about how the law defends its boundaries.

To rearrange his words just a bit, what Schauer concludes is that "if a judge has strong views, whether on morals, politics, personality, or economics, and where the case implicates those views, then . . . judges can . . . decide on the basis on non-rule factors . . . with the moral, political, psychological, or economic view dominating the desire to work out the best internally coherent answer. But where the decision-maker is more agnostic, either generally or about the issues presented in a particular case . . . [then a judge will] . . . struggle to reconcile competing rules or interpret them in such a way that the apparent conflict is eliminated" (Schauer 1991: 196–97). The implication of these words is that to a significant measure Schauer holds, as does Fish, that the law permits a judge, and therefore most certainly litigators on behalf of their clients, to use formalisms in ways that fit their respective conceptions of their respective judicial roles and interests within the context of legal battles. As a consequence, for Fish and Schauer, commentators should be extraordinarily wary of "employing the misleading and empty vocabulary of abstraction and formal principle, and . . . keep [an] eye on the true question of concern," which is the substantive policy consequences that accompany the use of the law's formalisms (Fish 1999: 148).

Therefore, following both Schauer and Fish, theoretical accounts that assume that judges are *always* free to impose their own views and those accounts that assume to the contrary that judges are *always* required to provide the most consistent and coherent rule or principled answer to legal questions are simultaneously overgeneralizations. No theory that postulates either that the law's formalisms constrain or that they do not constrain can capture what actual judges and lawyers as advocates for the law can and will do with it in actual cases.

An Efficacious and Inescapable Enemy

If formalism is an enemy, then it bears repeating: teachers and critics are in a fix. They must write about matters central to litigation and adjudication as if commentary could exert a significant practical and educational influence on them even though as commentators they ought to be skeptical about that result. And even if teachers and critics were full partners in the interpretive community, formalism would still close out in practice many of the intellectual methods—and the substantive claims they generate and justify—that would bring about changes in legal reasoning proposed, from the right and left, in the name of shaping tomorrow's results.[3]

The ideological self-discipline of agnostic skepticism requires, then, accepting the efficaciousness of the law's formalisms because it can be neither ignored nor escaped. If the law's efficaciousness can be neither ignored nor escaped then it is prudent to adopt a frame of mind that accepts being impelled by formalisms, yet resists their pressure through a commentary that questions their sufficiency as a means for understanding linkages between law and policies. This skepticism does not come naturally.[4] It must be learned by assessing legal formalisms, especially those one finds useful, in comparison to contextual and circumstantial conditions and relationships that they otherwise submerge into the work of the law.

These assessments do not come naturally, and the reason for that is straightforwardly a political one: as argued in the previous chapter, commentary on the left and right is not designed to be relentlessly skeptical of its own engagement with law and policies. In the final analysis, in order to treat formalism as an enemy, it is necessary to treat political and moral abstractions as enemies as well. Only then can a wider range of context-specific, circumstantial, and consequentialist considerations carry enough weight to bring into question whether, and to what extent, constitutional and legal opinions, as well as commentary, are sufficiently credible renditions of the politics of a case.

To put it another way, agnostic teachers and critics are to be likened to foxes, not hedgehogs (to borrow from the Greek poet Archilochus). Hedgehogs, on the left and the right, even self-critical ones, know pretty much in advance what needs to be argued. Their primary problem, although they do not always recognize it as such, is in working out the internal justifications of their argument with the appropriate degree of intellectual craft. The fox is more wary, knowing that context-specific facts inevitably impel colliding perspectives and consequentialist considerations to make the path, whether to the left or to the right, more justified.[5]

It is appropriate at this juncture to consider the first of this book's many case studies. This case study's primary purpose is to initiate the illustration of how intellectual jurisprudence about formalisms blocks out policies and what a more politically sufficient and agnostic commentary might do to narrow the gulf between the law and policies variously, and however, conceived. The point is that the gulf is to be *narrowed;* it cannot be closed. At a bare minimum law is not law if there is no gulf between it and conceptions of politics and policies. But beyond that (to return to Fish's point) there is the law's efficaciousness in rejecting anything it cannot absorb and use for the purposes of litigation and adjudication. Moreover, academic debates over what the pertinent politics and policies are that the law in its efficaciousness neglects will no doubt be interminable, and that makes closing the gulf still more unthinkable. Please note that all the case studies of this book are meant to reflect many of the central topics of those debates, but that they do not need to represent all of them to fulfill their respective purposes (nor do they). Granted those purposes, those case studies do not depend upon a deep survey of the legal or political science literatures on the topics discussed. For that reason, and others that will become self-evident, the case studies of this book are written not to persuade readers to one policy point of view or another, but rather to encourage academic debates about what politics and policies the law and intellectual jurisprudence efficaciously exclude. Let us begin then with a case that provides a clear illustration of how formalism might figure as an enemy.

Red, White, and Blue, I Spit on You

In 1984, during the Republican national convention, Gregory Lee Johnson burned the American flag while a hundred or so protesters chanted, "America, the red, white, and blue, we spit on you." He was arrested and subsequently convicted for violating a Texas statute making it a criminal offense to desecrate the flag in a manner known to "seriously offend" observers or those who learn of such an action second-hand (witnesses testified that Johnson's conduct seriously offended them). The Texas Court of Appeals upheld the conviction, but the Texas Court of Criminal Appeals overturned it, ruling that burning the flag was in fact "symbolic speech," protected by the First Amendment. Essentially the ruling was based on the principle that burning the flag was expressive conduct involving unspoken or nonverbal "actions" that convey a political message. Texas then appealed to the Supreme Court, where, in *Texas v. Johnson,*[6] Justice William J. Brennan, citing routine "symbolic speech" precedents,[7] confirmed that burning the flag is indeed expressive conduct.

The state had advanced two main arguments against Johnson's speech interests in political protest. The empirical argument was that Johnson's conduct (i.e., burning the flag) was offensive and a potential breach of the peace. The principled argument was that the Texas statute was not designed to limit speech but to protect the flag, as a venerated object, from desecration.

The Court simply dismissed the first argument as hypothetical and without sufficient supporting evidence. It rejected the second argument with the observation that the statute was, in effect, one-sided in protecting one kind of expression about the flag and punishing another. To permit the flag, as a cherished symbol of nationhood, to be burned as a manner of disposal but to prohibit its being burned in protest violates the "bedrock principle" that government "may not prohibit the expression of an idea simply because society finds the idea itself offensive or disagreeable."[8] Consequently, Justice Brennan concluded, Johnson "was prosecuted for his expression of dissatisfaction with the policies of this country, expression situated at the core of our First Amendment values."[9] This prosecution triggered the strict test of "most exacting scrutiny," and the statute, designed to protect the special symbolic character of the flag, was overturned.

In the major dissent (for the purposes at hand), Chief Justice William H. Rehnquist confirmed rather than denied Texas's empirical assertion that the potential for breach of the peace was sufficient to be punished. Moreover, at the level of principle, he denied that flag burning is political expression. The Chief Justice relied on the doctrinal distinction between speech and conduct to contend that the flag burning was "the equivalent of an inarticulate grunt or roar" and as such was conduct altogether lacking elements of expression and therefore not protected by the First Amendment.[10] For Rehnquist this prosecution triggered the less strict test of "important governmental interests," which permits regulations of nonverbal elements related to political expression even if such regulations have ancillary effects on expressive conduct.

It is significant that there was a considerable gap between the intense political attention that *Johnson* engendered and the immediate reaction of the scholarly community. *Johnson* was one of those few decisions that make front-page news. Public opinion was then, as it is now, overwhelmingly against the decision. The flag became a salient part of 1990 campaign politics (76 percent of those polled said that the issue was very or somewhat important for deciding how to vote in forthcoming House races)[11] as politicians attacked the decision, calling for revised flag-burning statutes and constitutional amendments to protect the flag.[12] This controversy over flag burning smolders on and on, in the polity and in the law reviews. Yet initially the major law reviews (there were something like twenty initial reactions altogether) considered the decision to be rightly decided and thus treated the case rather matter-of-factly, as typical of First Amendment adjudication (e.g., Loewy 1989; Stone 1989; Greenawalt 1990).

This type of matter-of-fact scholarly treatment always begs for more politically sufficient commentary. Consider then, as an illustration of this need, the *Harvard Law Review*'s (1989) summary of the term's cases, which read *Johnson* as a confrontation between liberal and communitarian political theories.[13] It is an excellent example of how law school students (not to mention undergraduates) learn to use theories like liberalism and communitarianism as abstract measures of "actual social costs" of freedom of speech. Its argument is that a liberal theory requires that the political community, more often than not, absorb the costs of whatever (social or psychological) harms ensue from conduct like Johnson's in order to protect the political interests of the individual and the pursuit of individual goals. A civic tradition of liberalism, the *Review* insists, recognizes that the Constitution is best understood as supporting the conclusion that "the government may not interfere with Johnson's ability to make political choices by dictating the value he must attach to the flag, or the respect he must accord it." Indeed, to do so is to confuse "loyalty to the flag . . . with loyalty to the country" (Harvard Law Review Association 1989: 254–59). Hence, according to the *Review,* Justice Brennan's opinion is both liberal and rightly decided.

On the other hand, the *Review* argues, a communitarian theory requires that greatest weight be given to the interests of the community. This means that what counts as appropriate individual interests and goals are determined and shaped by membership in "constitutive communities" (such as familial, racial, religious, ethnic, gender, or national groups). According to this view of the civic tradition, attacks on the shared social, symbolic, and psychological attributes of political identity and membership, as in flag burning, exact costs that are too high to be tolerated (Harvard Law Review Association 1989: 254–55). Accordingly, Chief Justice Rehnquist's dissent is labeled a communitarian one. This gives the *Review* an opportunity to bring into question whether communitarianism is compatible with the First Amendment, which implicitly encourages an "on-going debate" about the public good, rather than the "static notion" of it conveyed by a communitarian theory (Harvard Law Review Association 1989: 256–59).

So, by labeling the two opinions liberal and communitarian respectively, the *Harvard Law Review* transforms *Johnson* into a case study over which political theory and civic tradition better fit what the Constitution and the public good require. There are no surprises in this commentary. It is an altogether typical, even orthodox—albeit left-liberal—rendition of intellectual jurisprudence in commentary. Its treatment of liberalism and communitarianism follows from the presumption that it is appropriate and productive to read constitutional opinions not only for their legal implications but for their political theoretical ones as well. It should be said right off that the presumption behind this kind of commentary does in this case lead to interesting questions about civic behavior (e.g., "What reverence is owed to national symbols?"), participation (e.g., "What political actions are precluded because they violate fundamental social values?"), and civility (e.g., "To what extent is one free to think of oneself as independent of the national political identity?").[14]

Still, it must also be said that this presumption can lead to troubling obfuscations about law, politics, and policies in two different ways. The more obvious and not uncommon obfuscation occurs when analysis of this kind falls into philosophical conjectures about the strengths or weaknesses of formalisms at the expense of demonstrated linkages between philosophy and practical political and legal concerns. In this instance this particular distortion does not occur, but such distortion, symptomatic of the imposition of philosophy on law, has become so frequent that it prompts the now familiar complaint that philosophy puts itself first and provides precious little by way of law and politics in the bargain.

The no less common, but much more subtle, obfuscation occurs when political theoretical analysis like the one in the *Harvard Law Review* is convincing simply because it accords with the predisposition of intellectual jurisprudence to treat the law's formalisms with insider's affectionate deference. Consider the tacit political lesson this kind of commentary (re)teaches. We know very well that when Johnson burned the flag he was engaging in the politics of disdain: his actions were meant to signify disgust with and rejection of American civic traditions, symbols, and virtues (one might say its political formalisms). However, both Brennan's and Rehnquist's opinions in this case transform Johnson's politics of disharmony into the politics of harmony. Both opinions teach the lesson that even though Johnson is not bound by the fundamental values, sympathies, or loyalties of American citizenship, the polity is. They do this by "interpreting" (or transforming) Johnson's conduct, which attacks the form and content of political relations, in terms of formalisms like "bedrock principles" and "doctrinal distinctions" that confirm those relations.[15]

Justice Brennan uses those formalisms that protect Johnson and his speech, and Chief Justice Rehnquist uses those formalisms that punish him for his actions. But both Justices teach that what really matters in the case are shared public ideals: constitutional civility and a common political fate. Both opinions wash out the nastiness of Johnson's message, replacing his attack with formalisms that privilege the cultural norms of "unity and integration" (Levinson 1988: 17). In fact, both Justices go out of their way to confirm that their respective opinions seek "to preserve," as Justice Brennan concludes, "the flag's special role" and "cherished place in our community."[16] In doing so, both Justices decenter Johnson's politics and thereby defend the integrity of the law as the "glue" of social and legal relations.[17]

The *Harvard Law Review* echoes this decentering of Johnson's politics by arguing that what is important in the case is whether the liberal or the communitarian conception of civic virtue better explains what constitutional (not Johnson's) politics is about. Commentary of this kind recapitulates the view that legal formalisms, and their associated conceptions of civility, exhaust what is required to understand the politics and policies of freedom of speech.

But commentary that seeks to be more politically sufficient must challenge the practice of merely echoing, at higher levels of abstraction, the questions and answers generated by the law's formalisms and associated political theoretical abstractions. For example, in this instance what needs to be brought forward is the fact that principles of political obligation, participation, and civility are all part of "the language of citizenship" (Lasch 1991: 172). This language has its place: it can clarify issues by resetting specific controversies within larger, formulaic ways of thinking about U.S. constitutional history and civic tradition, and in so doing confirm, even when the threat of fragmentation is especially strong, a collective identity shaped by shared values and civic aspirations. Yet this language also has the capacity to obscure political issues, through its ever present tendency merely to recapitulate the political lessons of the past and to repress awareness of how the present differs or the future will differ from that past. This tendency should be reason enough to doubt whether formalistic articulations such as political obligation, participation, and civility always have such a good fit with actual political experience. Yet no such doubt is at work in the flag-burning case, where the shared civic traditions and values that Johnson's flag burning was meant to undermine are privileged legally and politically. In such ways formalisms do their work and manifest their power to obscure.

Because intellectual jurisprudence focuses so directly on the law's formalisms and the political theoretical language it prefers, those in the grip of it feel free to take solace in the conviction that ours is a polity in which conflict is understood to be reconciled by principles of right and not merely settled by forces of conflict. By contrast, a politically more sufficient orientation is driven to assess the benefits and costs of such assurances and on that basis subject them to stricter scrutiny. But that investigation cannot happen unless we stop sanctifying case studies and treating them within the narrow compass of intellectual jurisprudence.

Getting Our Bearings: Some Tenets for Commentary

Let us pause for a moment to get our bearings. I am not arguing that commentary should abandon case studies. Far from it. The next chapter will go more deeply into *Johnson,* and the rest of this book is a testament to my belief that case studies are the best avenue for understanding how the law's formalisms are used to construct and justify judicial policies. What I do suggest is that we have learned so well the lessons of the ideology of involvement and intellectual jurisprudence that it is very difficult to imagine ourselves resisting them. But just such an imaginative leap must be made in order for us to break away, as much as that is possible, from a habit of mind that, sometimes unintentionally, undermines or, even worse, supplants political interpretation by making the latter seem naive, superficial, anecdotal, or simply second-rate. To constitute an alternative habit of mind and to engage case studies in nonlegalistic ways that are attentive to common or ordinary social, economic, and political considerations, consider the following, rather familiar tenets to make legal commentary more frankly agnostic about the law:

1. Whether it is admitted by those in the interpretive community or not, legal interpretation is political and social judgments by more formal means (Kairys 1998). Thus, litigation and adjudication are to be interpreted as reasoning about competing and sometimes incommensurate claims about social necessities (Cardozo 1974: 122). These practical claims are transformed, in litigation and adjudication, into more abstract claims about legal rules and principles, precedents, and theoretical values (Strauber 1987).
2. These transformations are to be understood as judgments about the social foundations and the uses of power and force (Brigham 1987: 20–33; Posner 1990: 83). They are expressed in the determination of which facets of the political culture, which political interests, and which institutional practices of American politics are acknowledged as privileged (Brigham 1987).

3. These determinations are deemed to be "rightly decided" (or legitimate) only because a legalized political culture encourages the belief that courts, and a *Supreme* Court as the principal judicial authority, should render "final" judgments (Posner 1990: 79) about the role of legal formalisms and the text of the Constitution in resolving conflicts about political culture, interests, and institutional practices and processes.
4. The authority of the law thus arises out of its "social foundations" (Brigham 1987: 25). Agnostic skepticism's politically sufficient commentary challenges this authority by questioning: (a) the cultural privilege accorded the intellectual authority of legal elites; (b) the cultural privilege accorded the law's formalisms as the intellectual bases for interpreting law, politics, policies, and the Constitution; and (c) the cultural privilege accorded hierarchical judicial politics (i.e., the roles of the judicial system and Supreme Court discretion in conflict-resolution). Hence a more democratic ethos in commentary requires relentless skepticism about the legitimacy of the law in terms of the political credibility of its decisions.

It is self-evident that these tenets are to be associated, in a general way, with the ideas of sociological jurisprudence, legal realism / pragmatism, and critical legal studies.[18] More specifically, within the context of agnostic skepticism, they unmistakably situate teachers and critics on the outside, looking in on the law, its advocates, and its judges. The first tenet requires distance from thinking that legal commentary is solely about interpreting texts and it focuses on issues related to the fit between the law and social conditions and demands. The second tenet requires distance from thinking about power solely in legal terms, and it focuses on issues related to the law as an instrument of command and control, and even violence (Sarat and Kearns 1991). The third tenet requires distance from thinking about decisions in terms of being rightly or wrongly decided, and it focuses instead on the practical consequences of decisions that seek to shape political culture, interests, institutions, and processes. The fourth tenet requires distance from the tendency to take for granted the intellectual and political authority of courts; it focuses on the gulf between what legal formalisms imply and empirical considerations related to the distribution of political, social, and economic power in the polity.

In sum, these tenets encourage agnostics to acknowledge that they do *not* share the same intellectual agenda as litigators, adjudicators, and most teachers, critics, and students inside and outside law school. They should discourage the tendency, now ever present in commentary, to play advocate, judge, and "law professor"—that is, to plead for clientele groups, rewrite case law, reform legal reasoning, or make merely ideological "seat-of-the-pants social judgments" (Shapiro 1983: 542) about legal decisions. Freed from these agendas, teachers and critics, it is hoped, will make a central part of commentary those perspectives, experiences, values, standards, and socioeconomic conditions hidden by formalism (Kairys 1998; Brint and Weaver 1991) and discounted by advocacy and judgment.

It is here that agnostic skepticism and prudence reinforce each other to position commentary to take on a more contextual cast. For, even as agnostic commentary decenters case studies, it recognizes that it is only through them that one comes to understand, for example: how abstract legal rules, principles, and precedents are applied in legal opinions; how and why, over time, those rules, principles, and precedents are qualified and even transfigured; and how "principles determine decisions, [and how] decisions in turn modify and refine principles" (Walzer 1980: 169–71). Having come so far, teachers and critics and those who learn from them must go on to interpret these findings within the context of more politically sufficient commentary. When they take legal reasoning seriously in this way and discount the relative autonomy of the law's formalisms, they democratize the intellectual authority of the law. This is the Jeffersonian sensibility of being sufficiently observant of the law, yet tentative and suspicious of it, in order to recover the neglected policies the law and its advocates disdain.

What's Wrong with the Rightly Decided Orientation and Question

The tenets just recommended are not the only possible ones for recovering neglected policies. But they do have a singular virtue when it comes to putting a brake on intellectual jurisprudence: they challenge—and this is central—the problem-solving orientation of intellectual jurisprudence as currently presented in casebooks and commentary. (Hereafter, unless indicated otherwise, the term "commentary" refers to academic second-order interpretations.) Needless to say, this orientation, like the law's formalisms upon which it is based, is not easily challenged. It has a most prestigious institutional provenance—beginning with the law school at Harvard University under Dean Christopher Langdell—and case studies are so deeply entrenched that the problem-solving professionalism associated with them now marks "the official jurisprudence of lawyers and laypeople alike" (Posner 1990: 445).[19] Casebooks make this problem-solving orientation evident in their formats, as their materials are generally arranged so as to provide ways of answering specific questions, and the questions themselves are assimilated to various categories. Some formats stress *historical* questions such as "How did judicial review evolve?" and "How did the Court become a national policy-making body?" Others take a *conceptual* approach around questions about the justifications for the doctrines of "due process," "equal protection," and "fundamental rights." Some raise questions about the *function* of legal doctrines by grouping cases according to problems about the impact of judicial review on private property and the structure of the nation's politics. And there are formats that emphasize *modes of interpretation* and assimilate cases to questions about alternative models, metatheories, and theories of interpretation and judicial reasoning. But regardless of their variety, and no matter how they may appear to differ in other respects, all such formats defer equally to the idea that the vocabulary of legal reasons and arguments and the issues as they are defined by them are necessary and sufficient for solving the problem of whether opinions are rightly decided or not.

This deference reinforces intellectual jurisprudence by making it difficult to imagine legal commentary other than as an enterprise devoted to solving problems about textual and abstract "relations among legal ideas" (Posner 1990: 445). The unreflective presumption is that describing these relations means also simultaneously describing and assessing the colliding social, political, economic, and sexual realities that give rise to constitutional adjudication and to legal conflict generally. The image practitioners of intellectual jurisprudence thus have of themselves is that of the Herculean mind turned inward, struggling to find that one last metatheoretical, theoretical, or conceptual nuance that would justify the belief that a given legal argument is superior to another, and ipso facto that one policy result is superior to another. The tenets of political sufficiency and an agnostic habit of mind are meant to unsettle this self-image with a single prosaic question: Where is it written, except in legal commentary in the grip of intellectual jurisprudence, that there are necessarily any close connections between politics or good policy results, on the one hand, and the abstractions of legal commentary, on the other?

To make a question like this one central to case studies is to do more than worry about commentary's tendency to cut itself off from politics more commonly conceived and "to lose sight of . . . commonsense notions about justice" (Tribe and Dorf 1991: 109). Many legal scholars have come to worry about this tendency, but intellectual jurisprudence persuades them nevertheless that legal abstractions are worth their costs because they "push us constantly to check our practices against our principles" (Tribe and Dorf 1991: 109). This cost-benefit analysis ultimately maintains the presumption that legal formalisms ought to have privileged intellectual authority and that presumption is precisely what this book argues ought to be challenged, again and again, by circumstantial and context-specific considerations and not simply accepted as a matter of principle.

Indeed, when we turn outward to more than relations among legal ideas we remind ourselves that, even though law and commentary have their own abstract language that must be understood in their own terms, law and commentary as professionally conceived are nevertheless part of the family of political relations and are, in fact, inextricable from politics. Looking thus outward we are astonished that the ideology of involvement generally, and problem solving in particular, still lead one to forget the brute social fact that legal issues were originally political ones, transformed into legal formalisms by professional elites. And they lead one to forget that this transformation is deemed legitimate (i.e., lawful and definitive) solely because a political culture, partly based on the rule of law, has either elevated judicial institutions as supreme or casts the tension between them and legislative politics as the central morality play in democratic politics. One way or another, the addiction to formalistic and doctrinal case studies still leads commentary to repress the political side of things (e.g., Stumpf et al. 1983; Carter 1994).

Doubtless, many teachers and critics will be astonished in turn to hear that commentary today represses the political side of things. Has not the very scholarship that impels agnostic skepticism (as acknowledged in chapter 1) also forced commentary to confront neglected policies and the thoroughly politicized role of courts, lawyers, and the judicial process?[20] At one level the answer to that question has to be in the affirmative. But that is only half the story.

The other half is that the scholarly work mentioned above, even when it makes a bow toward pragmatism, or consequentialist considerations, or contextualism, proves to be no less given over than the usual commentary to problem-solving orientations. The orientations are different enough from those taught in mainstream casebooks, defined as they are by ideological abstractions and metaabstractions about alternative conceptions of self, society, and politics drawn from philosophy, political theory, and literary/aesthetic theories. Nonetheless, the basic *practice* of analyzing law politics and policies as relations among ideas remains intact; and conditions and relationships originally understood by participants in everyday political terms are still treated as mere conflicts of interests that cannot be really understood unless they are transformed into one prized mode of critique or another.

Since it is the ideology of involvement that pressures commentators to embrace the problem-solving orientations of intellectual jurisprudence, to break away from them requires giving up on the idea that only commentary that addresses how to transform law, lawyers, judges, and courts has practical significance. Teachers and critics willing to do so gain the intellectual space to consider what is necessary to recover neglected policies, including policies and politics about which participants may not be fully aware, in a way that is less given over to ideas about ideas.

As I have said, I think the way to do that is to recover conditions and relationships that are hidden by the clichéd ways that legal rules, precedents, and abstract values (like "bedrock principles" and political theories of civic traditions) are attended to. That means keeping a steady eye toward the data of political conflicts. And it means attending to specific, if (often) inconclusive, material about persons, institutions, policies, ideas, values, and the rest of it that are deemed (by the commentator) to be important for evaluating the purposes or repercussions of a constitutional or legal policy.

This kind of material appears in agnostic commentary by going through layers of reasoning about relations among law, politics, and policies. One layer of reasoning is about various circumstantial and consequentialist considerations that are relevant to the conflict at hand but are excluded or distorted by the law's efficaciousness. Another layer consists of descriptions and evaluations of prelegal and extralegal facts and values beyond the law that nevertheless provide a broader context for that law than the law itself efficaciously allows. A third layer develops doubts about any answer to the rightly decided question by illustrating how those answers depend upon constitutional and legal claims about conflicts that are at odds with competing and sometimes incommensurate claims that arise from the other two levels of reasoning.

These layers of reasoning do not require agnostics to abandon the role of legal or political principles in commentary or even philosophical abstractions about them. But they should lead agnostics to be more inclined to think about the extent to which principles and abstractions, like legal materials, are inevitably embedded in substantive policy predilections. Second, agnostics should be more inclined to evaluate the extent to which those circumstantial and consequentialist considerations lay open these predilections to disputes about their integrity. Third, therefore, agnostics should be inclined to judge the value of principles and philosophical abstractions in commentary solely in terms of how well they hold up to circumstantial and consequentialist fact disputes about their embedded policy predilections.

By way of summary, these three layers of reasoning encourage an agnostic to be a resourceful skeptic and to recover, in politically sufficient commentary, what adjudicators, litigators, and those teachers and critics who follow in the path of intellectual jurisprudence miss.[21]

As an illustration of what this recovery might produce, let us take another look at *Johnson,* this time reading it to discern how legal formalisms can systematically and relentlessly channel arguments so as to obfuscate any practical considerations other than those they embed.

· 3 ·
Skepticism and Neglected Politics

Chapter 2 argued that the flag-burning case should be read as an example of how adjudicators decenter Gregory Lee Johnson's politics. Now, in this brief chapter, I want to go one step further by showing (1) how, pace the *Harvard Law Review,* that decentering masks the extent to which the opinions of Justices Brennan and Rehnquist have the same, not different, political theory and conception of a constitutional civic tradition; and (2) that what these Justices disagree about is how judicial power ought to be used or not used to police what counts in their terms as political unity and integration.

I argued earlier that both Justices, in their respective appeals to bedrock principles and doctrinal distinctions relating to First Amendment adjudication, use the language of citizenship. And such language—and the decentering of politics like Johnson's that goes along with it—when taken for granted, leads one to forget that pluralist politics are just as aptly described in terms of "fragmentation and disintegration" as in terms of "unity and integration" (Levinson 1988: 17). Some rather commonplace political conditions can be cited to suggest that we are at risk. For one thing, it is now a common complaint that "the educational foundations of our society are presently being eroded by a rising tide of mediocrity that threatens our very future as a Nation and a people" (*Nation at Risk* 1983: 5). For another, our national political culture has disintegrated to the point where "there have to be doubts about citizens being able to reach some common understandings on complex issues" (*Nation at Risk* 1983: 7). Indeed, for some time there has been evidence that a disconcertingly large number of people have had doubts about their own civic capabilities (e.g., McCloskey and Zaller 1984: 77). The very record of such widespread doubts about the citizens' capacity to understand issues and to know what is good for them should make observers question the fit between the actual condition of our civic life and legal and political abstractions, understood as presupposing a body politic with a shared political identity.

The same question arises in the face of evidence that politics is actually shaped and constrained by the unequal distribution of political, economic, and social power. In a mass society, politics is controlled to a considerable extent by elites, governments, and bureaucracies, which manipulate the political agenda and distort policies in decidedly undemocratic directions. Such observations are not new to commentary. Indeed, they invite us to consider again to what extent opinions like those in *Johnson* and commentary on it ignore what is otherwise so plain about politics and policies merely for the sake of providing "an emotional safe-harbor for the educated classes" (Nagel 1989: 40) from the seas of political tumult and disorder in the polity.

Law and Political Theory in Agnostic Skepticism

This time we take up *Johnson* as a case study that uses the tenets before us and accepts the invitation to see how formalisms are able to turn us away from unpleasant politics in favor of safer harbor. When Justice Brennan states that burning the flag is a political message,[1] he is not interested of course in Johnson's political message. He is interested in situating flag burning within the context of a paradigmatic First Amendment question: "If the conduct at issue is expressive conduct, does the Texas regulation suppress it?" Because Texas conceded in oral argument that flag burning was expressive conduct, Justice Brennan indicates that the question arises whether flag burning falls within those precedents that allow for regulations of conduct so long as those regulations further a "substantial" governmental interest without directly suppressing political speech.

The landmark case in this regard is *United States v. O'Brien*,[2] where a conviction for draft card burning was sustained as a violation of a Selective Service regulation prohibiting mutilation of the cards. Regulations like that, serving "substantial or important governmental interests" and unrelated to direct suppression of political speech were deemed to be constitutional. To find that burning the flag is expressive conduct suppressed by state regulation requires giving reasons for rejecting *O'Brien* as the controlling precedent. Those reasons reveal themselves in Justice Brennan's rejection of two intertwined claims advanced by Texas in defense of the flag-burning statute. The first claim, that the regulation was intended not to limit speech but to protect the public from disruptions predicted to follow upon attacks against a venerated object, is, as indicated earlier, summarily dismissed. The second claim is that protecting the flag as a national symbol requires ancillary restrictions on communication activities. It is in the rejoinder to this claim that Justice Brennan offers up the images of shared values in place of a real engagement with Johnson's politics: although Justice Brennan acknowledges that Johnson was prosecuted for political dissent that he intended to be offensive, Brennan does so merely as an opportunity to address fundamental First Amendment formalisms.

I argue that Justice Brennan finds the political theoretical terms of his argument in *Boos v. Barry,* which references the landmark case *New York Times Co. v. Sullivan* as the ground for rejecting the applicability of *O'Brien.*[3] The words that are referenced from the *Times* case are as follows:

> Those who won our independence believed . . . that public discussion is a public duty; and that this should be a fundamental principle of the American government. They recognized the risks to which all human institutions are subject. But they knew that order cannot be secured merely through fear of punishment; that it is hazardous to disparage thought, hope, and imagination; that fear breeds repression; that repression breeds hate; that hate menaces stable government; that the path of safety lies in the opportunity to discuss freely supposed grievances. . . . Thus we consider this case against the background of a profound national commitment to the principle that debate on public issues should be uninhibited, robust, and wide-open, and that it may well include vehement, caustic, and sometimes unpleasantly sharp attacks on government.[4]

These words from Justice Brennan's *New York Times* decision offer up blind solace in the form of a political theory about political messages wherein the risks of harms from speech virtually always are outweighed by its benefits. I mean by the phrase "political theory" to direct attention, here and elsewhere, to the primary assumptions that are immanent in constitutional and legal opinions, especially as these assumptions determine which political interests, or which aspects of political culture, or what conception of institutional practices or processes are to be privileged when it is a question of what individuals and governments are entitled to do in politics.

Such political theory is either stated specifically in opinions or embedded in citations to precedent and represents a judge's conception of an "intelligible moral order" that "sustains a defensible scheme of human association" (Unger 1986: 2) for the polity. It is there to be analyzed in commentary on its own terms—not reduced or transformed into abstract political or legal theories (Strauber 1983: 72–73, 95)—for what it tells us about the image(s) behind legal formalisms and how these images may neglect politics.

The reference here is not the abstract theory of intellectual jurisprudence that is extrinsic to opinions and originates in the history of political ideas or is derived from contemporary theorists ranging from John Rawls to Michel Foucault and then applied in case studies. Rather, the political theory in opinions is to be recovered only by reading backward through layers of citations to precedent until one finds in them the materials for understanding a judge's political commitments to controlling legal rules and principles, as well as a snapshot of what a judge thinks about political principles, practices, and consequences. Inevitably, commentators will have competing conceptions of what those commitments are; or they will have competing conceptions about how well a political theory fits with practical political observations; or they will have competing conceptions about whether the law's formalisms adequately represent a political theory. All such disagreements serve the same purpose in skeptical commentary: they provide opportunities to identify the extent to which a retreat into such solaces as are offered by images of unity and integration (or disunity and disintegration) in case law and commentary as usual is justified.

Consider, for instance, the commitments implied in the *New York Times* precedent that is referenced in Justice Brennan's citation of *Boos*. The first three sentences of that passage establish the political theoretical principle that freedom of speech should be understood in terms of political means and ends. The political means are "independent" persons, who are characterized by a shared psychological attribute: a sense of public duty that they fulfill by political participation. The political end of that participation is stable representative government. The risks of such participation are readily acknowledged, but to repress speech is considered to confront even greater risks of political instability. The ultimate circumstantial and consequentialist reason that speech ought not to be regulated, then, is, in this instance, that the flag cannot be protected without repressing political messages, and the unacceptable political cost associated with that repression makes rejecting the *O'Brien* precedent the safer path to take.

This consequentialist line of reasoning is deeply embedded in First Amendment adjudication. Over time, the primary assumptions about what individuals and governments are entitled to do in politics have come to settle on very familiar interests associated with the idea of citizens as independent persons: for example, an informed citizenry, popular rule, freedom from external constraints, conduct compatible with one's political beliefs and self-development, equal access to information as a means to formulate beliefs and motivate actions, and maintenance of the health, safety, and welfare of the community (Strauber 1987: 520).

For the sake of analytic clarity let us consider these interests as belonging to three rough categories: *audience* interests (e.g., interests related to the benefits that citizens receive from being aware of the expression of, and deliberation about, competing political, social, artistic, and philosophical ideas and opinions), *participant* interests (e.g., interests related to the benefits that citizens receive from expressing, and deliberating about, competing political, social, artistic, and philosophical ideas and opinions), and *sovereignty* interests (e.g., interests related to the benefits that citizens receive from having an ultimate legal authority to preserve the common good, political stability, and popular rule) (Strauber 1987).[5] These three political categories are nothing more than (my) labels for interests that constitutional law has traditionally identified as salient for litigating and adjudicating competing claims in speech cases.[6] Yet they recommend an interpretation of Justices Brennan's and Rehnquist's opinions rather different from the one provided by the *Harvard Law Review.*

The *New York Times* precedent indicates that political messages are protected because participant and audience interests are secured by "the principle that debate on public issues should be uninhibited." This principle is interpretable not as an element of either a "liberal" or a "communitarian" theory. Rather, it is independent of both and is locatable in the category of sovereignty interests. Specifically, it is the creed, articulated in the *Times* case, that government is responsible for preserving the means whereby citizens are free to pursue the good of "public discussion as a public duty."

There are three political points to be made about this creed respecting public duty. Two of them repeat points made earlier. The first is that, from the perspective of Johnson's politics, it is a high-handed confirmation of what Johnson considered political cant and what his flag burning was meant to attack. The second is that the creed, as predicted, appeals to a political abstraction—"public discussion as a public duty"—which has, arguably, a poor fit with the reality of precious little political discussion and participation. In other words, it represents heedless solace in an image of unity and integration.

The third point is new and most important for the purposes at hand: from a skeptical standpoint, it is competing, yet ultimately parallel, conceptions of sovereignty interests, and not a confrontation between liberalism and communitarianism, that are at issue in *Johnson*. Here is why. The political abstraction of "public discussion as a public duty" provides a consequentialist justification for protecting audience and participant interests: in effect, these interests must be protected in order to maintain the stability and processes of representative government. It is this consequentialist consideration of what sovereignty interests require that warrants Justice Brennan's conclusion that the state may not protect one attitude toward the flag and punish another. The government must be neutral and permit all points of view the chance to be heard rather than acting as a gatekeeper for public morality.

Competing consequentialist considerations about sovereignty interests also characterize Chief Justice Rehnquist's dissenting opinion. His foremost practical political concern is to determine what may be done by the government to protect the nation's self-identity and image. But compared to Justice Brennan's austere formalism, Rehnquist's prose is virtually poetic in its discussion of audience, participant, and sovereignty interests, which he expresses via an historical account of the flag's place, in two hundred years of American history, as "the visible symbol embodying our nation."[7]

This account starts with the American Revolution, when the flag's function was "to unify" the colonies; it quotes from Ralph Waldo Emerson's "Concord Hymn"; it describes colonial and regimental flags; it cites the Continental Congress's resolution for a national flag and the first eight lines of the poem by Francis Scott Key that became the national anthem; it characterizes the flag's symbolic role during and after the Civil War, and cites John Greenleaf Whittier's poem "Barbara Frietchie"; it relates the story behind the Iwo Jima Memorial and tells about one of Roosevelt's presidential proclamations authorizing use of the flag on lend-lease shipments; it relates a Korean War story about the flag and the landing at Inchon; it retells a story about the passage of the Federal Flag Desecration Statute (1967) during the Vietnam War; it describes the flag's symbolic role in the military, judicial, and political systems; it centers the flag as the nation's most revered symbol; and it concludes with citations from congressional and state laws regulating the use of the flag.[8]

These sentiments represent Chief Justice Rehnquist's political theory, which also just happens to provide a version of solace in unity and integration. In this theory, it is the flag, rather than legal formalisms, that represents the collective identity of the polity. As Rehnquist puts it, quoting Justice Fortas in *Street v. New York*, the flag has "a special kind of personality [and for this reason] its use is traditionally and universally subject to special rules and regulations."[9] As proof of the applicability of that precedent to the facts of the case, Rehnquist reports that vast millions of citizens, of different social, political, and philosophical beliefs, by forty-eight acts of popular sovereignty, have determined that flag burning does not contribute to the discussion of governmental or social policies. Thus, Rehnquist locates the public duty in what, according to this analysis, can be recognized as sovereignty interests in governmental regulations to protect the flag as a means of preserving civic morality.

Chief Justice Rehnquist locates the unity of the polity in *Chaplinksy v. New Hampshire* to warrant the consequentialist argument that under specified circumstances like this one, certain kinds of conduct, and even speech, that may be deemed to be injurious or immediately inimical to social security, are "of such slight social value as a step to truth that any benefit that may derive from them is clearly outweighed by the social interest in order and morality."[10] This conclusion is clearly at odds with Justice Brennan's. But the parallels between the two political theories should nevertheless now be evident. First, both appeal to abstractions about "public discussion as a public duty" to characterize the political significance of flag burning. Second, both theories are at odds with an alternative and equally reasonable conception of the polity: Justice Brennan's argument that flag burning must be protected in the name of political participation is, to a considerable degree, at odds with the reality of a debased civic culture. And Chief Justice Rehnquist's creed that the flag is a symbol of national unity is, to a considerable degree, at odds with a polity that consistently reveals itself to be strained by competing interests absent any overriding sense of common interests or a public good.

Third, although the two opinions treat freedom of speech in terms of competing consequentialist considerations of sovereignty interests, they bespeak the same conception of a constitutional civic tradition in treating freedom of speech as an issue regarding what government must do to protect and preserve civic morality as the "bulwark of the public safety" (Meiklejohn 1965: 59). Examined apart from the competing abstractions they employ, Brennan's and Rehnquist's political theories and politics are remarkably alike, not different! They elevate sovereignty interests above the other two, and, as the rest of each opinion suggests, they differ only about whether the Court or state legislatures ought to have the authority to safeguard society and morality.

Political dimensions like these are ignored in commentary that focuses so emphatically on abstract political theoretical issues such as differences between liberalism and communitarianism, or doctrinal ones such as differences between Justice Brennan's formalism, which protects flag burning, and Chief Justice Rehnquist's historicism, which does not. Not that attention to such issues is inappropriate. Rather, it is that focusing on them exclusively precludes giving anything like sufficient attention to other political dimensions of the opinions: for example, the way they distort and re-represent the politics they address, and their proprietorship of the idea of what the rule of law and the nation require.

To deepen our appreciation of how a politically more sufficient commentary seeks to recenter neglected politics, let us pursue the point that, in *Johnson,* Justices Brennan and Rehnquist differ on how judicial power ought to be used, or not used, to regulate what counts from their respective points of view as political unity and integration. Here, the focus becomes *sovereignty* interests, specifically in relation to conflict over judicial authority and force in the polity. By interpreting *Johnson* in these terms rather than in the political theory terms of the *Harvard Law Review,* I may be seen as following the path of the new institutionalism, which calls for analysis of opinions in terms of how they reflect judicial perceptions of judicial duty and the norms of institutional practices. But I shall venture far beyond that path to say that no one opinion is superior to the other because both, in grappling with conflicts over sovereignty interests, confront an essential ambiguity about political power embedded in legal precedent.

The Neglected Politics of Sovereignty Interests

The creed of "public discussion as a public duty" and appeals to a national commitment to public debate are an implied statement of one of the most familiar of the law's formalisms: the marketplace of ideas. Both Justice Brennan and Chief Justice Rehnquist depend on it, for it has been central to First Amendment adjudication since Justices Holmes and Brandeis first used it in their articulation of freedom of speech. It received its most elaborate intellectual defense in 1948 by Alexander Meiklejohn (1965), and was rejustified as a central element in First Amendment doctrine by Justice Brennan himself in a *Harvard Law Review* essay (1965).

Thus, over time, the marketplace of ideas has become the formalism for representing the principle that pluralist political competition consists of a "free-flow" in the production, exchange, distribution and consumption of competing ideas. It shapes case law considerations of what I call audience, participant, and sovereignty interests in a number of ways: it requires addressing the ethical principle, borrowed from the economic sphere, that individuals ought to be free to maximize political choices; it requires addressing the political principle that political expression ought to be protected as a means of insuring "self-governing powers" (Brennan 1965: 11–12); and it requires addressing the consequentialist considerations that as long as expression contributes, directly or indirectly, to the processes of self-governance, it should be immune from governmental regulation.

As interpreted here, both Justice Brennan and Chief Justice Rehnquist agree that sovereignty interests—those that maintain the common good and popular rule—are the crucial ones involved in the flag-burning case. Indeed, they agree that individuals ought to be free to maximize political choices and that political expression should be protected as a means of insuring "self-governing powers." What they disagree about is whether flag burning contributes, directly or indirectly, to the processes of self-governance, and they express that disagreement in their characterization of competing conceptions of political choice-making and self-governing powers.

Justice Brennan's consequentialist conception of the marketplace is a process-oriented one: open competition between persons and ideas is the best means toward the end of maximizing political choice-making and political stability. As a consequence, according to this conception, except in extraordinary circumstances the role of the Court is to ensure that the push and pull of political conflict are unimpeded. Flag burning is "symbolic speech" because to understand it as such is the safest means of ensuring that sovereignty interests in "robust" political controversy are protected. Thus the Court, it follows logically enough, must use the First Amendment to oversee federal and state action to protect sovereignty interests.

Chief Justice Rehnquist's conception of the marketplace is an end-state-oriented one. He too holds to the principle that open competition between persons and ideas is the best means toward maximizing the goals of political choice-making and political stability. But the fact that the vast majority of states make criminal the public burning of the flag represents, for Chief Justice Rehnquist, the results of open political competition, and, as an end-state achieved, these laws constitute a condition of political stability. That is to say, First Amendment sovereignty interests in "robust" political controversy have fulfilled themselves in legislative conclusions that flag burning is not "symbolic speech" and there is no basis for using the First Amendment to invalidate the results of First Amendment politics.

What the *Harvard Law Review* picks up on is that Justice Brennan's opinion, as contrasted with Chief Justice Rehnquist's, weighs participant interests in political expression more heavily than audience interests in protecting the flag. But not only is this actually a very small part of the immanent political theory of *Johnson,* the contrast itself may be too simple. It could just as well be said that Rehnquist weighs participant interests as heavily as Brennan does—the difference is that Rehnquist treats participant interests at a different level of generality. That is, he characterizes them in the aggregate as inhering in the sovereignty interests of those citizens of states with legislatures that deemed flag burning a crime, whereas Brennan can be interpreted as characterizing them in terms of sovereignty interests in protecting individual expression.

The point is that, again, *Johnson* ought not to be treated solely as a conflict between liberalism and communitarianism, because it is more to the point to read the immanent political theory of the opinion as a conflict over interpretation of sovereignty interests and the use of the marketplace formalism. Even more important, treatment along the lines suggested here would make it difficult, if not impossible, to succeed in doing what the *Harvard Law Review* seeks to do, which is to persuade readers that *Johnson* can be read as rightly or wrongly decided.

One reason for that difficulty is that the marketplace formalism provides no legal criteria for justifying the claim that one interpretation of sovereignty interests in "public discussion as a public duty"—Justice Brennan's or Chief Justice Rehnquist's—is better than the other. The marketplace formalism only requires that litigators and adjudicators address its ethical and political principles. The other, and perhaps even more basic reason, is that both process and end-state arguments are equally lawful ways of relating those principles. Indeed, they share the same fundamental "intellectual and social form" (White 1990: 79), and there is no apparent legal reason for deeming judicial power rather than legislative power a better fit with the First Amendment and government's role in preserving public discussion.

This last point should call Fish to mind, for this channeling into intellectual and political forms is precisely what Fish predicts of the law (Fish 1994: 168–79). Still, let the positive function of such forms be celebrated. Formalisms do constrain legal reasoning by requiring judges to address a common ground of considerations about interests and ethical and political principles. It is true that they *may* breed solace in the law's power to create unity and integration at the cost of obscuring harsher political facts about the polity, but even then a skeptic is not interested in dismissing such solace out of hand. William Connolly put it best in *Politics and Ambiguity:* the "presumption in favor of the exercise of authority is supported by a background faith that over the long run its common acceptance will maintain and advance social progress and ends we prize the most. When that faith disappears the operation of authority unravels; it gives way to disorder or to other modes of social control or, more likely, to both together" (Connolly 1987: 137). That Justice Brennan's opinion protects political speech and Chief Justice Rehnquist's opinion protects the flag is something to be appreciated. The solace their opinions perpetuate is at least a "noble lie," situating the Court as a symbolic trustee for something other than legislative or judicial politics as usual.

Nevertheless, skepticism requires that solace, however functional, should not be allowed to hide from us the extent to which we are a nation of "resident aliens," separated by our heterogeneity and lacking deep and significant obligations to each other (Levinson 1988: 113, 17). In other words, skepticism requires that commentary should not hide the extent to which Supreme Court formalisms and intellectual jurisprudence can mislead us. Formalism, as critical legal scholars have pointed out again and again, "is a commitment to, and therefore also a belief in the possibility of, a method of legal justification that contrasts with open-ended disputes about the basic terms of social life" (Unger 1986: 2). This commitment and belief are shared by virtually everyone in the interpretive community—litigators, adjudicators, as well as citizens—and it must lead to practical and normative concerns about whether constitutional and legal opinions are rightly decided. But understandable and justifiable as such concerns may be, commentary does not fulfill itself when it proceeds as if affirmative or negative answers to that question tell us enough about whether constitutional and legal opinions are credible renditions of the open-ended disputes of a case.

Commentary unfulfilled is no better evidenced than in the conclusion that, given uncertainties about the effects of a decision regarding the flag's status as a symbol and the degree of honor it should have, the Court was well advised in *Johnson* "not to carve out an exception from ordinary First Amendment principles" (Greenawalt 1990: 45). A more politically sufficient and skeptical conclusion, given the same uncertainties, is that what the Supreme Court did, and what commentary as usual says about it, are beside the point in the face of disputes about the propriety of flag burning, which continue despite attempts by Brennan and Rehnquist, each in his own way, to use judicial power to close them out in a "right decision." Another way of making the same point is to say that agnostic commentary (re)awakens us to think more seriously about the quite ordinary congressional and state legislative and symbolic politics about the U.S. (and Confederate) flag, which the law's formalisms and commentary as usual neglect.

In sum, there is a very important level at which formalism and skeptical commentary must be seen as enemies. The unmerited solace in unity and integration; the multiple ways that answers to the rightly decided question obscure politics; the way also that facets of political power, such as reside in deference to the Court's intervention to shape sovereignty interests, and not just the formalisms themselves, can account for distortions of ideals and practices: concerns about all these separate the two kinds of commentary. This sketch also provides a baseline for understanding how an agnostic confronts the complexity, ambiguity, and inconsistency of constitutional conflicts and treats them as a check against premature judgments about the "right" and "wrong" of things.

The next step is to bring out some of the deeper implications of these concerns by reconsidering the marketplace formalism in relation to issues involving inconsistency and incongruity.[11] Inconsistency and incongruity provide two robust challenges to the belief that legal reasoning can provide determinate answers to the rightly decided question, and thus they arrive at center stage. And, because this discussion is applied and not theoretical, the stage is bare of almost all of the epistemological and all of the metaepistemological trappings that usually accompany an analysis of the indeterminacy of legal language, results, and systems. Their absence—which, I trust, will not be regretted—makes room for me to situate skepticism more precisely, which is to say somewhere beyond legal realism but not quite up to critical legal studies.

PART · II ·

· 4 ·

Formalisms: Facets of Political Power and Neglected Policies

Most teachers and critics regard themselves as legal realists, at least to the extent that they acknowledge that legal and constitutional judgments are not fully explicable in their own terms. They therefore agree that ambiguity in legal rules and principles, and partisanship in advocacy and judgment, are solid evidence that the law's formalisms cannot be put to use *mechanically* to solve legal, political, and social problems and that they cannot determine *single* right answers to those problems. They disagree about the extent to which formalisms do determine the law,[1] however, and about the criteria for determining, in theory and in practice, what constitute better answers among the multiple answers to the rightly decided question.[2] But few realists abandon answers to the rightly decided question altogether.

Because the tenets for politically sufficient commentary require agnostics to abandon rightly decided questions as a search for determinate answers, agnostics are bound more than legal realists are to the question of what to make of the skepticism about determinacy in the law that ambiguity and partisanship breed. In this regard, my inspiration comes from critical legal studies (CLS). I refer, of course, to that law school phenomenon, newly prominent in the seventies, when its advocates came to think of themselves as part of a movement that later evolved into a whole range of left "isms" (socialism, Marxism, feminism, various liberationisms, deconstructionism, even nihilism) and theories about law and social change. Today, notwithstanding significant differences among these isms, all CLS advocates agree that solace in the law's formalisms and in what they imply—falsely—about law and politics is to be attacked as a manifestation of the myth of the rule of law. Liberal legalists, as CLS theorists call advocates of liberal-democratic law, are said to depend on this myth. That is because liberal legalists are seen as committed to the distinction between reasoning about the law's formalisms, which are understood as a system of basically consistent rules and principles yielding rational and coherent doctrines, and the merely partisan, fuzzy, and open-ended disputes of politics. In demolishing this distinction, CLS takes skepticism as far as it can go without rejecting altogether the very idea of legal reasoning.

CLS advocates point to case analyses and doctrinal histories to demonstrate that legal reasoning is replete with logical, conceptual, moral, and political inconsistencies and incongruities. These arise from the incapacity of the law's formalisms to generate principled criteria for reconciling differences between legal and nonlegal claims. In fact, they say, liberal democracy itself, as theory and practice, is fatally flawed by internal contradictions or antinomies, such as those between liberal and communitarian concerns, or freedom and equality, or popular sovereignty and the rule of law, that simply cannot be resolved.

These internal contradictions usually guarantee that the law will be just "an endless and contradictory process of making, refining, reworking, collapsing, and rejecting doctrinal categories and distinctions" (Hutchinson 1989: 4). Likewise, it is said, liberal legalism is incongruous because the social forces of oppression and domination—which CLS associates primarily with racial, class, and gender distinctions—infect the legal process and results so that professed democratic aims and values (e.g., personal freedom, democracy, and egalitarianism) are always undermined. Consequently, neither in form nor in substance does the law separate itself from (degraded) politics or otherwise provide an intelligible conception of social order. Instead, the myth of the rule of law perpetuates false images of the polity, which sustain, through the cultural ethos of legitimacy that extends to the courts and legal reasoning, the oppression and domination of the ruling classes.

Many in the academy have come to learn quite a lot from CLS about skepticism toward law and politics. But there are also teachers and critics who find it uninteresting—just the old leftist wine in new bottles, an epistemological fad that has no practical significance or is too abstract to be useful. And still others dismiss it as misrepresenting liberal theory, or as failing to deliver the evidentiary goods against liberal-democratic law (Holmes 1987; Herzog 1987; Yack 1988; Altman 1990). I do not share in these dismissals.[3] But that is beside the point because, for better or worse, my agnostic skepticism owes a great deal to CLS.

But not everything: I have come to conclude that the similarities and differences between agnostic skepticism and CLS are complicated and subtle. I have learned that similar or even the same conclusions on one issue, such as the indeterminacy of legal formalisms, do not entail similar conclusions on other issues like the rule of law as a myth, the significance of the incongruity of the law's formalisms, or the rightly decided question. Because of the need to clarify these similarities and differences, I have taken the liberty of narrowing CLS to two camps, which I refer to as "radical rejectionism" and "revisionism." This is, naturally, a simplification but not an undue distortion of CLS, and it is justified if it serves to put into relief the range of issues under consideration here. Specifically, this chapter and the two that follow it explain why agnosticism owes a great deal to CLS when it comes to evaluating the inevitable ambiguity, inconsistency, and incongruity that attend law, politics, and policies. But they also explain why agnosticism breaks with CLS when it seeks its judicious check against premature closure in commentary and its appreciation of the unpredictability of politics and policies.

Basic Parameters: Rejectionism, Revisionism, and Agnosticism

Radical rejectionism insists that liberal-democratic law defeats all hope for social change. The law's indeterminacy may appear to offer opportunities for political democracy, social egalitarianism, and economic freedom, but it is so intermixed with flawed theory and inegalitarian practices that it can only obfuscate the severity of societal dysfunction. The slightly less disparaging camp of radical revisionism shares the position that liberal legalism is ultimately fatally flawed. But it holds, significantly, that the law can be used against itself: its inconsistencies and incongruities reveal hidden and previously uncharted opportunities to open up legal and political battles for the kind of democracy, egalitarianism, and freedom that liberal democracy otherwise represses or else eviscerates by piecemeal reform.[4]

Speaking very generally, it is not inaccurate to think of agnostic skepticism as an apostate subset of both rejectionist and revisionist versions of CLS. The latter two have their intellectual roots in legal realism (Kelman 1987), and so does agnosticism. All three arise from a habit of mind that denies a hard and fast line between legal and political reasoning. All share opposition to what I have identified as intellectual jurisprudence, at least as the term refers to deference to courts and the intellectual authority of the law (but CLS does tend to share intellectual jurisprudence's fancy for abstractions and answers to the rightly decided question). All three cast a skeptical eye on what happens when political conflicts are transformed into legal formalisms. All are skeptical about the consistency and congruity of formalist arguments, and all share the view that legitimacy is a function of institutional practices and political culture, rather than of the internal logic of the law.

Despite these similarities, agnostic skepticism differs significantly from both versions of CLS. Neither in principle nor in practice is agnosticism ideologically committed to the destruction or the transformation of liberal-democratic law and politics. That is because an agnostic does not prejudge case law as rightly or wrongly decided, politically or morally. And therefore an agnostic is prepared to accept, case by case, the results of analysis whereby formalisms may be found not to run into all the troubles attributed to them.

An agnostic is also more skeptical than either rejectionists or revisionists of what the consequences may be of trying to do something when the law is found to run into these troubles. Accordingly, at an appropriate point in this chapter I shift from the term "indeterminacy" to the term "underdeterminacy" (see Solum 1987: 473) to signpost two related ideas: that law justifies a multiplicity of results, and that when the goal is to recover neglected politics it is more credible for commentary to cut between conservation and criticism of those results than it is to commit itself to only one or the other of them.

Logic dictates that to cut between conservation and criticism puts agnosticism closer to revisionism than to rejectionism. But even if that dictate is a sound one it obscures more than it clarifies what an agnostic tries to do in commentary. Hence the goal of this and the next chapter is to clarify the virtues of a skeptical habit of mind in undertaking case analysis based on the tenets of political sufficiency. The present chapter prepares the way by picking up again on the marketplace formalism and facets of political power related to two issues: regulations of public broadcasting and the Internet. The primary lesson to be learned from this analysis is not theoretical, and its decisive appeal is to common sense: an agnostic habit of mind fosters a commitment to circumstantial facts and consequentialist considerations,[5] and this makes for a commentary that has to be always skeptical of grand-scale generalizations about the strengths and weaknesses of liberal-democratic law and politics.

In the next chapter, a similar appeal to common sense is the basis for explaining how it is that skepticism about rejectionism does not entail underestimating the significance of the flaws attributed to facets of liberal-democratic power. This explanation provides the wedge into two issues that all constitutional commentary must address: the text of the Constitution and the political structure of the polity. My discussion of these two issues—via the core formalism of sovereignty interests, federalism (the core formalism for understanding those interests), and the cases of *McCulloch v. Maryland* (1819),[6] *National League of Cities v. Usery* (1976),[7] *Garcia v. San Antonio Metropolitan Transit Authority* (1985),[8] *United States v. Lopez* (1995), *Printz v. United States* (1997), and *United States v. Morrison* (2000)[9]—closes out my defense of politically sufficient commentary and agnostic skepticism and opens up the rest of the book to more case studies that explore the uncharted courses of neglected politics.

The Marketplace Formalism Redux: *FCC v. League of Women Voters*

The marketplace formalism is an especially fertile one for pursuing the implications of indeterminacy. It covers some of the most basic public policy issues—the pluses and minuses of governmental intervention and nonintervention, the adequacy of political processes, and the nature and limits of the rights of individuals. Clearly, when such a crucial formalism for conceptions of the public good runs into such troubles as will be described here, it makes sense to ask whether and to what extent the same troubles repeat themselves with other legal formalisms. Because the political implications of this analysis are complicated and not easily summarized, they are best left to unfold over the course of case studies.

Meanwhile, our focus is the marketplace formalism in adjudication. Although we began with *Johnson,* it does not deserve further analysis here. It served well enough as a case study for introducing the tenets of political sufficiency at work in agnostic doctrinal analysis. But the problem with *Johnson* is that, despite the uproar the issue of flag burning continues to produce, its significance is primarily, if not altogether, in the realm of symbolic politics, a politics that raises notoriously abstract issues about freedom and democracy.[10] To get at more material issues, it is useful to have a case that depends as much as *Johnson* on the marketplace formalism but has broader implications for the polity: *FCC v. League of Women Voters* (1984),[11] a major First Amendment case in political communication.

League of Women Voters is about government-sponsored political expression, public broadcasting specifically. Its interest for us lies in the fact that the legal and political issues involved in its litigation and adjudication required the Court to apply typical marketplace considerations to the atypical situation in which the government sponsors political communication. Likewise, ongoing legislative efforts to defund public broadcasting and reconfigure the role of the Federal Communications Commission in the communications industry attest to the long-term significance of the issues of the case. Yet nowhere has conventional constitutional commentary made *League of Women Voters* a thematic centerpiece, even though it is politically more significant than the much discussed *Johnson* for suggesting "how far the Justices are prepared to go in adapting constitutional doctrine . . . to the realities of the modern regulatory state" (Harvard Law Review Association 1984: 205). (Law reviews sometimes can put down potentially politically sufficient tracks.)

The facts of the case are as follows. In 1979, the Pacifica Foundation (owners of various noncommercial broadcasting stations around the country), the League of Women Voters of California, and Congressman Henry Waxman challenged the constitutionality of section 399 of the Public Broadcasting Act of 1967, which prohibited the management of public stations from broadcasting editorials or endorsing candidates for office. Although the Senate filed an amicus brief in defense of section 399, the Carter administration refused to defend the ban, and the suit was dismissed for lack of justiciability. The Reagan administration, however, did choose to defend section 399, and Congress responded by amending section 399 so only public stations that received funds from the Corporation for Public Broadcasting, that is, "public broadcasting stations," were forbidden to broadcast editorials; only the ban on political endorsements was to apply across the board for all public stations.

Justice Brennan, writing for a five-to-four majority, concluded that section 399 violated the First Amendment. Although broadcasting regulations are ordinarily subject to less strict standards of First Amendment review than the "compelling governmental interest" invoked in cases involving other kinds of political expression, the Court found editorial opinions per se weighty enough to sustain the stricter doctrinal test for section 399.

The Court concluded that section 399 failed the stricter test at three levels. At the level of legislative history and purposes, the Court found section 399 superfluous given the range of other provisions of the Broadcasting Act.[12] At the level of social facts, the Court found that section 399 was unnecessary because "the character of public broadcasting suggests that . . . a risk [of its being used for propaganda purposes or becoming a privileged outlet] is speculative at best."[13] The Court put great weight on the localism of public broadcasting: the very number of local stations, and the probability that editorials would be concerned with local matters, were said to make it unlikely that the federal government would see fit to retaliate politically against the whole system on the basis of some local hassle. Moreover, the Court deemed it just as likely that general programming would be as inflammatory as editorials, and that whatever risks were said to be involved in one would also be involved in the other obviously protected expression of views.

And, at the constitutional level, the ban was read as overbroad. The Court argued that editorials preceded by a disclaimer that distinguishes management's opinion from that of funders (including the government) is sufficient to satisfy the purposes of section 399. Ergo, an outright suppression of editorial opinion was determined to be unnecessary, and consequently, to be a content-based restriction on editorial expression.[14] These judgments firmly situated noncommercial public broadcasting editorials alongside commercial ones at the center of a process of mass political communication that is protected expression under the First Amendment.

It is my contention that the same marketplace formalism we saw at work in *Johnson* did indeed shape an inconsistent and incongruous rendition of legislative purposes, social fact considerations, and constitutional conclusions when it came to public broadcasting. To find this effect is not by itself so astonishing. To understand it, however, we must subject it to a politically sufficient analysis, so we turn, again, to the immanent political theory embedded in *League of Women Voters*. Access to this theory, as it relates to audience, participant, and sovereignty interests, comes via a citation to the landmark political communication precedent, *Red Lion Broadcasting Co. v. F.C.C.*[15] This citation is used to warrant the consequentialist conclusion that under specifiable circumstances, the sovereignty interest in an unregulated marketplace of ideas in which "truth" will ultimately prevail outweighs the competing sovereignty interest in protecting against potential abuses of the power and privilege of broadcasters.

The one sovereignty interest outweighs the other because audience interests in having "suitable access to social, political, esthetic, moral and other ideas" need to be protected,[16] first to assure the means of informed "decision-making in a democracy"[17] and second to guard conduits of information against "abuses of power by government officers."[18] The consequence of this line of thinking is that participant interests of broadcasters prevail as a means toward the ends of political communication.

This way of bundling audience and participant interests conforms to the liberal-democratic conviction that political order and stability require that the production, exchange, distribution, and consumption of economic and political goods be insulated from governmental intervention. Accordingly, *League of Women Voters* is to be placed in that group of precedent-based arguments that prohibit prior restraints on news publications,[19] punishing the mere advocacy of seditious political ideas,[20] punishing political expression that is offensive to an audience,[21] and punishing those who burn the flag as an expression of political protest.[22]

Still, there is another way the *Red Lion* citation can be used to warrant consequentialist conclusions about competing sovereignty interests like those at play in *League of Women Voters*. This alternative and contrasting way to bundle interests is located in the *Red Lion* decision itself. There, sovereignty interests in licensing procedures were deemed to outweigh competing sovereignty interests in a marketplace free from governmental interference. In this case the Court allowed such things as broadcast licensee renewal provisions for judging whether stations have served the "public interest" and honored the (now defunct) "fairness doctrine" requiring broadcasters to conduct themselves "as a proxy or fiduciary with obligations to present those views and voices which are representative of [the] community and which otherwise . . . would be banned from the airwaves."[23] As decided, then, *Red Lion* confirmed the consequentialist conclusion, and the liberal-democratic convention, that political order and stability require governmental intervention to rectify distortions in the marketplace and to redress inequalities of power. Both, if not confronted, would violate sovereignty interests in an efficient marketplace for the unimpeded flow of ideas.

Thus, in instances where *Red Lion* is used to justify government intervention, broadcasters are understood not in terms of participant interests but as power holders and brokers who control a scarce resource.[24] The primary reason for this is the fear that they might take undue advantage of the communication processes in ways that conflict with audience interests in political communication. This way of bundling interests shapes arguments about judgments in accordance with precedents that justify government intervention to protect the polity from clear and present dangers of any given political evil,[25] to prohibit the burning of a draft card,[26] to justify the time, place, and manner of restrictions on political speech,[27] and to regulate obscenity.[28]

League of Women Voters is particularly interesting for the fault line it reveals in the marketplace formalism of its precedent. *Red Lion* embeds the ideological ambivalence that liberal democracy always betrays when it comes to deciding whether, in both politics and the economy, the marketplace does, or does not, require governmental intervention. This ambivalence about how to weigh competing sovereignty interests works itself out through arguments about how to bundle audience and participant interests so as to justify conclusions about governmental intervention. This is yet another way in which the marketplace formalism does not, in and of itself, predetermine a legal result, does not provide criteria for rightly deciding which sovereignty interests should prevail, and only sets the parameters of the contest.

There is nothing controversial in what I have just pointed out. Mainstream legal scholars have long realized that *Red Lion* simultaneously endorses intervention and nonintervention, with equally compelling arguments on both sides. Some have gone even further, challenging the marketplace formalism as having a bad fit altogether with the realities of political communication. They worry about the extent to which the "flow" of political ideas is constrained by the unequal distribution of political, economic, and social power. They worry that in a mass society elites manipulate and distort political communication and that the electorate is neither very well informed about politics nor in control of either policy agendas or choices.

Challenges of this sort raise an important question that litigation and adjudication ignore: Can the marketplace formalism fulfill its putative function in the rule of law as a way of warranting conclusions about governmental intervention? They thus also bring into question the solace in messages of unity and integration that First Amendment adjudication is meant to convey. Commentary driven by intellectual jurisprudence can answer that question by drawing on legal and/or political abstractions about pluralism and the adequacy of liberal-democratic theory. But those answers will not be skeptical enough for politically sufficient commentary.

That is because the main, if not sole, function of legal and political abstractions is to justify conventional criticisms of either intervention or nonintervention. These criticisms can be persuasive only if they are steadfastly adhered to as the correct, or at least demonstrably better, ones for answering the rightly decided question. Being steadfast in turn means treating ambiguous, and protean, circumstantial fact considerations as enemies in that they inevitably cast doubt on the consistency and congruence of the criticisms being advanced. But, of course, treating circumstantial fact considerations as enemies is something that is politically insufficient and something which agnosticism cannot abide.

What follows is an attempt to produce more politically sufficient commentary by mixing and merging abstract legal and political analysis with context-specific social fact and/or social-scientific commentary, even anecdotal information if that is more practicable. This kind of commentary transforms the self-evident rhetorical function of abstractions: claims based on abstractions will be found to be persuasive only if their use is compatible with the commitment to distrust categorical answers to troubling questions.

This commitment to politically sufficient commentary is a two-edged sword when it cuts between abstractions that breed solace in criticism and those that breed solace in the conservation of law and politics: it produces a persistently relativistic, or "shifty,"[29] point of view about what law and politics generally, and rights and powers specifically, require. Needless to say, then, skeptics and their audiences have to be broad-minded enough to reconcile themselves to points of view that do not inevitably advance their own policy predilections.

Skepticism, Relativism, and the Marketplace Formalism

The point of departure for this, more relativistic, analysis is Justice Brennan's conclusion in *League of Women Voters* that "the government's interest in ensuring balanced coverage of public issues" is outweighed by the public good that arises from protecting broadcasting as "an independent form of communicative activity."[30] His historical account of public broadcasting, and associated social fact determinations about government intervention,[31] are (it need be shown), an astonishingly selective, and one-sided, justification for bundling sovereignty, audience, and participant interests in opposition to such intervention.

As retold by the Court, the history of public broadcasting is marked by its struggle to withstand life-threatening economic and political constraints.[32] Government funding is designed to rescue public broadcasting on the consequentialist grounds of securing a public interest in "programming excellence and diversity that the commercial sector could or would not produce."[33] Section 399 was part of a package of statutory regulations, and in this context Congress saw it as an intervention designed "to ensure the autonomy of the Corporation and to protect the local stations from governmental interference and control."[34] Nonetheless, in *League of Women Voters* the Court aligns public with commercial broadcasting editorials and those precedents protecting participant and audience interests in producing and consuming news to warrant its conclusion that section 399 fails the "compelling governmental interest" test.[35]

To be sure, to nestle public editorials with commercial ones, and to shield them both from government regulation, accords with the ideological reflex to protect political expression from abuses of governmental power. And the legislative history, social fact considerations, and legal claims that the Court provides are logically, and perhaps rhetorically, sufficient to justify the conclusion that traditional conceptions of journalistic freedom are compromised by congressional legislation. As it does in *Johnson,* this type of conclusion in *League of Women Voters* encourages solace in the belief that principles of unity and integration will be upheld by the Court against partisan political attacks on ostensible First Amendment freedoms.

However, it is almost appallingly easy to show that this solace obscures the actual conditions in which public broadcasting subsists. First and foremost, there is the conjunction between money and governments. Smaller stations tended to rely far more on federal funds than larger stations, with the overall federal contribution ranging from almost 40 percent to as low as 4 percent. But in the aggregate, in 1983, 60 percent of public radio's income came from tax-based sources generally, including federal, state, and local authorities. At the time of *League of Women Voters,* somewhere around three-fifths of public radio stations were owned by government instrumentalities (Lee 1986),[36] so focusing on federal funding alone obscures actual and potential political threats to a system becoming more and more dependent on decreasing tax-based income and audience-sensitive sources of funds (Giovannoni 1995: 16). Indeed, even then, if not to the same degree as today, public broadcasting stations were alive to the need to find alternative ways to finance themselves in the face of the eventual elimination of federal financing.

Then there is the issue of programming. Well before *League of Women Voters,* scholars had documented "numerous examples of federal agency interference in program content [and] pressures on the system from congressional and administrative sources." They had also noted the "widespread apprehension in the system [in the face of] what it perceived to be threats to its survival" (Carnegie Commission 1979: 57, 101). There were questions as well about public broadcasting's responsiveness to local participant interests. While it was true that only about 25 percent of public radio broadcasting was nonlocal, radio's peak listening hours (6:00 to 8:00 A.M. and 4:30 to 6:00 P.M.) were dominated by programming from National Public Radio (Carnegie Commission 1979: 60). And, though the nationalization of programming results in quality programming, it also discourages programming independence, as does the fact that the "best vehicles for fund-raising have been programs that do not threaten the audience's sense of well-being." In other words, the need to appeal to various funders and underwriters "has created little incentive for local public affairs programs, for programs that serve small or less affluent audiences, or for controversial programs that may offend" (Carnegie Commission 1979: 60).

There are experts who agree with Douglass Cater, special assistant to President Johnson during the drafting of the Public Broadcasting Act (1967), that the claim of localism, which the Court perpetuates, "goes directly against the laws of broadcast economics, and has set public broadcasting at war with itself in trying to budget its scarce resources" (Cater 1976: 3). Indeed, a public broadcasting system must struggle to survive at any level of federal funding, and that, along with the "centralization of program decisions," creates the risk that public broadcasting will become "an instrument of the state, and this is surely contrary to the principles of freedom of expression" (Owen 1975: 132).

The linkages that have evolved between public broadcasting and the federal government are of course extremely subtle and complex. Therefore it is not always self-evident what is to be made of the fact that an entity is "an instrument of the state." Consider the way perceptions of public radio have changed over time: When *League of Women Voters* was litigated, the impression was well established, in and outside Congress, that public broadcasting was biased to the left,[37] and that it had sacrificed appeals to mass audiences and minorities to maintain its base of support with its elite audience—that is, predominantly male, white, educated, and affluent baby boomers. Now, nearly two decades later, in the wake of budget freezes and then cuts by succeeding administrations, and threats by Congress to oversee it for its political content, public broadcasting provides opportunities for prominent conservative voices to be heard. And, although local stations rarely air editorials per se (Kleiman 1987),[38] National Public Radio/Public Radio International does continue to produce controversial stories about issues that commercial broadcasting systematically avoids. Supporters of public broadcasting persuasively interpret this evolution as evidence of public broadcasting's having become "the equivalent of Andrew Carnegie's public libraries."[39] Detractors, just as persuasively, interpret it as evidence that public broadcasting has always been, as politicians like to put it, an upper-middle-class entitlement program that sustains, if not liberal elitist views, then its tastes.

Now, from a consequentialist perspective it may not be altogether a bad thing that public broadcasting is to be seen as "an instrument of the state"—

as both a public library and an upper-middle-class entitlement program. But there was no reason when *League of Women Voters* was being litigated, nor is there much now, to suspect that elite producers of public broadcasting are any more inclined than commercial broadcasters to alienate their audience. The point is that public-sponsored communication for an elite hardly fits with the marketplace ideal of public broadcasting for "the people." So even if the uncertain view is a good thing, that surely does nothing to close the gap between a characterization of public broadcasting as a process of public education and the reality of a communication practice that may do no more than manipulate or reinforce existing elite opinions. In short, protecting public broadcasting editorials may mean no more than protecting government-sponsored political speech for those who benefit from the unequal distribution of resources in society.

And, if this is the case, if the marketplace formalism can lend itself so easily to an image of political communication that simply does not square with readily known political and economic facts, it can just as easily be said that section 399 was not a violation of the First Amendment but a prudent way of protecting a fragile system. From this it is but a step to the conclusion that public broadcasting editorials are quite unlike commercial broadcasting ones, and, despite the Court's professed confidence in the localism of public broadcasting, or things like broadcast disclaimers, an interventionist interpretation of *Red Lion* is warranted.

There are good reasons then to bundle interests in support of legal claims about public broadcasting as an instrument of social control (Hurst 1982), in which case sovereignty interests justify government intervention. But there are equally good reasons to conclude that public broadcasting actually is part of a marketplace of ideas wherein intervention undermines sovereignty and audience interests in a free flow of ideas. This collision of perspectives provides ample circumstantial reasons to be skeptical about how well the marketplace formalism in *League of Women Voters* clarifies the politics it is supposed to be about.

And if the marketplace formalism is of no great help in determining whether government intervention is justified, then there is reason to doubt that it can help with the rightly decided question, or that it can warrant the solace it provides to First Amendment advocates about unity and integration in the polity. At worse, as applied in *League of Women Voters,* the formalism perpetuates an image of political communication that merely serves the ideological and practical interests of left-liberal elites and their clients. At best—as public broadcasting scrambles for funds from this or that quarter—

the formalism only leaves us with inconclusive empirical lessons when we use it to make sense of political communication in the modern regulatory state.

A Radical Revisionist Interpretation of the Marketplace Formalism

The skepticism about the marketplace formalism first identified in the discussion of *Johnson* and seen to go even deeper in *League of Women Voters* is to be set off from the treatment the formalism has received from mainstream legal scholarship. There, inconsistency in the application of noninterventionist and interventionist images of a free flow of ideas, as well as their lack of fit with actual conditions and relationships, has been commented upon often enough to invite any number of recommendations. Among these, notably, are suggestions that litigation and adjudication using the marketplace formalism ought to depend more on social-scientific claims to offset its indeterminacy; or that litigation and adjudication ought to depend on alternative images of politics and political communication drawn from philosophical conceptions of autonomy, or self-dignity, or community, or republican politics.

These are reasonable theoretical recommendations. But—quite apart from a skeptic's reluctance to make recommendations to lawyers and judges about how to reformulate formalisms—given the analysis we have just gone through, they cannot help but be regarded as premature, even superficial. They are to one degree or another insufficiently attentive to more politically significant nuances and implications of the inconsistency and incongruity of the law's formalisms. And, in fact, to get to these more nuanced implications, we need to delve ever more deeply into a radical revisionist take on the marketplace formalism as it might be understood to apply to issues of political communication, freedom, and democracy.

The version of radical revisionism that suits the purposes of this comparison is that of Roberto Unger, arguably CLS's most accomplished philosopher. His earliest legal and political works, *Knowledge and Politics* (1975) and *Law in Modern Society* (1976), provided CLS with one of its first full-blown philosophical attacks on what he saw as the antinomies of liberal political theory. In what might be called the second stage, *The Critical Legal Studies Movement* (1986), Unger refined that attack by directing it specifically against liberal-legal reasoning. The third stage, for my purposes, is represented by *Unger's Politics: A Work in Constructive Social Theory* (1987–88), and *What Should Legal Analysis Become?* (1996) that go beyond critique to map out how liberal legalism, turned against itself, can provide for social and political change. The analysis that follows depends primarily on materials from the second and third stages (and not at all on Unger's latest writings).[40] Even then it is highly selective, with an emphasis on those aspects of Unger's work that I have found to bear directly on how his "revisionism" and skepticism's relativism differ over what to make of the indeterminacy of political formalisms.

When Unger reads liberal-democratic case law, he finds it to be both constituted and justified by two commitments. The first is formalism, by which Unger means the belief that there is a distinguishable difference between the rationality and objectivity of the materials of the rule of law and the open-ended and merely partisan disputes of politics which it ostensibly pushes aside. (This conception of formalism resonates with my use of the concept and the earlier discussion of the law's efficacy.) The second is objectivism, the commitment to the idea that precedents and statutes, and doctrinal abstractions such as rights, freedom of contract, due process, equal protection, the speech/conduct distinction, and the marketplace, "embody or sustain [a] defensible scheme of human association" (Unger 1986: 2). (Formalism and objectivism are deeply intertwined, and to reduce unhelpful complications I do not follow Unger by distinguishing between them but treat them as coincidental: consequently, hereafter, when I refer to formalism, I invoke the commitment to objectivism as well.)

Unger argues (and I concur) that the marketplace formalism ought to be understood not only as one of the most important liberal-legalist formalisms (among them representative government, separation of powers, and federalism), but as a prototype for the functioning of liberal-legal formalisms generally (Unger 1986: 5–6). Like them, but even more so, the marketplace formalism, he says, blinds its devotees to the fact that it cannot provide principled arguments for reconciling its competing and contradictory commitments to liberal-democratic ideals and practices about governmental intervention and nonintervention. Because there is no distinction between law and politics, and because legal reasoning cannot rest on objective and principled arguments, Unger refers to that portion of liberal-democratic law shaped by the marketplace formalism as mere "hocus-pocus" (Unger 1986: 13).

It is this "hocus-pocus," Unger says, that gives liberal legalism much of its intellectual authority: the myth of the rule of law makes it appear that adjudication bespeaks high ideals for the polity. But, again and again, he says, CLS case analysis reveals that the marketplace formalism (like the others) lends itself to arbitrary factual and normative premises, social fact characterizations and determinations, and legal conclusions that favor the interests of those who control and/or benefit from the unequal distribution of political and economic power. What is more, the law's formalisms distort and render hollow potentially positive elements of liberal-democracy such as commitments to personal freedom, democracy, and egalitarianism.

A revisionist would say that liberal legalisms are "radically indeterminate:" they permit any number of ways of arranging arguments about facts, interests, the role of government, and constitutional law (Unger 1986: 67). Yet the commitment to the marketplace formalism—and by implication all the other formalisms—is so strong, says Unger, that despite obvious "conflicts between the available ideals of social life . . . and their flawed actualizations in present society" (Unger 1986: 18), the "hocus-pocus" of the law prevails in legal reasoning. Moreover, as he sees it, mainstream legal commentary is incapable of coming to grips with this indeterminacy, or with the impossibility of predicting when formalist ideals will be used to correct for actual conditions, or when current conditions will be used to benchmark what counts as the realization of those ideals.

To make matters even worse (from Unger's point of view), liberal-legal ideology relentlessly represents this indeterminacy as a virtue of the adaptive capacities of law rather than as a fatal flaw. And it is true that some, for example, might argue, along with Fish, that indeterminacy is evidence that the law has the capacity to grow with changing conditions (Fish 1994: 155); and, going even further than Fish, that it does not serve only singular interests. But a revisionist would dismiss these apologies: given the forces of capitalism, sexism, and racism, and the interests of various elites in maintaining power, the law can only be an instrument of those who command or benefit from those forces and interests. Revisionists are unrelenting about this: the indeterminacy of the law, and the efficaciousness of the law's formalisms, drive just enough political change to forestall severe conflict and to maintain existing patterns of hierarchy.

Unger's relentless skepticism about the marketplace formalism runs so deep that he discredits the usefulness of any academic left-radical debate about the extent to which the law is indeterminate. He views that debate as a diversion from the intellectual work that needs to be done to lay cornerstones for genuine democracy and institutional change. The debate over the relative or extreme indeterminacy of the law cannot provide those cornerstones, according to Unger, because it only succeeds in demonstrating the finesse by which those engaged in the debate can manipulate formalisms for their social and cultural criticisms (Unger 1996: 45, 119–22). Such intellectual finesse, he complains, does not really take the law seriously as a form of power because it only recapitulates liberal legalism's idea that the law is a kind of language game of justifications.

From this CLS perspective, it is no surprise then that there are readily available political and economic facts to justify both an interventionist and noninterventionist reading of the *Red Lion* precedent for *League of Women Voters;* the situation is simply compelling evidence of a failed liberal legalism and radicalism that cannot provide principled criteria for deciding between legal claims that actually further extend democracy in the polity. As for the shifty, or even worse, distorted, images of political communication and politics that the marketplace formalism provides: these are examples of a vicious rhetoric that refers to ideals of citizenship and informed democratic decision-making but in practice protects the interests of the powerful. In sum, *League of Women Voters* is, from the perspective of radical revisionism, a prime illustration of how belief in the marketplace formalism encourages the treatment of public broadcasting as a process of civic education through which political "truth will prevail" and situates the issue of government intervention as crucial when in practice all that is involved is just another way of organizing elite belief systems and political agendas (Yudolf 1983).

Yet Unger's radical revisionism is optimistic. It encourages revisionist critics of liberal law to put the law's distortions to good use as part of a political strategy he calls "expanded doctrine" (Unger 1986: 4). Although not all radical revisionists would embrace Unger's philosophical defense of expanded doctrine, they would agree with its aim of exposing formalist inconsistencies and incongruities, tearing them open, as it were, to show how hollow formalist promises really are. Having embraced this goal, revisionists are free to follow their preferred philosophical "isms," to interpret in their terms existing ideals and practices in order to "reveal deeper individual and collective identities, and liberate productive and creative powers" (Unger 1986: 23). By such means, radical revisionism fulfills its goal to push liberal-democratic promises about state and society, and pluralist political conflict, to the point where those promises reach beyond themselves to merge into larger, (always) left-radical ambitions in the struggle over power and rights (Unger 1986: 4; Unger 1987: 454–80).

Unger recommends that expanded doctrine should develop into what he wittily, and perhaps too innocently, calls "superliberalism." Superliberalism seeks to transform liberal democracy into something freer, more egalitarian, and more democratic than it has been, by instigating "perpetual conflicts and deals among more or less transitory and fragmentary groups" (Unger 1986: 41–42). As it turns out, most revisionists share, however they may differ in regard to details, the short-term goals of superliberalism: to reorganize the economy, to break the hold of welfare capitalism, to build a system of rights which is not property-based and does not inhibit the government from getting at the causes of social division and hierarchy, and to establish the accountability of political parties and processes (Unger 1986: 53; Unger 1987: 441–539). But only those revisionists who are enthusiasts of postmodernism share the purported long-term goal of superliberalism: to guarantee that there is no single conception of law or politics that is held to be necessary, historically or naturally. These postmodernist enthusiasts believe that people will learn to challenge connections between theory and practice so as to be always prepared to undo the social world they construct (Unger 1986: 19, 26, 40–41, 60, 108–9; Unger 1987: 356–64).

Apparently, taking Thomas Jefferson's recommendation for occasional revolution to a postmodern boiling point, revisionism like this seeks a law and politics capable of persuading one and all "that no one scheme of association has conclusive authority" (Unger 1986: 19). This ambitious revisionist politics has its enemies: the conventional ways and agents of analyzing political and legal reform in the polity (e.g., litigators, adjudicators, teachers, and critics). Unger claims that conventional analysis is an enemy because it locks imaginativeness about reform into dominant formalisms, like those about the marketplace, the welfare state, representative politics, and political participation. Formalisms like these purportedly constrain conceptions of social change to a range of possibilities limited by the criteria inherent to what is "actually" practicable in law and politics (Unger 1996: 51). The "actual" then is the enemy of "true" social democracy, freedom, the mobilization of citizens, and equality because the "actual" truncates the possible implications of these ideas for "genuine" self-determination and social change (Unger 1996: 140).

Judges and scholars are no less the enemy for Unger (as they were for Tushnet). They are the enemy because they constitute an elite, and therefore they are the agents of antidemocratic thought, politics, and law. To Unger, the law's formalisms and elite politics reinforce each other to perpetuate a "conservative reformism" (Unger 1996: 51, 80) that pits the ideal against the "actual." Judges and scholars also perpetuate a "progressive pessimistic reformism" that rationalizes away arguments for authentic social change in a corrosive shower of arguments about why the unintended consequences of reform will make things worse rather than better. In sum, conventional law, courts, and scholarship are an enemy of the "ideal" because they are the political instruments that maintain the form, content, and pace of truncated social change.

The (only) friend, Unger contends, that a politics of the ideals of expanded doctrine, superliberalism, and open-ended thinking about associations and institutions could have is the citizenry (Unger 1996: 113). Evidently, citizens, and judges and scholars who attend them as (mere) technicians for citizens, would have to engage in a form of thinking that Unger thinks about as "the mutual correction of abstract ideals and their institutional realizations" (Unger 1986: 19; Unger 1987: 454–80). Unger's writing about what this thinking would be like has always been rather abstruse, and the best that I can make of it is as follows.

Citizens would give free reign to progressive ideological ideals by engaging in something that Unger calls "purposive analogical reasoning" (Unger 1996: 114). This kind of reasoning would release the imagination to experiment with abstract ideas about progressive ideals. Unger does not have much to say about how citizens would go about this kind of reasoning, but he does characterize what he has in mind for judges. They would engage in an eclectic, even inchoate, rumination about a mix of things like political conflict, public opinion, everyday life experiences, legal doctrines, and public policies. The purpose of this kind of judicial experimentation would be to lay the groundwork for a legal analysis of the similarities, inconsistencies, and incongruities between progressive ideals and actual legal doctrines (Unger 1996: 78, 113–14, 133).

Unger intends for this kind of judicial thinking to be arbitrary from the perspective of conventional adjudication. Its virtue is that it would render conventional techniques of legal analysis anomalous and elevate transformative ideals as the primary source of legal and political possibilities. Then legal and political doctrines could expand to fulfill their potential to encompass ideals, democratic innovations in institutional arrangements, and their forms of collective political participation. Any other kind of thinking, says Unger, capitulates to hierarchy and domination.

Indeterminacy Should Be Understood as Underdeterminacy

Now we come to the crux of the matter: given all the inadequacies of the marketplace formalism analyzed in *League of Women Voters,* and the obvious similarities between that analysis and a radical revisionist treatment of those inadequacies, what can possibly account for my reluctance to characterize the marketplace formalism as fatally flawed? The basic answer is, by now, apparent: any blanket conclusion is politically insufficient because it represents an unjustifiable confidence that judgments are rightly decided. Therefore the blanket conclusion that indeterminacy, and the obfuscations, contradictions, inconsistency, and incongruity associated with it, entail the bankruptcy of liberal-democratic law is politically insufficient.

The first, and most mundane, thing to be said in defense of this answer is that there are—liberal-democratic ideology aside—commonsensical, yet quite robust, facts about choice-making that help explain indeterminacy. Judges judge, Stanley Fish rightly reminds us, by coming down on one side or another of a legal question (1994). Judging inevitably means that judges have to embed in their justifications selective normative and social fact considerations that will appear to be, from the opposing side, at least arguable if not ambiguous, equivocal, or just downright false. CLS revisionists write about this as if it were impossible to believe what litigators and adjudicators are well enough aware of: that indeterminacy is attributable, to some significant degree, to the use of abstract concepts to integrate that complex bundle of context-specific and circumstantial factors that go into relating principles to practice generally. By necessity the use of these concepts is colored by a person's own biases and values, policy considerations, the prevailing standards of legal exposition and narration, historical sensibilities, attitudes toward the role of precedent and courts, and innumerable other factors that make judging difficult (Strauber 1987: 522–28). It is difficult to imagine the situation otherwise, and therefore difficult to imagine why liberal-democratic law should be considered any more or less indeterminate than any other kind of law that depends upon abstractions, including law under the direction of expanded doctrine and superliberalism.

Second, it seems always prudent, Unger's revisionism notwithstanding, to inquire to what extent indeterminacy may be a matter of degree. Then it falls to case law commentary to determine whether indeterminacy might be attributed to a lack of judicial craft, specific styles of case law litigation and adjudication (which exhibit more or less indeterminacy), intellectual styles associated with the recruitment and socialization of judges, bargaining and negotiation between judges or Justices, or nothing more profound than rank partisanship. It is simply an ideological reflex to presume, in all cases, that the problems of formalism are fatal flaws intrinsic to liberal-democratic ideology and law rather than attributable to these other dimensions of legal and political reasoning in general.

Finally, the concept of formalism's "fatal flaw" may miss the mark altogether. Consider an alternative to a CLS interpretation of the indeterminacy of the *Red Lion* precedent: that indeterminacy efficaciously acts as a constraint on the power of litigators and adjudicators. Because *Red Lion* and the marketplace formalism *require* legal arguments about audience, participant, and sovereignty interests, they guarantee fixed points of discursive contact (or a common battle ground) between competing arguments about freedom of speech and political power and policies. These arguments about interests provide all parties, including advocates of CLS, a shared basis for evaluating the significance of legal claims in terms of commentators' concerns about the uses and abuses of political power. Not to put too fine a point on it, unless one is prepared to reject completely the role of marketplace formalism as a check on the uses of power in a democracy, these fixed points of contact are in turn efficacious criteria for legal claims.

This is not to deny that formalisms are prone to inconsistencies and incongruities, or that their efficaciousness makes for arguments that are resistant to the realization or revision of liberal-democratic values, or that they eclipse competing images for understanding law and politics, or that they fail to provide determinate answers to the rightly decided question. Rather, it is to suggest that we stop thinking about indeterminacy only within the framework of fatal flaws. It is to suggest that we begin to evaluate how formalisms function not only by acknowledging the apologies they allow for the status quo distribution of benefits and harms in the polity, but also by examining their political *virtues*—for example as boundaries and constraints on the ever present abuses of intellectual and political power.

In CLS boundaries and constraints are almost (or so it seems) inevitably associated with what they obscure or repress, and the rejection of them is deemed a virtue and rarely a vice. But at least one important consideration for weighing the political *virtue* of boundaries and constraints is that marketplace indeterminacy forces us, in politically sufficient commentary, to focus on sovereignty interests and the effect—good or bad—of government intervention on the public welfare. It thereby also forces us to confront a very important fact: there are *always* costs and benefits to the polity, regardless of the winners and losers in adjudication. These costs and benefits are determined by means that are more practical and prudentially arrived at than would be the case with a CLS revisionist politics of perpetual conflict and destruction of fixed structures. What is more, yesterday's legal and political winners may be today's losers and just as subject as yesterday's losers to the command, control, and (sometimes) violence of law, politics, and governmental policies.

It is within the context of such relatively unpredictable considerations that agnostic skepticism, still mindful of legal formalism's potential to obscure politics and perpetuate the interests of those in power, references "underdeterminacy" rather than indeterminacy of the law's formalisms. "Underdeterminacy" refers to the law's efficaciousness in shaping an "outcome [that] must be chosen on grounds other than the law itself—for example, on grounds of policy, principle, or even personal preference—from a range of possible results that [may or may not be] consistent with and limited by the law (Solum 1987: 473).[41] By using the one term in preference to the other I mean to draw attention to a central point: the substantive difference between (on the one hand) making blanket assessments of (a) the political implications of the law's formalisms, (b) the "myth" of the rule of law, (c) political or moral principles, (d) social facts, and (e) facets of political power, and (on the other hand) looking to specific case studies to assess the virtues and vices of the range of formalism's plausible, often variable, implications. I repeat this point about virtues and vices, which I have made (and will continue to make) in a number of different ways, primarily because of the tendency in commentary, whether informed by revisionism, rejectionism, or intellectual jurisprudence in general, to make blanket assessments as if the burden of proof were always on the other party. As I hope is clear, I try my best to avoid such assessments in this book.

The habit of mind I am recommending does not preclude attempts to expose hocus-pocus in the law. Nor does it preclude endorsements, in a given situation, of some aspect of expanded doctrine or superliberalism, or any other partisanship, as long as those endorsements are made skeptically. Rather, it alerts commentators to the political insufficiency that results when, under the influence of doctrine, they presume what requires to be demonstrated—when, that is, they tear open underdeterminate reasoning knowing in advance that solace in messages of unity and integration is always unmerited. It thus reminds them to be as nonideological, nondoctrinaire, and pragmatic as possible when thinking about relations between law and politics. Naturally, agnostic skepticism will disappoint those who are committed, as all revisionists are, to a predetermined agenda of change. But my ultimate justification for this skepticism is that it is prudent to maintain some confidence in fixed social images of conservation, whether they issue from the left or the right, without which there is no bulwark against social disorder and potentially authoritarian appeals for social control. Here, skepticism underscores the point that being able to embrace colliding political perspectives is essential to achieving more nuanced understandings of the difficulties arising from legal and political abstractions.

If some more nuanced defense for this position is insisted upon, I enlist the support of those, even in CLS, who would argue for the possibility "that the existence of the particular pattern of contradictions in theory and practice is itself functional, either in the traditional sense, responsive to social needs or particular interests, or, in a more critical sense, constitutive of the sort of society we live in" (Kelman 1987: 260). In other words, to some extent inconsistency and incongruity may be both a matter of practical necessity and an intrinsic, irremediable, characteristic of (at least) our political culture. This was the point I was trying to make when I recommended that we evaluate the problems arising from the use of the marketplace formalism in *League of Women Voters* by taking into account factors such as resource and demand constraints, elite control of communication and political agendas, and technology and bureaucracy constraints, which are forces at work in all polities, not just liberal-democratic ones.

There have been some even in CLS (Trubek 1984) who point up the need to integrate circumstantial empirical evidence relating to these factors into legal analysis, but there is precious little of it in either traditional or radical scholarship (Griffin 1989). Unger's objections to what he calls "conservative reformism" and "progressive pessimistic reformism" (as discussed above) are indicators of why revisionist legal analysis avoids such evidence. If such evidence gives rise too readily to argumentative iterations about the practicality and effects of progressive ideals that serve only to undermine those ideals then, naturally enough, such evidence will be absent in radical legal analysis.

But a commitment to politically sufficient commentary requires such evidence to evaluate the underdeterminacy of legal formalisms; moreover, the task of politically sufficient commentary is not the preservation of (progressive) ideals. Therefore in these respects—even though agnosticism and Unger's revisionism are, at one level, one and the same in being at odds with intellectual jurisprudence and in seeking to recover politics neglected by it and the legal formalisms—agnosticism and revisionism are far apart. In point of fact, agnosticism is prepared to pit the "ideal" against the "actual," and to consider the unintended consequences of policies in order to have politically sufficient commentary—as revisionism is not.

To help us understand why that is so, in the next chapter we pick up where we left off with the case study of *League of Women Voters*. There I began to define the virtues and vices of the underdeterminacy of legal formalisms by means of two circumstantial fact-based investigations. One focused on the role of money and politics in public broadcasting in order to suggest the extent to which the marketplace formalism may obscure the role of resource and demand constraints and the distribution of power in mass communications. The other focused on the extent to which the marketplace formalism does help shape and limit commentary about competing concerns over bureaucratic intervention—as we understand it in this instance in relation to public broadcasting. The central point, that facets of political power and not just the formalisms themselves may account for distortions of ideals and practices, is important enough to warrant a bit more elaboration. In the next chapter we will consider in this regard (and as an indicator of other problems) the initial controversy over sexually explicit materials on the Internet.[42] This case study serves two purposes: it provides material for fleshing out what politically sufficient commentary about underdeterminacy can be in regard to unjustifiable confidence in judgments being rightly decided, and it further clarifies differences and similarities between such commentary and CLS revisionism in regard to the unpredictability of law and politics.

· 5 ·

The Internet: Distorted Ideals and Practices

In June 1995, the Senate, prompted by electoral politics, user complaints (especially by parents), a highly controversial study of computer users at Carnegie Mellon University, and mass media exposure, set out to regulate sexually explicit communications (i.e., written materials and images) available on the public Web sites and private bulletin boards of the Internet. The House initially resisted regulation, but ultimately the outcome was a major legislative attack on these materials via the Communications Decency Act (CDA), which was attached to the Telecommunications Act of 1996 (a deregulation bill for the broadcasting, cable, and telephone telecommunications industries). The CDA amended title 47 of the U.S. Code to permit heavy fines (as much as $250,000) and prison terms (of up to two years) for anyone who uses a telecommunications device in interstate or foreign communications to knowingly distribute "obscene or indecent messages to anyone under eighteen years of age or sends or displays patently offensive messages in a manner available to anyone under eighteen years of age."

The CDA was framed as an extension of existing regulations having to do with telephone harassment and commercial enterprises such as dial-a-porn. So, just as a telephone company is not liable for illegal activities that are without its knowledge transacted on its lines, the CDA exempted from its antismut regulations those operators who provide "mere" access to the Internet and shielded from prosecution those who make a good faith effort to protect minors from exposure to regulated materials. Here the act borrowed from FCC regulations of television and radio broadcasting prohibiting "indecent" materials and sexually explicit images and words from being transmitted during times of the day when minors may be watching or listening.[1] Meanwhile, a significant number of states were framing regulatory measures of their own in an attempt to insinuate local politics and legal standards into the controversy. These measures focused primarily on restricting the distribution of obscene materials, materials deemed indecent or "harmful" to or exploitive of children, and lewd electronic mail.[2] In response to all this regulatory fervor, commentary opposed to the CDA in particular, and to regulation of the "information highway" in general, abounded in the mass media, scholarly journals, and, naturally, on the Internet.

It was readily apparent and widely commented upon that the CDA was troubled on traditional First Amendment grounds. Primarily, the act ran up against the doctrinal distinction between obscene and indecent materials. *Obscene* materials *are not* protected by the First Amendment. These comprise sexual materials that a jury, applying the standards of both an average person and the community, deems to appeal to prurient interests, to depict or to describe sexual conduct in a patently offensive way (as specified by state law), and to lack, as a whole, serious literary, artistic, political or scientific value.[3] *Indecent* materials *are* generally protected by the First Amendment, but the broadcast of patently offensive materials—descriptions of sexual or excretory activities and organs[4]—may be regulated to protect the privacy of individuals and to make such materials unavailable to minors. It is generally recognized by lawyers and scholars that the legal character of both obscenity and indecency is vague, as is the distinction between them.

The CDA, by meshing language about indecent and patently offensive materials with language about community standards, ran into all this doctrinal vagueness in at least three significant ways: (1) it appeared to be unconstitutionally broad and intrusive by sweeping into its net traditionally protected (indecent and even harassing) communications along with those obscene ones that may be vulnerable to regulation; (2) it appeared, in the process of attempting to restrict indecent communications with persons under eighteen, to infringe on protected communications between consenting adults; and (3) its provision for sexually explicit materials raised the question whether communications that are protected in some venues, such as letters, are unprotected in venues like electronic mail and public or private electronic bulletin boards.

The ACLU, the lead plaintiff, along with a wide range of other interested groups, challenged the portions of the act that made it a crime to knowingly transmit indecent communications and to send or display communications that are patently offensive, as measured by community standards, to any one under eighteen. The District Court for Eastern Pennsylvania ruled the act unconstitutional on its face. It found that the provisions shielding providers from prosecution were either economically or technologically impracticable, and it judged the act's indecency provisions as overly broad and unconstitutionally vague under the First and Fifth Amendments. Ultimately, in *Reno v. American Civil Liberties Union* (1997),[5] Justice Stevens, deciding the case solely on the First Amendment issue, confirmed that the CDA was an unconstitutionally vague and content-based restriction on free speech.

Quite apart from the details of this ruling, what is to the point in *Reno* is the difficulty—and the difficulty was, to some degree, apparent early in the controversy—of relating the law's formalisms and their conjunction with facets of political power to the problem of sexually explicit materials on the Internet. Not surprisingly, these difficulties were not addressed by the government in defense of the CDA, as its defense revolved around precedents about radio broadcasts of indecent speech.[6] Nor did the ACLU brief address these difficulties: its challenge to the CDA was based on traditional First Amendment telephone doctrine requiring strict scrutiny of regulations,[7] although it did present, as findings of fact, the creation of the Internet and the nature of Internet and World Wide Web access and communication. What this chapter will argue is that these findings together with other more significant ones cast a dark shadow of doubt over all the First Amendment formalisms contending here because none of them is sufficient to encompass the range of circumstantial fact relating to crucial sovereignty interests in communication on the Internet.

For a start, there are salient incongruities between the traditional legal frames of reference of telephone, radio, and television for regulating communications and a cluster of political, social, and technological conditions and relationships associated with Internet telecommunications. During oral argument, Justice Scalia briefly touched on an implication of these incongruities when he asked whether technological change was not so "enormously rapid" that it was possible for a statute like the CDA to be unconstitutional when framed, or when adjudicated, but yet to be constitutional the following week, or year, or two years. For an agnostic, a question like Justice Scalia's cannot be answered without considering four conditions and relationships: (1) the interactive capacity of the Internet—in particular, opportunities for users to structure the form and content of communications—simultaneously integrates and goes beyond elements of telephone, radio and television communications; (2) Internet interactions (e.g., email, public/private bulletin boards) blur the public/private distinction in communications because of the openness of file transfers; (3) the capacity for users to be simultaneously publishers of materials makes it unclear who controls the Internet; and (4) the Internet comprises a global, not national, telecommunications phenomenon driven by complex multinational technological and commercial influences.

Despite these incongruities between traditional legal frames and the Internet, these four conditions and relationships can be related to the telephone, radio, and television frames of reference in at least two different ways. Each of these leads to opposite conclusions about whether the government should intervene in Internet communications. One way is to interpret the interactive capacity of the Internet—its blurring of the public and private distinction, the dynamics of user capacities, and the international technological and commercial influence—within the context of a political theory of anarchistic social and technological change. Here, most especially, the perceived threat is that absent political intervention, commercial competition and technological changes in computer software and hardware will shape the future in socially undesirable ways. From this perspective, sovereignty interests in regulation appear to be a reasonable response if future communication needs and social relations are to be determined by the polity rather than by technological, commercial, and international interests.

Justifications for governmental intervention place great weight on the fact that the Internet is a product of the government. The basic internal structure of the Internet was designed by the Department of the Defense in the late 1960s and the National Science Foundation in the late 1980s. Once opened to the public, it was intended to provide users with a legal high-speed path to communicate with each other. Arguably, the Internet, like the radio, telephone, and television before it, could be considered a common carrier of traffic—a public resource held in trust by its users—which the government has a compelling interest to regulate. Such regulations might require the least restrictive federal and state means to accomplish compelling governmental interests. For example, on-line providers could be treated as publishers with editorial responsibility and liability for illegal activities (e.g., *Stratton Oakmont Inc. v. Prodigy Services Co.*)[8] in order to forestall transactions (like those proscribed by the CDA) that are at odds with the public safety, welfare, and morality.

A second way to correlate these four conditions and relationships with traditional legal frames is to consider them in the context of a practical political theory of community building. Here the Internet's "cyberspace" transactions are theorized as present and future opportunities to generate electronic communities born free and independent of any architectonic political and/or economic authority. These transactions, interpreted as triumphs of voluntarism, flow from users' choices about where to go and what to do when they get there.[9] Interference in these users' choices, themselves an architectonic of sorts, thus may be perceived to promote sovereignty interests that encourage citizen autonomy and protect processes whereby that autonomy is realized.

Theorizing the problem in this second way warrants the conventional First Amendment conclusion that federal and state governments lack a compelling governmental interest in regulating materials on the Internet. Even apart from this concern, such an approach triggers hard questions about whether state-by-state regulations will produce First Amendment violations when materials legal in one state turn out to be illegal in another (Salbu 1998).

It follows from this second way of theorizing the Internet that it is neither legal nor technically feasible to regulate it. On-line information service providers should be treated as carriers of information like telephone companies and, like them, not be held liable for illegal activities unless they have been or should have been aware of them (e.g., *Cubby Inc. v. CompuServe Inc*).[10] And whatever control there is to be should come from voluntary content-rating fields that allow users to know the nature and content of materials (and warn them that materials may be deemed "obscene" or "pornographic" by the standards of their community); or software lock-out mechanisms that permit parents to restrict access to specific sites and materials; or validation systems that require proof of age and subscriptions to access sexually suggestive materials.

Conventional wisdom favors addressing the Internet in terms of community building. But even some First Amendment advocates have been quick to admit that the novel nature of the Internet makes the rightly decided call much closer than they would like. Unfortunately, this admission is not enough: it takes a little more effort to see why legal judgments drawn from both anarchy and freedom-community building theories suffer from incongruity precisely because they close out the underdeterminacy surrounding regulating novel technologies. The history of technology is instructive here, and that of the social changes associated with the telegraph, telephone, wireless and broadcast radio, television, and microwave is especially complex. But a few generalizations can be stated with some degree of confidence: Telecommunications technologies are never socially and politically neutral. More often than not new technologies and their sociological implications are not understood until after they have been in use for a considerable period of time. It is rarely certain whether, and how, telecommunications technologies are under control, scientifically, politically, economically, and socially. It is rarely self-evident, until after the fact, whether the problems new technologies create are self-correcting or require some mode of political, social, or economic intervention. Also, it is almost impossible to say whether technological and social change is deliberate or accidental. Therefore it is hard to evaluate what the role of government ought to be in managing the course of technological changes because government is pushed by those changes even as it pushes them by being the biggest user of telecommunications technologies (Brock 1981; Dizard 1985).

Commentaries from these two theoretical perspectives seek to be definitive on the sovereignty issues involved in regulation or free expression. Hence they ignore the underdeterminacy involved in technology and social change in favor of the solace to be had from arriving at the relevant sovereignty interests. Note that this goal can be reached only by treating audience and participant interests in terms of a conflict between free expression and regulation. Here, however, the incongruity between the law and Internet technology runs even deeper than that associated with public broadcasting issues. That is because the radio, telephone, and television frame of reference, and conventional First Amendment reasoning, cannot provide strong enough criteria for deciding what the relevant sovereignty interests are in regard to the Internet.

Why not? There are many widely recognized factors, two of which are sufficient to make my point. One is that the Internet is, for the present at least, economically and technologically decentralized. It thrives because it piggybacks on existing telephone networks. In the future it will take advantage of cable networks and satellite links as well. This development, coupled with design advances in computer central processing units and advances in fiber optic delivery systems, will allow for exponential growth in future capacities of one or a number of Internets. But the cable and satellite delivery systems are far less decentralized, economically and technologically, than the Internet itself. This means that telephone, cable, and satellite providers are potential competitors, at least in regard to levying entrance fees to Internet providers and users. As the number of Internet users multiplies, providers could charge higher access fees for those who want faster connections; or offer menu services at different fee rates the way cable companies do; or charge, as the telephone companies do, for the amount of time a service is used.[11]

No one knows for sure how telephone, cable, and satellite delivery services will react to increased use of the Internet. But if they do go into competition with the Internet providers in order to restore the distribution, pricing, and profit structure of their own technologies, then Internet providers might go their own way rather than pay higher access fees. That scenario would result in a multiplicity of telecommunication networks of varied quality, an unsystematic distribution of telecommunications technologies, and increased costs in that distribution. And, outcomes like these always prompt debates about whether the market or governments should structure the distribution of social overhead capital.

On the other hand, following this second scenario, competition in a deregulated environment shaped by the Telecommunications Act of 1996 might well encourage the trend in the telecommunications industry toward mergers and acquisitions among various technological and corporate competitors.[12] In 1998, a proposed merger between ATT and the TCI cable television system encouraged speculation about the implications of a high-speed network for sending telephone, video, and Internet services into the home. A network of converged digital technologies could threaten still evolving stand-alone Internet technologies and make competition very expensive. If so, and if prices should rise in the absence of rate regulations, or if market mergers and acquisitions should limit consumer choices, or if access were limited, then public policy imperatives for governmental regulation and consumer protection would more likely be revisited.

Another facet of convergence to consider is the potential for competition between the Internet, with its capacity for advances in video and telephony technologies, and the telephone business. To date, the FCC has decided to let the Internet's computer processing technologies develop unchecked. But if small or rural markets should receive inferior services because they are not profitable markets for telephony technologies, or if issues of competition and price controls become prominent, then the FCC will become involved in regulatory issues.

A second factor making it difficult to identify the relevant sovereignty interests is that the Internet is a global, not national, technology. It is therefore highly susceptible to international and corporate interests beyond the control of any one polity. There are governments that are far more involved than ours is in administrating both the technologies and the content of expressive activities as they may relate to commercial fraud, drug advertising, privacy protection, obscenity, and restrictions on political speech. The Clinton administration's position on such matters was that self-regulation and privately implemented technological solutions are the preferred approach. Who can predict what position future presidential administrations will take?

If the present globalization trend continues, as it appears it will, then international nonprofit groups, along with national and international computer and communications companies, will push, or be pushed, to develop standards on the issues mentioned above, as well as on issues of taxation, tariffs, intellectual property, data protection, and liability. So, at a minimum, given the social and technological changes already registered by the Internet, politically sufficient commentary must not overlook the limits of domestic legal formalisms and facets of power for analyzing the extent to which international cooperation and technological alternatives to governmental regulation are truly feasible or desirable.

Such complications make the controversy over the CDA and the Internet a valuable opportunity for agnostics to address the law's formalisms within the context of the social, cultural, and political facets of continuing technological change. Under these pressures conventional conceptions of sovereignty and other interests may well be altered, along with the conception of citizenship, the role of the rule of law for constituting public good in the polity, and the relation between one polity and another.

To take advantage of such an opportunity is first to refuse to get lost in the clamor about censorship and free speech. Instead, if one seeks to reveal how formalisms and facets of political power distort a deeper appreciation of social ideals and practices, then a likely place to look is the issue of regulation. Regulation has proven to be one of the most efficient ways to provide for social and political control of innovative applications for new technologies. It also appears as an entry barrier to those same innovative applications and their diffusion throughout the polity. The dilemma of control versus innovation is reason enough, I think, for us not to expect, now or in the foreseeable future, that any one political theoretical frame of reference—anarchistic or community building—can be applied sufficiently to the issues involving the Internet. Like Hegel's "owl of Minerva" (1942: 13)—a symbol for philosophy that casts its wings only when the events have grown old—today's decisions will tend to reflect past conditions and relationships that are of limited value in understanding the present or the future.

Here, then, is a place for political agendas like superliberalism. Their virtue is that they encourage commentary that breaks with conventional ways of interpreting the past, present, and future by encouraging us to look more deeply into the political significance of the law's incongruities. Such a break most certainly is appropriate in trying to analyze the issues involved in attempting to control the Internet.

Consider the incongruity that arises between, on the one hand, the First Amendment ethos that currently dominates the law and, on the other, the culture of the Internet and the widely shared perception that technology has the potential to replace domestic law in shaping telecommunications. Conventional commentary about the Internet, which recognizes this incongruity, addresses one big question: What is practicable and best in considering how far the Internet should be governed by the market and technology, by federal or state law, and by international agreements? An agenda like superliberalism, by contrast, invites a deeper question: To what extent do the Internet and the social forces that it engenders threaten to unravel conventional ideas about what is practicable and best, and therefore to require novel reconstructions about the present and future of democracy and state power?

We will pursue aspects of this question later. To raise this compelling question now is to foreshadow the recognition that superliberal agendas have a vice: their presumption that it is easy to see how liberal democracy can be pushed beyond itself. It is not that agnostic skepticism is dead-set against arguments that call for novel thinking about democratization, commerce, capitalism, and individual rights, or for alternative ideas about the accountability of governments. It is rather that agnostic skepticism resists—and this is worth reiterating—endorsing any undiscriminating presumption about politics, of the left or of the right. If anything, the dilemma of regulation underscores the prudence of this resistance, just as, from another direction, the inadequacy of the marketplace formalism does also. But if superliberalism is freed from its shackles in intellectual jurisprudence, then both its recognition of the underdeterminacy relating to regulation and sovereignty and other interests, and its focus on the uncertain consequences of government intervention for the public welfare, can provide one particularly apt paradigm for thinking about unpredictable technological and social change.

As it happens, however, radical agendas like superliberalism tend to trigger the suspicion that radical revisionism is an expression of intellectual jurisprudence. A radical revisionist commitment to destroying fixed social structures exemplifies unreflective devotion to the intellectual resources and political prestige of philosophers as agents of social change. This commitment is hard for an agnostic to accept, and the dilemma of regulation is a good example of why it is so hard. For one thing, most persons, whether academics (including the elite audience committed to developing their Jeffersonian sensibilities) or others, will not easily listen to superliberalism's postmodernist soundings about things like "purposive analogical reasoning." For another, superliberalism, like all revisionism, arises out of academic considerations and determinations, and textual arguments are the primary instrument of radical revisionist politics. From a skeptic's perspective, radical revisionism has reduced the law and its politics to relations between ideas. In opposition to that conceit, agnosticism encourages one to find contingent social fact, and sometimes just good common sense, as reasons for arguing that when social change occurs in the law, as it eventually must when it comes to technology, politics, and policies that change will arise from forces most certainly outside the control of academics. Change is, at best, only accidentally correlated with, if not altogether incidental to, their ideas. In short, it is not legal theory or Unger's intellectual jurisprudence about mutual correction of abstract ideas, but political and legal conflict and technological change that shape and constitute social conservation and change.

Finally, agnostic skepticism encourages a habit of mind that makes one suspicious about whether there is, or ought to be, any general theory or political agenda, superliberal or otherwise, on the left or on the right, which would purportedly settle on a predetermined basis (that is, absent empirical investigations, reasons, and arguments) the extent to which it is the law's business qua law to accommodate changes in social conditions.

Similarly, agnostic skepticism encourages a habit of mind that cannot be satisfied with abstract ideological prescriptions to determine when liberal-democratic law runs into trouble. To be politically blunt, unlike radical revisionism, agnosticism means not necessarily being opposed to capitalism and politics ordinarily conceived. Admittedly, from the perspective of Unger's revisionism this bluntness opens agnosticism up to the accusation that it concedes to the "conservative reformism" and "progressive pessimistic reformism" that undermine genuine efforts at democratization. There is no rejoinder to this accusation except to say that this "agnostic take" on the troubles of formalism and politics leaves us where I think we have to be, even if we may not want to be there: confronting questions—questions about the obfuscation inherent in politics, about when a decision is rightly decided, and about inconsistency and incongruity—with only contextual and tentative answers.

Recently a few, very prominent legal (e.g., Tushnet 1999; Sunstein 1999) and political science (e.g., Kahn 1994; Graber 1999, 1996) scholars have become strong advocates for interdisciplinary approaches to the law and the Constitution, approaches that are compatible, in one respect, with agnosticism's contextual take on the law's formalisms. These scholars also stress that commentary should come in closer contact with political, social and economic fact considerations. However, those inclined toward agnosticism should read these scholars carefully to evaluate the extent to which their work actually breaks with the ideology of involvement and intellectual jurisprudence.

For the sake of illustration, consider how Cass R. Sunstein, in *One Case at a Time* (1999), addresses some of the issues related to applying traditional First Amendment formalisms to regulating a new technology like the Internet. His discussion stresses the complications and uncertainties that arise when applying these traditional legal formalisms to a social and economic context that is changing rapidly and in unpredictable ways, in good part because of the unforeseeable future of computer technologies. Sunstein concludes that these formalisms can still be well applied in some instances. But in those contexts where "changing issues of fact" (Sunstein 1999: 205) have the most unpredictable implications, Sunstein advises judges to avoid the comprehensive rule making and ambitious abstract reasoning that are often associated with First Amendment formalisms. Instead Sunstein advises judges in these contexts of high social fact unpredictability to take "one case at a time" by making narrow and incremental decisions that fit with the principle that, at least presently, there is no better fully articulated formalistic way to resolve these issues.

Certainly, apart from the advice to judges, Sunstein's contextual and tentative approach to First Amendment formalisms and social fact considerations is what one would expect from politically sufficient and agnostic commentary. But the implications of the ideology of involvement's grip on commentary should never be underestimated, for intellectual jurisprudence often follows in its wake and that limits or undermines contextualism and tentativeness. For example, in his concluding remarks, Sunstein goes out of his way to pledge allegiance to the First Amendment canon by expressing his contentment with comprehensive rule making on a "wide range of free speech issues [that] . . . are quite clear" (Sunstein 1999: 205). A pledge like this makes perfect sense if one is concerned with commentary that will be persuasive to judges and judges-to-be. But Sunstein's pledge is premature, and therefore incompatible with politically sufficient commentary, because agnostic commentary seeks to test the canon against social fact considerations. These tests are likely to include several plausible, competing political and moral points of view, and, hence, these tests will bring into question just what should count as "quite clear" considerations of free speech issues.

Returning to the agendas of radical revisionism, they too are invaluable for politically sufficient commentary because they can make commentators mindful of these kinds of tests. I do not share the view of those who reject radical revisionism out of hand. A remarkable volume, *Utopian Thought in the Western World,* captures exactly the idea that I want to express when it says that utopians sometimes provide remarkably trenchant observations about practical matters which others have either only "vaguely sensed or have refused to recognize" (Manuel and Manuel 1979: 28). Jean-Jacques Rousseau and Karl Marx did that in political theory. I think the legal realists did that for classical jurisprudence, and CLS revisionism on formalism does that for constitutional and legal commentary. Of course, a revisionist will find my treatment of revisionism perverse since the lessons I have taken away from it certainly complement ones learned from Fish. And while these lessons may deepen suspicion of the solace that the law's formalisms may breed, they also deepen suspicion that left-wing interpretations of the law are not all there is or ought to be.

The foremost conclusion I draw from *Johnson, League of Women Voters,* and *Reno* is that the troubles associated with the law's formalisms and facets of political power are best treated as intrinsic to the routine of pluralist political conflict. This is, you might recall, an injunction of the new institutionalism. This injunction compels a companion conclusion: Solace in either the law's formalisms or facets of political power are unmerited apart from commentary that arranges circumstantial and consequentialist facts along with partisan and ideological considerations, so that these arrangements reveal the strengths and the weaknesses of law and power. These two conclusions do not so much "save" liberal-democratic law as encourage teachers and critics to ask more hard-to-answer questions about how it functions. Such a stance does not mean a retreat into the comfortable idea that liberal-democratic law is a complete or definitive rendition of interests, politics, and policies. The lessons taught by radical revisionism mean that somehow teachers and critics must learn to shuttle back and forth between two points: commentary that is more understanding about the conservation of law, politics, and culture in a democratic polity and commentary that is more critical of these factors.

I hope to have made clear by now why mixing and merging empirical claims about facets of power with formalistic ones reveal the extent to which the subject matter of legal commentary ought to be thought about in terms of underdeterminacy. I hope it is also clear that the extent to which that subject matter is deemed to be underdeterminate is also the extent to which one should be skeptical about blanket condemnations or celebrations of the law's formalisms, even though that skepticism (especially in regard to condemnation) may in fact confirm inconsistency and incongruity in the use of legal formalisms.

What remains to be made clear is how agnostic skepticism can be defended against the charge that its more relativistic analysis underestimates the worst-case scenario depicted by radical rejectionism regarding inconsistency, incongruity, and the distortions of ideals and practices attributed to facets of liberal-democratic power. To do that we revisit the work of Mark Tushnet and the canonical federalism case, *McCulloch v. Maryland,* to see how politically sufficient commentary comes to grips with the accusation that a fundamental formalism for routine politics in the polity is merely a sham. Going there provides additional material for understanding why agnosticism tries to steer something of a middle course between skepticism about the law's formalisms and about facets of political power, on the one hand, and analysis that respects some degree of solace in them, on the other.

· 6 ·

Agnostic Skepticism about Radical Rejectionism

According to the worst-case scenario, as it is painted by CLS radical rejectionists, liberal-democratic law and politics defeat all hope for positive social change. There are as many versions of this rejectionism as there are "isms" in CLS. But they all come down to a root idea that once its flaws are described and evaluated, it becomes clear that there are no norms—not the rule of law, nor superliberalism, nor anything else—that can revitalize liberal democracy, in either theory or practice. Many of us hold that liberal democracy is beyond redemption when now and again a political, legal, or constitutional judgment profoundly disappoints our perception of justice. The difference between radical rejectionists and agnostics, however, is that rejectionists *always* believe that liberal democracy fails and that, given the evidence, it is politically immature to expect "true" justice *ever* to be served by it. In the final analysis, the rejectionist rejoinder to revisionists especially is that little can be done to offset the legal and political advantage that allows the haves to fare better than the have-nots. Consequently, it is politically and morally more prudent to oppose liberal democracy altogether and to seek, somehow, to achieve alternative politics and cultures.

The version of rejectionism that I have chosen as a foil to agnosticism belongs to Mark Tushnet, certainly one of the most widely known of CLS scholars. Once again, we will examine here only a tiny fragment of an author's work, in this instance Tushnet's rejectionist critique of the crucial liberal-democratic formalism of federalism (Tushnet 1981a, 1985a, 1988, 1990, 1996). Tushnet's examination of Federalism sets the framework for a case study of *McCulloch v. Maryland*,[1] and together they provide material sufficient to take a number of steps toward a fuller appreciation of the implications of an agnostic approach to commentary.

Step 1 elaborates on, and, hopefully, deepens appreciation of, a continuing theme. That is, if there are no single right answers to constitutional questions and no conclusive reasons for choosing between multiple right or even "better" answers, then the law's inconsistency and incongruity do not require, or even necessarily imply, the conclusion that the law is always politically incorrigible. Step 2 reveals why features of the social fact and formalistic claims in *McCulloch* provide a rationale, from the perspective of politically sufficient commentary, for a more forgiving conception of the law's formalisms and routine politics. This rationale holds despite the fact that a rejectionist criticism of *McCulloch* is partially credible. Therefore it can be said that there are reasons for a more forgiving reading of *McCulloch:* even where *McCulloch* is strong, there are reasons to be very suspicious of it. Step 3 indicates why agnostics ought to take seriously yet skeptically, what litigators and adjudicators have to say about the law's formalisms and routine politics in order to recover neglected politics and policies. This third step positions us for the next chapter, which illustrates some of the main elements of an agnostic approach to doctrinal analysis, with federalism as its centerpiece.

Liberal-Democracy: Plain Bad Law and Politics?

For Tushnet, the fatal flaws of both liberal legalism and federalism radiate from the same place: at the conjunction of two companion commitments, liberalism and constitutionalism (Tushnet 1981a, 1985a, 1988). Liberalism, as he characterizes it, refers to faith in the politics of will: the aggregating of conflicting individual interests, through the political process of checks and balances, to arrive at the common good. Constitutionalism refers to faith in the politics of reason in the form of legal rules—what we have been referring to as the rule of law via formalisms and political principles—to control the inevitable abuses of power and rights violations that attend the political process.

Tushnet considers federalism—the formalism for the structure and functions of U.S. politics—as one of the primary, if not the primary, manifestations of this dual liberalism-constitutionalism commitment and fatality (Tushnet 1985a, 1990). In politics as it is ordinarily conceived, federalism is understood as the principle that there ought to be constant political competition between the national government and the states. To divide powers, or competing political wills, between and among the states, and between the states and the Union, is essential to liberal politics. Constitutionalism's contribution to federalism is a written constitution that enumerates powers belonging to competing governments and grants to the judicial branch the authority and discretion to identify any intergovernmental usurpation of those powers.

According to Tushnet, liberal legalism is committed, fatally as it turns out, to the ideal that liberalism and constitutionalism—faith in political will and faith in political and judicial reason—can be integrated and reconciled. Tushnet does look past its flaws to recognize in federalism and the diffusion of governmental power "a major innovation in political theory" (Tushnet 1988: 9; 1996). But he also contends that liberal legalists are guilty of a number of presumptions about liberalism and (judicially abetted) constitutionalism in federalism—namely, that they promote greater opportunities for political participation and competition generally and for policy experimentation at the state and local levels; they limit opportunities for abuses of power and make overseeing governmental officials easier; and, most important, they provide a guarantee against the centralization of political power (Tushnet 1985b: 691). Against liberal-legalist presumptions Tushnet asserts that liberal and constitutional conceptions of political power contradict and undermine each other at every point, and that therefore the putative benefits of complementarity are illusory.

For Tushnet, the primary problem is embedded in the political theory of liberalism. This theory derives its sanction from the arguments of Thomas Hobbes and John Locke, which, Tushnet asserts, have "gone essentially unchallenged in the dominant institutions of this country since the framing of the Constitution" (Tushnet 1981a: 412). At the core of liberalism, Tushnet argues, is an antinomy, or irresolvable conflict, between the will and reason. (Many have pointed out how contentious this claim is, but for our purposes it will go unchallenged.) Liberalism, says Tushnet, teaches that the roots of political conflict lie in the individual desires and interests of persons whose freedom depends on their acting in accord with the will to fulfill them. It also teaches that acting *solely* in accord with the will is potentially self-destructive, and inevitably harmful in some degree to others. Liberalism thus has to seek limits on political conflict to avoid a war of all against all or of the many against the few (Tushnet 1981a: 415). This limit on conflict is what constitutionalism is all about: it teaches liberal democrats that there exists a system of rationales, principles, and policies that can justify legal rules which will manage political conflict and avert political disaster.

But nothing, says Tushnet, can save liberal political theory from its own contradiction without undermining it as a political theory. To impose limits on the expression of the will in order to constitute the public good—which is to impose restrictions on the vox populi (the voice of the people) in the name of *salus populi* (the welfare of the people)—is to undermine the liberal foundation of the good. All attempts to integrate and reconcile the theory of liberalism with itself, and with constitutionalism (or, by the way, to push liberalism beyond itself as Unger recommends) result in arbitrariness.

What Tushnet's critique means in practical terms is that constitutionalism cannot reconcile liberalism to itself because the job of integration and reconciliation falls to judges. And, judges, from Tushnet's rejectionist perspective, are solely political actors. Judging has to be, at the end of the day, an act of will, not reason, given judges' legal socialization and recruitment, the lack of any substantial difference between legal and political reasoning, the indeterminacy (it is appropriate to use that strong variation of the term in this context) of legal formalisms, and the prevailing economic ideology of the polity. Not only that: judicially constructed limits on the politics of will amount to nothing less than judges' political rule over the will of the people, and that only doubles the arbitrariness of constitutionalism. (Hence Tushnet's commitment for taking the Constitution away from courts and his preference for a populist constitutional law.)

From Tushnet's rejectionist point of view, then, in practice federalism is a sham. Its formalisms are used arbitrarily to secure what liberal legalism's political integration requires: a strong enough national government to protect and promote private property and capitalism's economic growth with just sufficient autonomy remaining to the states and local governments (Tushnet 1988:9) to keep the system from disasters of too much command and control. For instance, the marketplace formalism, a companion formalism to federalism, lacks a fixed set of substantive values shaping the government's approach to speech issues, and therefore decisions about when it is proper to intervene are unpredictably up for grabs (Seidman and Tushnet 1996: 186). Just so with federalism: the Court that decides victories and defeats among national, state, and local governments is bound to constantly revise and distort their doctrines so that they fit with the changing needs of the economy and power. Moreover, in a contemporary industrial economy it appears that political power can work no way other than in terms of its incessant expansion. Thus, for Tushnet and rejectionists, liberal-legal federalism, as one of the cornerstone formalisms of U.S. politics, cannot constrain power—economic or political—and, consequently, solace in it is hardly ever merited.

Tushnet's steadfast rejection of federalism is offset to some extent by his saying, here and there, that perhaps law and commentary that endorse the results of the economics and politics of socialism might make things authentically better in the polity. He also appears to believe that the effects of culture, the economy, politics, and law on national and subnational local relations are sufficiently dynamic as to allow for some possibility of a more authentic federalism, say in Europe, which has some national experiences with socialism. On the other hand, he also believes that hope for an authentic federalism may be implausible because the vectors of historical forces are against it (Tushnet 1990: 139–51).

Tushnet's expression of apparently conflicting beliefs is typical of rejectionists. Whatever their "ism," those who express optimism do so within the context of grave doubts about the possibilities for authentic social change through law, politics, and commentary. Even when they have no doubts about what it means to rightly decide political and moral questions, they reject (for a variety of reasons that need not concern us here) as implausible any hope of reorganizing the economy and diminishing hierarchies based on class, race, sex, and gender. In other words, rejectionists rarely articulate a positive program for social change of their own.

Rejectionists do though engage in intellectual jurisprudence, and they do offer up programs for revising or transforming legal argumentation. The most accomplished, and some say notorious, program is mounted by radical feminists and critical race theorists to tell stories that reject conventional academic standards for evidence, objectivity, and the like. Rejectionists advance programs like narrative jurisprudence not in the hope of having a significant impact on the academy or the polity but to attack conventional scholarship and to create solidarity among themselves.

On this last point, Tushnet's rejectionism is closer to Unger's radicalism than it is to narrative programs. Although he is sympathetic to its goals, Tushnet has expressed concerns about narrative's lack of intellectual integrity (Tushnet 1992) and its tendency to suffer from some of the same faults as conventional legal arguments (Seidman and Tushnet 1996: 195). Consequently Tushnet's preference is to use conventional constitutional arguments against themselves. His goal is to persuade those in the middle of controversies who "are more open to argument" (Seidman and Tushnet 1996: 199) to develop an ironic sensibility about constitutional claims based on the understanding that all claims are inevitably contingent and flawed. "Adherents to skeptical commitment would reach out to opponents while also confronting them. They would combine anger with empathy, faith with agnosticism, action with reflection" (Seidman and Tushnet 1996: 201).

These last sentiments about civic education appear to be similar to those of agnosticism, and that complicates the relationship between it and rejectionism. Later we will see that this similarity is only a superficial one, but in order to do so we first need to pursue an agnostic defense of federalism against the rejectionist charge that it is a sham.

McCulloch and Federalism

McCulloch v. Maryland is the classic statement of federalism, and, as interpreted here, it is its own best defense against the idea that federalism is a sham. It also provides reasons why agnostics should reject rejectionism, Tushnet's in particular. This is a lot of weight to put on a single constitutional opinion, but *McCulloch* can bear it.

McCulloch's defense of national power and of the Union's control of the economy is a weave of legal arguments about federalism. It is also a weave of pragmatic and political theoretical arguments about underdetermined sovereignty interests that mute the force of arguments for state and shared sovereignty[2] without, however, altogether undermining claims for state power. Each strand of this weave of arguments about sovereignty and federalism is not in itself strong; but each merges with the others to strongly confirm the political sovereignty (or will) of the Union. Together they confirm, at both the theoretical and practical level, the destructive effect of state machinations on federal spheres of power and on the security of the new nation. Together they drive constitutionalism and legal reasoning into an enduring argument for limited governments, with each sphere plenary within its own ambit and the Union supreme over all.

From an agnostic perspective, in *McCulloch* sovereignty interests and federalism are coordinated to teach three lessons. First, principles such as the principle of sovereignty, political conventions such as "power derived from the people," and sovereignty interests create but cannot by themselves decide specific political and economic problems about the distribution of power. Second, consequentialist and context-specific political judgments about principles, conventions, and interests are essential for deciding issues about the distribution of power. Third, judicial discretion alone, quite apart from the ambiguities of the materials of judgment, ensures that whatever image of politics arises from issues about federalism will always be underdetermined. Each of these lessons provides reasons for being skeptical about radical rejectionism.

Most importantly, radical rejectionism, and Tushnet's in particular, fall short of what any commentary, agnosticism especially, needs in order to make sufficient sense of persistent and inevitable conflict over what governments may do. It is true that Chief Justice John Marshall's words, as a whole, seek to constitute a political community and culture out of solace in popular sovereignty as a source and a promise of unity and integration. But Marshall's words also tell the truth that there are no formulaic solutions for fleshing out what the public good is or for determining if the states or the Union should prevail. These words confirm moreover that such lack does not mean "anything goes" when it comes to political power. Federalism always requires arguments about the fit between conventions and plain politics to integrate sovereignty and constitutionalism. In effect, federalism promises the development, over time, of a self-reflective, self-corrective body of discourse about political power. For an agnostic, this body of discourse is something that *McCulloch* represents as always a matter of close calls because criteria for the distribution of power are intrinsically underdeterminate.

McCulloch thus teaches that underdeterminacy ought to be judged as a means for treating law and politics as never beyond rejoinder. Underdeterminacy, taken advantage of the way it is in *McCulloch*, could provide opportunities to perpetually construct competing images of the politics of federalism, in commentary if not necessarily in legal practice. To think along the lines of *McCulloch*'s jurisprudence in commentary is to learn how, from the vantage point of a habitual skepticism about *any* justification for the use of political power, to manipulate the law's formalisms while always paying requisite attention to consequentialist readings of the Constitution.

It helps here to remember that the First Bank of the United States was chartered by Congress in 1791 as a means for promoting economic development and was rechartered in 1816 to meet the financial crises that followed the War of 1812. Both the First and Second Banks were marked by financial corruption and mismanagement, with banks in the South and West suffering the most. Many states passed taxes in an effort to destroy the Second Bank of the United States (BUS). The Maryland tax was to be imposed directly on the BUS, but not on other banks not chartered by the state. From the perspective of Maryland, the BUS had achieved an intolerable competitive financial edge over state institutions. From the perspective of the federal government, the Maryland tax on the BUS was simply another odious effort by a state to counter what the government considered the necessary growth of national power.

The cashier of the Baltimore branch of the BUS refused to pay the tax, whereupon a suit was commenced in state court and won by the state. The decision was appealed to the Supreme Court, where Maryland contended that Article I, Section 8 of the U.S. Constitution, which enumerated the powers of Congress, did not give that body "the necessary and proper power" to incorporate the BUS and that, in any case, Maryland had the sovereign power to tax the bank. Maryland's argument depended primarily on three points. First, federalism does not require a rule of law conception of sovereignty as popular. Second, the Constitution provided for precisely limited federal powers and the states retained all power beyond those expressly granted to the federal government. Third, Maryland was exercising its co-equal positive law authority, in other words, legislative independence and discretion, in taxing the bank.

Chief Justice Marshall, writing for the Court, overturned the state decision by interpreting Article I, Section 8, and the Constitution as a whole to require the conclusion that the BUS was indeed constitutional and that the Maryland tax was not. To do so, he had to settle the dispute about which government was sovereign in this case, the Union's or Maryland's. This was no simple matter, given the ambiguity of the concept of sovereignty, the lack of legal—though not practical—precedents, and the strength of the case Maryland made for its right to exercise power over the bank.

As my analysis will show, Chief Justice Marshall worked a way out of this dilemma by means of consequentialist considerations subtly woven into his legal formalisms. A great deal was at stake in his ruling: the adequacy of federalism and the future of the Union, the meaning of the rule of law and liberal democracy, and a great property. All of these cruxes (except the last) and Chief Justice Marshall's rhetorical strategy, are implied in the first paragraph:

> In the case now to be determined, the defendant, a sovereign State, denies the obligation of a law enacted by the legislature of the Union; the plaintiff . . . contests the validity of an act which has been passed by the legislature of that State. The Constitution of our country, in its most interesting and vital parts, is to be considered; the conflicting powers of the government of the Union and its members, as marked in that constitution, are to be discussed; and an opinion given, which may essentially influence the great operations of the government. No tri-

bunal can approach such a question without a deep sense of its importance and of the awful responsibility involved in its decision. But it must be decided peacefully, or remain a source of hostile legislation; perhaps of hostility of a still more serious nature; and if it is to be so decided, by the tribunal alone can the decision be made. On the Supreme Court of the United States has the constitution of our country devolved this important duty.[3]

These words clearly indicate that *McCulloch* is about conflicts over the distribution of power between the states and the Union as these conflicts bear on the means toward maintaining the common good, political stability, and popular rule. These words also stipulate that conflicts over sovereignty interests can be resolved only by the imposition of the Court's discretion and, by implication, the rule of law. One must remember that, while "sovereignty" is a commonplace eighteenth- and nineteenth-century political term, it does not appear in the Constitution. It takes on rule of law properties only from construction of the document as a whole. Chief Justice Marshall's words, then, bespeak the urgency of the case and his awareness that a nation is in the making.

In *McCulloch,* "sovereignty" carries two implications about state power, one political, the other legal. The political one is not contentious: to speak of Maryland as a sovereign state is to convey its positive law authority, which resides in a state's exclusive and indivisible legislative independence, or monopoly of power within territorial limits. It follows from this that a state has ultimate discretion (that is, the last say) regarding the proper use of that power. However, the constitutional structure of American politics provides for a Union that represents national legislative independence and discretion—based on popular sovereignty—*within* a context of state legislative independence and discretion.

This contextualism is a problem in liberal-democratic political theory and practice, because sovereignty is understood to be indivisible, and for the Union and states to be both sovereign would appear to be a political contradiction. Nonetheless, Publius, in *The Federalist* No. 31, argued that just such a division of sovereignty is a consequence of states' having divested power to the Union and that that division is therefore implicit in the text and tenor of the Constitution. As Publius saw it, the Constitution resolves this contradiction and creates a more perfect union in the bargain, by the powers enumerated in Article 1 that augment a union's authority without destroying state sovereignty.

But, of course, advocates for the states denied that the politics of federalism requires a rule of law conception of sovereignty as popular. They agreed that the Constitution, as the rule of law, represents the "constitution" of a political community (the nation); but their view of federalism was closer to a "compact" between states that shared power, within limits, to "reconstitute" a union and a nation from sovereign states.

In this context, then, Chief Justice Marshall's "sovereign state" resonates with the uncertainty of one of the root legal problems of American political theory of the nineteenth (and twentieth) century. It also begs the question whether federalism embodies or sustains a defensible scheme of human association when it extends to the Union vast authority yet leaves the states distinct and independent entities that it is nonetheless to superintend.

One might very well go under in the face of such a question. Yet Marshall does not succumb. Rather, he uses the underdeterminacy about sovereignty in the Constitution to confirm Maryland's positive law authority (and to that extent its sovereignty) while denying the appropriateness of state sovereignty theory for describing constitutional politics. That is, he transforms ambiguities about the constitution of the nation and what governments may do into (seemingly) unequivocal rule of law talk about what the Constitution requires of them. And he does this not so much by defending the premises of popular sovereignty as by attacking the political consequences of the theory and politics of state sovereignty.

Thus the important thing to note about these first sentences is how subtle they are. Especially when, having identified the competition between the states and the Union as the source of both the theoretical and the practical problems of sovereignty, he then points to the Court's adjudication of the rule of law as the solution. Without the Court (and Tushnet's rejected "thick Constitution") there would be war of all against all. Now, nothing in the preceding lines explicitly justifies this generalization of Court sovereignty over the rule of law. It is just that by this time the Court's judicial independence and discretion were well established, despite state sovereignty objections, and Marshall must speak of the Court's authority in the somber confident tones of one who expects no rebuttal.

And, having introduced the Court in this way, Marshall can quietly put into play his controlling political theoretical premise implicit in the words about duty: If the Court, as a part of the tripartite whole that is the Union, has the duty, and therefore sovereignty, to arbitrate between competing judicial and legislative wills, as *Marbury v. Madison* (1803) indicates, then the whole (the Union) must perforce have the authority to settle sovereignty disputes between the Union and the states as well. Thus, juxtaposed to Marshall's explicit reference to Maryland's status as a "sovereign state" is the reference to the role of the Court and Union indicating, in effect, a background and political precedent for the Union's rule of law sovereignty.

Chief Justice Marshall's whole first paragraph, then, provides a consequentialist choice: a community glued together by the Court's rendition of the rule of law and the Union's version of sovereignty interests, or, the politics of all against all. Readers would have recognized a similar choice offered in *The Federalist* papers, among anarchy, democracy, and a republic, where the first two guarantee disorder and only the third can break and control factions. This need to choose between order and chaos is the ultimate warrant for a rule of law version of sovereignty that allows for no middle ground, and Marshall uses it at every crucial turn to vacate sovereignty arguments contrary to his.

But simple as this logic is, and as artfully as it has been made to impose itself on the reader, it must still confront Maryland's conventional political and constitutional wisdom that "shared sovereignty" is a middle ground. Divided sovereignty as shared sovereignty embodies a distinction between the origin and the extent of power. The origin of all power in the nation is "the people" and, as Madison puts it in *The Federalist* No. 46, the "federal and state governments are but different agents and trustees of the people, constituted with different powers, and designed for different purposes" (Wills 1982: 237).

Advocates of shared sovereignty contend that because the origin of power is the same for both the Union and states—power is derived from the people—it follows that the extent of power is also shared between the two. Chief Justice Marshall's response here is to weave together liberal-democratic conventions about property and power and their associated consequentialist considerations to show why divided sovereignty does not entail shared sovereignty.

The groundwork for the attack on the shared sovereignty doctrine is located in the account of how the BUS came to be. In this move Marshall invests the BUS with considerable, albeit not total, rule of law legitimacy by recalling "the practice of the government": "The bill incorporating the bank . . . did not steal upon an unsuspecting legislature, and pass unobserved. After being resisted, first in the open field of debate, and afterwards in the executive cabinet . . . it became law. . . . It would require no ordinary share of intrepidity to assert that a measure adopted under these circumstances was a bold and plain usurpation to which the constitution gave no countenance."[4]

Marshall's appeal to plain politics generates three interrelated claims. Overtly, it bestows on the BUS the same positive law legitimacy denoted by the expression "sovereign state" as it has been assigned to Maryland. At the very least, this places the bank on the same political footing as any positive law act that a "sovereign state" might promulgate. Second, and more subtle, is the intimation that practices that pass as plain politics could not possibly be construed as a "plain usurpation" of the conflicting powers of the Union that are constituted, moment by moment, by debate. To put it another way, the language intimates that a close, but not complete, connection exists between the plain politics of incorporating the BUS and rule of law authority. Finally, the remark about bold usurpations of power not going unnoticed signals the use of social fact claims as appropriate rejoinders to (Maryland's) theoretical state sovereignty claims.

In context, Marshall's appeal to plain politics seems commonsensical, yet it is as contentious as it is crowded with intimations. Remember, from the perspective of state sovereignty, the Congress lacks authority to incorporate a bank, notwithstanding the promulgation of the positive law act of incorporating it. "Plain usurpation" or not, the incorporation, as Maryland sees it, violates the rule of law of federalism.

Moreover, if plain politics is a criterion of the legitimacy of acts of sovereignty, that criterion cuts both ways: the Maryland tax did not "steal upon the scene" either. If both the BUS and the tax have a degree of legitimacy on the grounds of practices, then the criterion of practices suggests shared sovereignty. So, the appeal to practices does not, nor is it meant to, undercut state sovereignty directly; rather, it fulfills its purpose merely by shifting attention to plain politics.

Chief Justice Marshall uses this shift to set up a linkage between property, power, liberalism, and the rule of law. In his oral argument, Daniel Webster, as litigant, brought to the Court's attention the financial value of private property implicated in a state challenge to the BUS. By insisting that an "exposition of the constitution . . . on the faith of which an immense property has been advanced, ought not to be lightly disregarded," Marshall echoes Webster's concern that upcoming appraisals of congressional capacity and sovereignty have plain economic consequences which are not to be ignored. This has the further effect of making political and economic considerations at least as central as formalist doctrines about sovereignty. Altogether, Marshall is suggesting that it is neither ideologically sound nor practical to "lightly disregard" the plain political fact that there would be no bank if, in theory and practice, it did not serve the property interests of the people. As a rhetorical package, appeals to practices, property, and the BUS connect up with the liberal-democratic convention that the rule of law arises out of political processes that settle conflicts over principles and interests.

But the question is, "Which political process?" To answer this question, Marshall must undermine the claim that state sovereignty theory enjoys a closer fit with plain politics than popular sovereignty does. To do so he pushes his opinion deep into liberal-democratic questions about political agency: who acts fundamentally in politics, states or "the people"? Here Marshall depends on a reiteration of a Lockean version of the origin of power (Faulkner 1986: 103–06). Not the states, but "the people," acting in "perfect liberty," constitute the political community through their "final" consent, a consent made conclusive by virtue of their independence and discretion.[5] This version of the consent of the governed, and participant interests, is no definitive knock-out punch against state sovereignty—and no such punch exists. But it suits Marshall's purposes to suggest that popular sovereignty has a superior fit with national sovereignty interests, as well as with liberal conventions about the origin of power, liberty, and the consent of the governed. For by doing so he can make Maryland's argument appear one-sided because it rejects the sovereignty of the people in its own name,[6] whereas popular sovereignty is identified with both national power and states as the agents of ratification. In effect, advocates of state sovereignty would destroy the power, liberty, and consent of the people as specified by liberalism. The elegant twist of all this is that it makes popular sovereignty appear to be a middle course, if not a compromise, and state sovereignty an extreme and destructive doctrine!

Now, having thus positioned Maryland's claim to equal if not greater sovereignty, Marshall can move from his consequentialist account of the origin of the rule of law to the "universally admitted" (Lockean) convention that government is limited by enumerated powers. This convention, he allows, means that questions about the extent of powers are "perpetually arising, and will probably continue to arise, as long as our system shall exist."[7] His admission that the character of power is fuzzy lends an air of credibility to his account, but he must still use all his rhetorical skill to link enumerated powers to the sovereign positive law authority of the Union. This he does by reference to the Supremacy Clause: the "Union, though limited in its powers, is supreme within its sphere of action."[8] The effect of such talk is to picture American politics divided by somewhat ambiguously structured spheres of Union and state positive law powers, each politically sovereign within its ambit. But the Union, the government "of all; its powers delegated by all," is the only one that "represents . . . and acts for all." It is supreme as long as it acts within its sphere.

Invoking the textual authority of the Supremacy Clause allows Marshall to transform what is otherwise contestable about the extent of limited government into still another apparently justified appeal to the rule of law. It also allows him to play once again on the issue of agency: whereas states act for themselves, the Union, though limited, serves, and acts, for all. That this is so allows Marshall to return to the plain political consequences of treating states as if they were sovereign: any one state in the Union is willing to control the nation, but no one state is willing to let other states control it. Thus the convention of limited government, like the others that have already gone through Marshall's hands, becomes an instrument to contrast popular sovereignty, attached to a liberal picture of government that serves all, to the politics of divisive states that puts the people at risk of the war of all against all.

It is worth reiterating that the primary force of these arguments resides in their foregrounding political facets of power not legal facets. The argument for the supreme authority of the Union depends on a liberal-democratic image of the birth and growth of power immanent in the Constitution. A nation, an extraordinary political creation of "the people," born out of conflict and strife, endowed by the people with independence and discretion, struggles to survive the tendencies of state governments to disrupt the peace, endanger the union, and threaten the blessings of liberty.

The conclusion to be drawn from this image of power is that the only way to preserve the Union and bind up its parts is to weigh competing theories of sovereignty on the basis of their compatibility with liberal-democratic conventions and their practical consequences. It is this image of power that grounds Marshall's transformation of language about agency into rule of law language about the Supremacy Clause. With the recitation of this clause, the groundwork of *McCulloch* has been completed. Now he can go on to the BUS.

The attack on the bank was premised on the idea that its incorporation was not among the enumerated powers of the Union. In his customary way, Marshall uses this point to further develop a consequentialist conception of power phrased as a construal of the legal terms of the Constitution. The right to incorporation, though not specified in the Constitution, can be "deduced" from "a fair construction of the whole instrument" and the "ample" powers it provides to secure the objectives that are specified. In other words, "fair" constitutional construction requires the rule of law that powers required to secure the enumerated ends of power include the nonenumerated means. Behind this conception is a plain political threat: if Congress does not have the power of incorporation, because it lacks sovereignty over such means, it could not long sustain the authority to pass other laws to accomplish its objects. Hence, the incorporation of the bank is an act of sovereignty, a "necessary and proper" legislative act carried out within the proper ambit of congressional power.

These remarks open up to a rejoinder to Maryland's rule of law claim that the enumeration was designed to restrict congressional power for the sake of maintaining the integrity of the remainder of sovereignty not delegated to the Union. Maryland's reading is that the word "necessary" controls the clause as a restriction on power. Marshall refuses to get drawn into the issue at this level and reaches instead to "ordinary language," wherein "necessary" connotes that which is "convenient, or useful, or essential."[9]

The word, he says, implies discretion over means incidental to ends; it is not used to express absolute exclusion but matters of degree determined by "the subject, the context, and the intention" of actors. For this reason, any interpretation of the rule of law about congressional legislative means must be consequentialist. This is to say, as Marshall does, that the interpretation must not "deprive the legislature of the capacity to avail itself of experience, to exercise its reason, and to accommodate its legislation to circumstances." Such flexibility is essential to the Constitution, which was "intended to endure for ages to come, and consequently, to be adapted to the various crises of human affairs."[10] Obviously, it was not meant to function as a "legal code."

Thus, the rule of law conclusion that "necessary" obtains to those means appropriate for executing sovereign powers, and that such means are "a right incidental to [those powers] and conducive to [their] beneficial exercise," is crucial to a nation of citizens engaged by a common constitutional language and common political practices.[11] The founders, Chief Justice Marshall recounts, would consider "any means" constitutional "which tended directly to the execution of the constitutional powers of the government."[12] Now referring directly to the text of the Constitution, Marshall observes how the Necessary and Proper Clause appears in the context of the powers, not the limitations, of Congress; how the form and effect of its words are not restrictive; and how, if the intention was to restrict congressional means, the convention would have done so explicitly. Ergo, the clause does not enlarge or restrict powers, it simply relates to powers incidental to enumerated ones.

Not that "any means" implies unbridled discretion. Marshall reiterates that the limits of government "are not to be transcended."[13] He specifies that the rule of law regarding supremacy in the Union's sphere requires the conclusion that only those means are constitutional that "are not prohibited," and then only if the "end be legitimate," and the means "appropriate [and] plainly adapted to that end."[14] Given all that has come before it, "plainly" connotes plain consequentialist politics: that which is politically reasonable or compatible with settled liberal expectations about what governments may do (including chartering corporations). With this, the means-ends argument for the BUS is completed and the issue of the tax can be confronted directly.

It is noteworthy that nothing in the defense of the BUS, in and of itself, yet excludes the legitimacy of Maryland's tax of out-of-state banks. As it stands, although Congress has the sovereign authority to incorporate the Bank, divided sovereignty leaves Maryland free to tax it within its rigid sphere. To void the tax, the rule-of-law argument for congressional plenary power and the Union's supremacy has to be positioned to bar the way against shared sovereignty without at the same time undermining divided sovereignty.

Politically and legally, divided sovereignty leaves both the Union and states their share of respective sovereign powers of taxation. However, there are also constitutional specifications where the power of taxation is withdrawn from state control. These instances, Chief Justice Marshall says, are analogous to the Supremacy Clause principle that state sovereignty may be limited (even within its ambit) whenever it interferes with "necessary and proper" federal governmental activities.

Chief Justice Marshall generates two corollaries from the clause to distinguish between state and congressional functions. The first corollary is a plain political one out of positive law: Webster's famous dictum that "a power to create implies a power to preserve," and "a power to destroy, if wielded by a different hand, is hostile to power to, and incompatible with these powers to create and preserve."[15] This formalist dictum summarizes all that has come before it. Power originates in the people, who, for the sake of stability, security, and peace, delegated power and consented to a Constitution that constitutes a union. The power of this union is fiduciary, and

Congress has the right and duty to create and preserve itself, and the union, in the name of the people. The power to destroy that unity comes from hostile and divisive states, which must be kept in check.

That check comes from the other corollary as a rule for constitutional construction: "[T]he very essence of supremacy [is] to remove all obstacles to its action within its own sphere, and so to modify every power vested in subordinate governments, as to exempt its own operations from their own influence."[16] That is, shared sovereignty and the rule of law are incompatible, because the former prevents the Union from fulfilling its legislative duties by making it dependent on the states. Yet again, state sovereignty implies the theory and practice of war of all against all. Thus, only the rule of law of popular supremacy protects the Union from the states, and counters their odious use of political power.

Chief Justice Marshall, though, does not let the opinion rest at the Supremacy Clause. Instead, he goes on to mount an even broader political defense of his version of federalism and in the process reinforces the impression that the question of taxation is at least as important in that regard as the constitutionality of the BUS. This final assault then is an attempt to close out Maryland's assertion that its absolute positive law power of taxation is sufficient for the state to "exercise [its] acknowledged powers" on the BUS.[17]

To that end, Chief Justice Marshall takes pains to distinguish the kind of political sovereignty being exercised. The power of each state, he asserts, arises from the people within it. The authority within each sphere is plenary and absolute because of the exigencies of government. He then reminds us, playing off liberal anxieties over property and abuses of power, that the only protection the people of a state have from "erroneous and oppressive taxation" is the "structure of government."[18] By "structure of government" Marshall means plain legislative politics.

The origin and extent of the taxation power of the Union within its ambit are the same as for a state: its power arises from the people, its power is plenary within its sphere, and this power is subject to the same abuses. But the Union's politics is structured differently than for a state, by the power delegated to it as the government of all the people. This structure implies the plain politics of the separation of powers between the Senate and House, not that between the states and the federal government. That being the case, only a coordinate branch of the tripartite government, not the states directly, can control Congress's power of taxation. It is therefore appropriate that the constitution "devolved" on the Court "this important duty" of policing the rigid spheres of taxation sovereignty.

With this argument Chief Justice Marshall has transformed the issue of sovereignty into the issue of whether liberal-democratic conventions for the origin and extent of national government, with its separation of powers, are to be sustained in practice. Federalism, as a political and rule of law doctrine for divided powers, requires the conclusion that taxation sovereignty cannot be shared because no state can extend its sovereign authority beyond the structural limits of its respective public and its politics. The bank is an instrument of the Union's taxation power, it serves national interests, and only the Union has the authority to protect or destroy it.

The implications of this argument cannot be overemphasized. Apparently, neither implied power nor supremacy is sufficient to protect the interests involved. It is ultimately plain politics that dooms the tax. Daniel Webster, in another context, observed that to "confer . . . such [tax] immunities as may induce individuals to become stockholders, and to furnish . . . capital" is to "control an economy" (Wheeler 1905: 40). The power to tax is a crucial exercise of political and economic power, and *McCulloch* is meant to ensure that states do not have the power, nor privilege, to check the Union's independence and discretion over the development of capital in the nation. At bottom, consequentialist considerations about the plain consequentialist politics of sovereignty—stability, security, peace, and the wealth of the nation—are behind *McCulloch*'s conception of federalism.

McCulloch and Federalism Are Not a Sham

To focus only on its political credibility, *McCulloch*'s jurisprudence is dazzling. In form, it is so brilliantly executed that the initial issue of the sovereignty and the extent of congressional power is lost in its glare. Read in its own setting, the opinion as a whole appears to be axiomatic, deductive, and textual, even though it might be said that in strictly logical terms the consequentialism of its reasoning prejudices the issue of sovereignty. It is, at this level, a classic example of what Stanley Fish referred to as the law's efficaciousness at settling controversies.

All this is not to say that because *McCulloch* credibly addresses economic issues and the reality of power relations, it is rightly decided. For one thing, there are strong arguments on both sides about whether *McCulloch* provides an adequate examination of the relationship between Article I, the actual powers of the bank, and the principles of sovereignty and limited powers. For another, as Tushnet rightly points out, *McCulloch*'s formalistic treatment of sovereignty provides for checks and balances between state and federal power only by opening up to the tyranny of judicial discretionary power (Tushnet 1988: 76–77). And, finally, there are mainstream doctrinal reasons on both sides for arguing whether *McCulloch*'s consequentialism adequately addresses the possibility that a nondiscriminatory state tax on all banknotes would have been constitutional. That all said, though, does not make *McCulloch* a sham.

By logical extension then, *McCulloch* teaches some important lessons about why one ought to be skeptical of answers to the rightly decided question. One lesson is that there is no formulaic way to determine whether to give social fact claims more or less weight than formalistic ones in judging whether a decision is rightly or wrongly decided. Second, it is plausible that there may be a scholarly consensus that a decision is rightly decided on political or moral grounds yet is formalistically weak. A contemporary example of this weakness is *Brown v. Board of Education*. Conversely, politics being what it is, it is almost inevitable that some commentators may have good and strong grounds for asserting that this or that decision is formalistically sound but objectionable on political or moral grounds; *Texas v. Johnson* fits that characterization. Third, the underdeterminacy of the law's formalisms, and their relation to liberalism as embodied in the Constitution, make it just as inevitable that there will be multiple ways of reading what the Constitution requires.

It should be evident by now that *McCulloch,* which construes the Constitution in favor of the Union and a national economy, can be turned against itself. The decision is an occasion for shuttling between political and legal language. Underdeterminacies are dealt with by means of a prose which is itself shimmering with imprecision: it is this strategy that makes *McCulloch* more than the sum of its parts. Reading it makes one aware that a shift to a decision expanding state power in the scheme of federalism would require only its own set of consequentialist considerations portraying national power as a threat to the common good, political stability, and popular rule. This possibility does indeed suggest that "the language of the Constitution, and hence the language of the law generally, is continuous with ordinary language and capable of the same richness, complexity, and variation—indeed of the same capacity for inconsistency" (White 1984: 260). Later on, we will pursue the substantive implications of this claim more fully. For now it is enough to see that, at a more mundane level, it means that political and formalistic claims can be made in more or less persuasive ways, and if the present state of constitutional commentary is any indication, teachers and critics will not agree about any of them.

This array of considerations helps warrant an agnostic's skepticism about all answers to the rightly decided question, but it also helps warrant a rejectionist's determination that controversies are never rightly decided. So, the decision to be skeptical about rejectionism cannot be dictated by logic alone. However, and this is important, skepticism about rejectionism is not necessarily dictated by partisan political preferences either. Whatever these partisan preferences may be, skepticism about blanket criticisms of law and politics based on philosophical criteria, or on absolute moral and political convictions, breeds still more skepticism regarding the association of those criticisms with a disrelish for contingent fact and contextual considerations of plain politics. When there is an appreciation for these considerations, then agnosticism appears to be the preferable choice because those considerations so often dictate attention to the practical implications of those blanket criticisms.

If so, a rejectionism like Tushnet's that lacks a positive political theory or program of its own, other than to attack liberal legalism as fatally flawed, or to seek to dejudicialize the Constitution, seems to be even more arbitrary than the liberal democracy it attacks. At least with liberal democracy and the "thick Constitution," we know what the core conventions are and therefore we can ask questions about their practical implications. As for a rejectionism that has a positive program of its own, it too is as arbitrary as the commentary it attacks if it always comes down on the side of the losers rather than the winners or the "good" versus the "bad" guys.

The arbitrariness of commentary that teaches skepticism and empathy arises, in Tushnet's case, when he says that constitutional argument, like federalism, is really just a sham that he and his fellow skeptics engage in it solely because there is no rhetorical alternative to it (Tushnet 1996: 193–200). Here the similarity between rejectionist skepticism and agnosticism is only skin deep. If commentary is a sham then persuasion is a sham. If so, it is the skepticism of a rejectionist that makes it a sham. The agnostic point here is that any skepticism is a means toward an end.

From an agnostic's perspective, to read *McCulloch* for what it teaches about how to go beyond blanket generalizations is to learn that it is difficult to be persuasive about who the winners and losers ought to be in a controversy. Compare this with the relative simplicity of Tushnet's approach to a case study where one is supposed to be compelled to conclude that federalism is a sham because of the antinomy between the will and reason (e.g., between sovereignty and constitutionalism) that is (said to be) endemic to liberal legalism. What is lost, or ignored, or blindly denied, in the fog of this abstraction is the capacity of an agnostic's more politically sufficient commentary to plausibly show that plain politics is simply more fuzzy and a matter of close calls than rejectionists care to admit.[19] Naturally, a rejectionist refutes this point about plain politics. But perhaps any refutation is beside the point.

It is all too easy, but nonetheless appropriate, to turn Tushnet's remarks against liberalism against rejectionism itself. Whether rejectionism has a positive program or not, its "arbitrary character . . . means that the sword of Damocles will drop, perhaps at random or perhaps for invidious political reasons, without having broader implications for the exercise of power generally" (Tushnet 1981a: 422). From an agnostic's perspective, rejectionism depends upon an image of persons shackled in a cave of political values, captured by a parade of shadow arguments and, absent some kind of liberation or consciousness-raising, without real choices about what can be done with language and politics. This image not only denies the possibility that more social fact-based commentary can show plain politics to be more dynamic and constructive than rejectionists make the law out to be. It is literally at odds with *McCulloch,* which shows itself in its many parts to have reformulated political beliefs and practices as much as it has mirrored them.

Finally, and ironically, but not surprisingly, rejectionism also takes much of the political sting out of its own critique by depriving itself of—or excusing itself from—any kind of programmatic efficacy. The civic education consequences of a lack of programmatic efficacy can be significant. As a case in point, consider what might be made of the consequences of Tushnet's summons for a populist constitutional law and its focus on a thin Constitution. Tushnet admits that the practical policy implications of this summons are, at best, slight. His primary purpose, he says, in writing about taking the Constitution away from the courts is to encourage a "conversation [among scholars, teachers and students] about some fundamental aspects of constitutionalism and politics" (Tushnet 2000: 551). In the spirit of such a conversation, we might well ask what might be the positives and negatives for undergraduates who would take his summons seriously?

Perhaps one positive is that a break with the thick Constitution might make students more open to speculate about what thin Constitutional values are about, how they are related to progressive political legal and political agendas, and how one might conceive institutional and cultural strategies for realizing those values and agendas. To the extent that this might happen, the study of constitutional law and politics might become more democratic. But there is a negative here: if students keep away from a serious study of thick constitutional issues—like a study of the strengths and weaknesses of *McCulloch*—what context will these otherwise untutored students have for self-critical examinations of the weaknesses of their speculations, except for their own personal policy predilections? Is it a positive for the polity to have more weakly tutored students who are uncritically committed to their own personal policy predilections, even if they are progressive and democratic ones? Or is it a positive to have more Jeffersonian students, prepared to challenge themselves and others that there are better and worse answers to questions about judicial review, and that even the better answers have weaknesses that must be recognized as such?

However, it has been said here that the law's efficaciousness is an enemy to alternatives. If so, it is a positive to have students shy away from studying the thick Constitution. It is a positive because, all things considered, if students shy away from the thick Constitution then, ipso facto, it cannot lead them to reject populist constitutional law as an insignificant alternative. But if those students who understand the thick Constitution on its own terms are then better prepared to combat it, then shying away from it is a negative.

One could go on like this. But eventually the point would be that Tushnet does not, and would not consider anything like a review of the positives and negatives of his own account. In his own defense perhaps Tushnet would say, justifiably, that "it is hardly the case that every author must take on every aspect of every issue relevant to the one he or she chooses to write about" (Tushnet 2000: 552). He might also say, less modestly but no less justifiably, that it is enough for an author to have the ingenuity and the craft to construct this thesis about rejecting the thick Constitution and taking the Constitution away from the courts in the first place. Therefore, it is not up to an author but to those of us who want to join the author in a conversation about his thesis to address its positives and negatives.

Fair enough. Nonetheless, from an agnostic perspective rejectionism neutralizes its critique of the status quo by excusing itself from any programmatic efficacy. That is because any conversation that takes place about Tushnet's work will not likely be concerned with its practical policy implications but will become a debate about why the status quo is wrong and rejectionism is correct. At the risk of putting too fine a point on it, as Tushnet says, "I understand that the most that can be said for my work is that it is right. And I am satisfied with that" (Tushnet 2000: 552). To the extent then that rejectionism pushes away deep skepticism about itself, and is confident in its "rightness," it neutralizes its own political sting by leaving others to just cast it aside as "wrong," and being satisfied with that.

All in all, from an agnostic perspective, rejectionism like Tushnet's presumes too much and explains too little even as it provides the agnostic an absolutely crucial reminder that, in a liberal-democratic polity, constitutional law and politics are vulnerable to a variety of inconsistent and incongruent obfuscations about itself in defense of the political and intellectual status quo. In the next chapter we will consider an agnostic take on federalism that integrates doctrinal analysis with social scientific considerations in the pursuit of politically sufficient commentary.

· 7 ·

Agnosticism, Federalism, and Constitutionalism

Admittedly, agnosticism is tricky business. In keeping with Marshall's jurisprudence, and H. N. Hirsch's advice that constitutional commentary benefits from due regard for both doctrinal analysis and the materials of social reality, agnostics must be scrupulously attentive to the Constitution as well as to formalisms and social fact considerations (Hirsch 1992, 1995). For Hirsch, due regard for the text of the Constitution and doctrinal analysis requires a theory of fundamental rights and liberty. Hirsch prefers a political and historical theory of "liberty" as an organizing idea for commentary rather than the more promoted "equality," because of liberty's historical and theoretical pedigree as a core textual and structural element of the Constitution.

Since I share Hirsch's preference for liberty as an organizing idea, this and subsequent chapters will present an agnostic conception of liberty and will explore its implications for doctrinal analysis and social fact considerations. An agnostic version of liberty must nevertheless break with Hirsch's companion commitment to advance minorities' rights, because that substantive commitment contradicts an agnostic's resolve that nothing, even minorities' rights, is certain or beyond rejoinder. Agnosticism must also break with Hirsch's commitment because politically sufficient commentary seeks to include issues of power and sovereignty interests equal to considerations of rights.

Here is where the skepticism of revisionism and rejectionism is particularly helpful. They help break the grip that traditional interpretations of rights and powers have on us. At the same time, agnostics must still be skeptical of revisionism and rejectionism because of the politics and policies both neglect. Therefore agnostics inevitably find themselves unmethodically balancing formalisms, social fact considerations, and the Constitution as they try to craft a commentary that fulfills agnosticism's mandate for neglected politics and policies.

Undertaking such a tricky business can be immobilizing, but it is a necessary risk if we are to break with intellectual jurisprudence. Fortunately, the risk is significantly diminished if we remember that we are expounding a Constitution. Despite the problems associated with constitutional commentary, the Constitution and its formalisms do provide dependable footholds for some measure of constancy in recovering neglected politics and policies. The risk is also diminished if we remember that the new institutionalism provides another foothold for a measure of constancy. It does so by asking teachers and critics to analyze the diverse social forces that constitute conflicts over the law. From such an analysis arise (multiple) constructions of the law. These constructions provide competing ideas about how society is, and should be, organized and how citizens do, and should, interact with one another to shape their politics and policies. To illustrate this point, we turn now to a consideration of how such doctrinal analysis can produce a commentary that is self-reflective and self-correcting about power and policies associated with it.

Neglected Politics and Doctrinal Analysis

Gibbons v. Ogden (1824)[1] and *Willson v. Black-Bird Creek Marsh Co.* (1829)[2] are two classic, post-*McCulloch* Commerce Clause cases. Read in the light of *McCulloch,* they instigate agnostic considerations about the political theoretical implications arising from sovereignty interests and federalism beyond those Chief Justice Marshall articulated in *McCulloch.* In *Gibbons,* a federal navigation law granted national coasting licenses even as a New York State commercial law granted a steamboat monopoly for travel between New York and New Jersey. Daniel Webster argued here, as he did in *McCulloch,* to the effect that if the state law were to prevail, the power of the Union over commerce would be in jeopardy. He also argued that Article 1, Section 8 vested Congress with exclusive power to regulate commerce. Although Marshall's opinion voided the constitutionality of the New York state law, only in dicta did Marshall indicate his approval of the textual soundness of the exclusivity thesis. The *Gibbons* doctrine is that under the Supremacy Clause, federal laws are preeminent when they collide with state laws.

In *Black-Bird Creek,* a Delaware law provided for a public improvements dam to be built on the tidal Black-Bird Creek, which flowed into the Delaware River. A boat in interstate commerce, with a federal license, smashed through the dam that obstructed navigation to pass down the creek. Marshall ruled that absent a collision with federal laws, measures calculated to improve conditions within state borders are compatible with power constitutionally reserved to the states even if such measures impinge on interstate commerce. This is in apparent contradiction to the *Gibbons* doctrine, according to which a federal coasting license would prohibit state constraints on interstate commerce. *Black-Bird Creek* also appears to be legally and politically incongruous with the *McCulloch* doctrine that state constraints on interstate commerce (be they a state monopoly or a dam) threaten the consolidation of national power.

Some scholars explain *Black-Bird Creek* as a rank political retreat from *McCulloch* and *Gibbons* in the face of the 1828 election of Andrew Jackson and Court-curbing efforts by Congress. Others explain it by drawing doctrinal distinctions about significant and insignificant obstructions of commerce. Or they parse *Gibbons* for Commerce Clause criteria that demarcate permissible state health, safety, and welfare functions from impermissible infringements on congressional authority. Alternatively, *Black-Bird Creek* is read to explain that if there are tangible economic benefits of state regulations (e.g., the improvement of property values) and if there is no conflicting federal law, then that may be sufficient to outweigh otherwise dominant federal authority over commerce.

That so many explanations are possible gives weight to the view that there is no single theory of the distribution of power under the Commerce Clause, and that in consequence there will inevitably be political conflict over what the clause means in terms of sovereignty interests in political integration. The *McCulloch* interweave of plain politics and consequentialist consideration drives this conflict and makes it impossible to maintain doctrinal "consistency." In other words, Court opinions will perpetually produce social fact incongruities, and they will never be rightly decided.

It is on this premise that *Gibbons* and *Black-Bird Creek* are to be read as being about colliding conceptions of power and sovereignty interests that do not seek to utterly destroy one another. I have in mind ways of commenting about the text of the Constitution, the Tenth Amendment in particular, that can produce a dynamic between federal and state power that is sufficient to realize the intimations of *McCulloch, Gibbons,* and *Black-Bird Creek.* This is the sort of commentary that radical rejectionists cannot abide because they have so much at stake in finding only the destructive elements of liberal-democratic law. But it is commentary compatible with finding a politics and policies of programmatic efficacy that others have neglected, or vaguely sensed, or have refused to recognize.

The jumping-off point for this commentary is the Tenth Amendment as it appears in *National League of Cities v. Usery* (1976)[3] and subsequent Commerce Clause adjudication. The Tenth Amendment says that "powers not delegated to the United States, nor prohibited by it to the States, are reserved to the States respectively, or to the people." Most constitutional historians agree that the original purpose of the Tenth Amendment was to check the power of the federal government, Congress in particular. But Court rulings during the New Deal that legitimized expansive congressional legislation in the economic domain rendered the amendment "a mere truism." Then, in *National League of Cities,* the Court, in a five-to-four decision, struck as unconstitutional a 1974 congressional statute that extended the maximum-hours and minimum-wage provisions of the Fair Labor Standards Act to state governments and their political subdivisions. One of the central elements in Chief Justice Rehnquist's majority opinion was a Tenth Amendment finding that traditional state governmental functions, related to such duties as police protection and public health services, were exempt from federal regulations. The justification for this finding was that these functions had attached to them attributes of sovereignty of states as states that could not be legitimately violated. In dissent, Justice Brennan argued that Chief Justice Rehnquist's opinion violated *Gibbons* and the principle that the sole constraint on national power under the Commerce Clause is congressional politics and not judicial review.[4]

Nine years later, after what five Justices, and many scholars, found to be a futile and unprincipled exercise in trying to draw lines between "traditional" state governmental functions and federal power, the Court in *Garcia v. San Antonio Metropolitan Transit Authority*[5] reversed *National League of Cities.* In doing so the majority made but one glancing reference to the Tenth Amendment. Then, in 1995, in *United States v. Lopez,*[6] another five-to-four decision, the Rehnquist Court indicated its willingness to revisit line drawing, traditional state governmental functions, and passive acceptance of the idea that national power ought to grow in proportion to the exigencies of an integrated national and international economy. For the first time in over half a century, the Court ruled an act of Congress, the Gun-Free School Zones Act (1990), unconstitutional.

The core issue in the *Lopez* case was whether the act satisfied the substantive effects test of Congress's Commerce Clause authority: that is, an activity, taken alone or in its aggregate consequences, must have a substantial impact on economic enterprises or market activities involving interstate commerce to be regulated by Congress.[7] In promulgating the act, Congress did not indicate, through legislative findings, specific relationships between firearms in and immediately adjacent to schools, and interstate commerce. Instead it depended on the legal convention that earlier legislative enactments may be relied on to establish that an activity (here possession of a gun within one thousand feet of a school) has an adverse effect (in this case on education) that in turn has a substantial negative impact on interstate commerce.

The Court, in upholding the appeals court, agreed that the act exceeded Congress's power because Congress had not provided prima facie evidence that possession of a firearm in a local school zone was an economic or commercial activity that affected interstate commerce. The Court concluded that absent such evidence the act had to be judged unconstitutional if there were to be any judicially enforceable limits on congressional power. The Court also confirmed that firearms and schools relate to "noncommercial" activities that come under the umbrella of general police powers of the sort held only by the states. It made not a single reference to the Tenth Amendment.

But in *Printz v. United States,*[8] the Rehnquist Court, in yet another of its five-to-four decisions, did address the Tenth Amendment explicitly. *Printz* ruled that the provisions of the Brandy Handgun Violence Act, which commanded state officers to fulfill the act's provisions by performing background checks on potential handgun gun purchasers, violated the reach of the Commerce Clause. The majority opinion, by Justice Scalia, cited the Tenth Amendment as a companion to its adjudication of the Commerce and Necessary and Proper Clauses to indicate that the Constitution established a system of dual sovereignty within which states retained an inviolable residual power.

But the Tenth Amendment did not play an explicit role in the more recent *United States v. Morrison* (2000).[9] There, a five-to-four Rehnquist Court struck as unconstitutional that portion of the Violence against Women Act (1994) that provided a federal civil remedy for victims of gender-motivated violence.

All these inconsistencies about what federalism and the Commerce Clause require, and the relatively indifferent treatment of the Tenth Amendment, might well be taken to corroborate claims that formalisms are plainly bankrupt when it comes to principled ways to abate national economic and political power. Alternatively, they also provide space for agnostic commentary about a shifting dynamic between federal and state power. To make our way toward such a commentary, we would do well to begin with Justice Clarence Thomas's concurring opinion in *Lopez* about the original meaning of the Constitution and the effects test.

Justice Thomas concurred with the majority of the *Lopez* Court when it held that in principle the federal government lacks any police power functions whatsoever. He also agreed with the principle that congressional power is limited under the Commerce Clause, and that there is at the same time no formulaic way to determine whether an activity substantially affects interstate commerce such that it comes within the Commerce Clause authority of Congress. However, Justice Thomas broke with the Court on the legitimacy of social and economic facts and the effects test to determine whether an activity falls within the ambit of congressional power.

For Justice Thomas, the effects test is a mistaken judicial creation that does violence to the original meaning of the Commerce Clause as well as to the Tenth Amendment. Basically his argument proceeds as follows: At the time of the ratification of the Constitution, the meaning of "commerce" was distinguishable from manufacturing and agriculture. The enumerated powers of Congress under Article 1, Section 8 further verify that congressional power ought not to be plenary over just any or all productive activities.

Justice Thomas admits that today determinations about which activities fall under congressional power are not so self-evident. Nevertheless he contends that to interpolate a modern meaning of "commerce" as "business generally" into the Constitution, or to read the Necessary and Proper Clause to include all matters that substantially affect commerce, effectively renders the limiting function of Article I and its enumerations superfluous. In fact, he says, the effects test obliterates federalism by eviscerating the Tenth Amendment's provision that powers not delegated to the Union nor prohibited to the states are reserved to the states.

A strength of Justice Thomas's position is that it stands alone in its *McCulloch*-like commitment to the text as the insertion point for adjudicating the plain politics of commerce and federalism. All the opinions in *Lopez* do pay their obligatory respects to the spirit of *McCulloch,* but their insertion point is a defense of the effects test, at the level of precedent and/or social fact claims about "activities" and a national economy. These insertion points fail where Thomas's succeeds: Thomas's originalism, like *McCulloch,* makes the Constitution itself the theoretical root of the rule of law.

Justice Thomas alone teaches the *McCulloch* lesson that it is a Constitution that is being expounded, and not (just) precedents, social fact claims, or some thin version of it that serves political interests in the rightly decided question. Unfortunately, Thomas fails to teach the lesson that the Constitution cannot be read absent attention to plain politics and consequentialist considerations. Instead, his originalism leads him to the conclusion that line drawing "may ignore 'economic reality' and thus seem arbitrary or artificial to some," but "we must nevertheless respect a line drawn 'true to the Constitution.' "[10]

The point has merit, of course, but there are at least three reasons to be skeptical about this line-drawing originalism. For one, it depends on metaphysical commitments to reduce, without remainder, the law to textual claims about the political structure. Likewise, it confers legitimacy on distinctions between federal and state power that deliberately ignore colliding perspectives about sovereignty interests that give rise to Commerce Clause litigation and adjudication. Last, it disregards the view that because there is no single theory of the distribution of power under the Commerce Clause, persistent and irresolvable political conflict is inevitable over what the clause means in terms of sovereignty interests in political integration.

Indeed, to determine what the Commerce Clause and federalism require solely via the original meaning of the words of the Constitution, along with semantic or logical claims about the text, puts abstraction in control of understanding law and politics. And with what result? Looked at from the perspective of Marshall's ambiguous and consequentialist conflation of prudent policies and the rule of law, Justice Thomas's originalism is indeed arbitrary and artificial because it obscures the politics and policies of prudence—something, by the way, not to be attributed to all originalisms. Debates about federalism, it must be said, are always policy debates, and they are always about which institutions and which political elites ought to have control over a policy.

No less an originalist than Hadley Arkes, in his celebratory analysis of George Sutherland (1994), arguably this century's most sophisticated Court advocate of constitutional limits on federal power, makes a similar point. Arkes is persuasive, I think, when he insists that any test about federal and state relations must go beyond the text to configure "rigorously moral arguments" with textual ones (Arkes 1994: 141). "Moral arguments" must include those about liberty which are secured by the separation between federal and state power. The course of federalism and Commerce Clause case law demonstrates, moreover, to almost everyone's satisfaction, except Justice Thomas's, that anything less than merging formalistic and empirical considerations will always prove to be too mechanistic, both legally and politically, to accomplish the goal of explaining the connection between legal principles and what is required by way of preserving liberty. That is why I say that Thomas's originalism comes off, from an agnostic's perspective, as undermining itself. Its dependence on historical meaning and logic alone is too mechanistic to be an adequate defense of the rule of law over against the politics and policies of centralization of federal power. To reject what the past and present indicate the rule of law requires—that is, prudential consideration of extratextual matters—is to treat federalism as a sham.

However, and this is a very large qualification, commentary cognizant of a politics of capital development and mobilization is well advised not to reject originalist predilections out of hand. Suitably integrated with prudential considerations (although not the ones Arkes has in mind),[11] originalism has something to contribute to closing a gulf (which I am about to identify) between the effects test and the politics and policies of federalism. What I have in mind is commentary that merges Justice Thomas's dictum that the meaning of commerce and the limits of Congress and national power are intrinsic to the very language of the Constitution with the dynamic about power I referred to above. This much, at least, follows the path of *McCulloch,* already described, that recognizes both the necessity and uncertainty of textualism.

An Inconstant Dynamic: Federalism and the Constitution

In this regard, we might recall that we took from *Gibbons* and *Black-Bird Creek* a root idea: textual limits of national power under the Commerce Clause must be linked to consequentialist considerations in order to defend conceptions of power that do not seek to utterly destroy one competitor or the other. Today, the politics and policies of development and mobilization, and changes in political economy generally, recommend that rigorously serious arguments return to the text. Hence any return to the text should be based on the premise that commentary involving the Commerce Clause and federalism, given their nature, is not well served by timeless or time-bound abstractions about things like the effects test or command-and-control conceptions of politics. Rather, my premise is that the Constitution needs to be read within the context of context-specific considerations about sovereignty interests as they play out in the various politics and policies of cooperation and competition.

For instance, the effects test is incompatible with my premise to the extent that the test focuses on "activities" because that focus obscures important, and common-sense, considerations about circumstantial facts and sovereignty interests. Ironically, a focus on "activities" has its roots in legal realism and its commitment to conceptions of sovereignty interests and a national marketplace subject to federal control. As this commitment has worked itself out in adjudication in this century, the national government has come to be seen as the pinnacle of an administrative state (Horwitz 1992). Thus, despite agnosticism's debt to legal realism, agnostics have to be skeptical of it at just this point.

Under federal command and control, "activities" left to state and local governments are those that do not interfere with sovereignty interests to consolidate national power. Consolidation is deemed necessary to redress market failure, create equitable conditions between citizens, limit the influence of private wealth and business and corporate power, and reform the political process (Elazar 1991: 106–09). This agenda dovetails with the presupposition that if negative effects of activities on the national economy are demonstrable, then overriding state and local power is warranted. The agenda served by the effects test shapes a way of thinking that is wary of competition between the national and subsidiary governments.

A potentially more dynamic conception than federal command and control is cooperative federalism, as it is known in plain politics. Cooperative federalism allows for either the centralization or decentralization of power, depending on fact determinations about how this or that activity fits into the larger picture of sovereignty interests in national power. Yet there is no mistaking the general trend toward increasing integration of the nation's economy. President Richard Nixon's version of cooperative federalism recognized this. His New Federalism, as he called it, attempted to combine elements of centralization and decentralization by instituting management reforms to improve federal program efficiency, block grants, revenue sharing, and the nationalization of public sector activities, such as welfare. All this was tried in the name of economic efficiency and in the hope of reviving the power of state and local governments. The results of the New Federalism were mixed: a dramatic increase in federal expenditures for domestic spending and greater, rather than lesser, centralization of power; but the polity also experienced a "burst of state and local policy innovation . . . in the declining dependence of states and localities on federal assistance" (Conlan 1988: 228).

By contrast, President Ronald Reagan's New Federalism was ideologically opposed to Nixon's pragmatism. It used budget reductions, tax cuts, and deregulation, not to make the federal government more efficient but to diminish its role in intergovernmental relations, to retract the reach of the modern welfare state, and to discourage governmental intervention at all levels. The jury is still out on the long-term consequences of Reagan's policies. Nevertheless, the short-term results of the Reagan agenda are somewhat clear. First, although it appears to have amplified elite and mass ambivalence, if not hostility, toward government generally, it left specific governmental services at any level basically undiminished. Second, it made the federal government more efficient and, some would argue, *stronger* in the bargain (Conlan 1988: 221–37), without at the same time seriously decreasing state and local activities.

Prudence dictates caution in drawing any conclusions about the implications of such mixed results for the future politics of federalism. Still, it does not seem rash to say that these two political experiments in cooperative federalism indicate the complex interrelatedness of government activities and public sector economics, as well as the inertia of national power. Fold into the mix international economic and technological forces of the kind at work in the Internet and it seems plausible to ask whether legal realist faith in the effects test provides an adequate grasp of the sovereignty interests of federalism.

Confidence in a negative answer to this question increases when we put the present in the context of the past and the future. The conventional wisdom is that since the founding there have been three major shifts in the "character" of federal-state relations: "the era of national infrastructure development (1848–1913); the period of federal intervention (1913–1977); and a new period beginning in 1977 whose character is not yet clear" (Elazar 1991: 77). The uncertainty of this new period is nevertheless sufficient to make us want to measure the effects test against the results of cooperative federalism and the circumstantial facts of late-twentieth-century political economy.

Here I follow those social scientists (e.g., Dye 1990; Elazar 1991; Ostrom 1991) who conclude that cooperation alone has not provided for a sufficient degree of division among powers, given "the centralizing consequences of cooperative federalism" (Elazar 1991: 112). They suggest that there needs to be a dynamic cooperation and competition between states and states, and between states and their localities, as well as between them all and the federal government. At least in principle, competition should yield, so these social scientists argue, a greater range of public policies than cooperation alone has been able to produce; as they see it, policies would be driven by the comparative costs and benefits of state and local services versus federal ones, rather than by command and control. If encouraging tax policies were in place, if state and local budgets were less reliant on federal programs and financial aid, and if the potential mobility of citizens and capital increased, then, to the extent there was an oversupply of public goods, certain outcomes could be expected. For example, "consumer-taxpayers [would] have the opportunity to register their policy preferences by moving into or out of government jurisdictions . . ." (Dye 1990: 23); and, correlated to an expansion in the range of available public policies, an increase would occur in the economic and political power sites in the polity.

Encouraging these power sites is not easily accomplished. At a bare minimum, it requires the baseline policy of the social-gain rule which says that "governments should refrain from policies if costs are not exceeded by gains" (Dye 1990: 22). But if governments lack the right or sufficient information, officials "have no accurate mechanism for weighing these [consumer-taxpayer] preferences, for finding the preferred balance between benefits and costs, and for estimating the equilibrium level of government activity" (Dye 1990: 22). What the social-gain rule introduces into the discussion of federalism is underdeterminacy, both for balancing interests and for predicting desirable distributions of economic and political power. This underdeterminacy is hidden from view by the frame of reference of the effects test and "activities." The social-gain rule would encourage a more dynamic and comprehensive, and therefore more adequate, reference point for thinking about sovereignty interests than the reference point of "activities" alone.

To understand this dynamic we need to loop back to the *Lopez* opinions. All of those opinions, in one way or another, conceive education and economics in terms of a balance between two categories of mutually exclusive "activities," that is, areas of traditional state concern and areas that have come under national government command and control. It is at least debatable that categories of mutually exclusive "activities" are at odds with circumstantial facts associated with the history of public sector economics, the history of cooperative federalism, and the potential of competitive federalism. Let us begin with public sector economics.

The social-gain rule recommends that issues of violence and education be moved from the context of "activities" into the context of human capital investment and economic development. In the latter context, violence and education are to be associated with "a wide range of human resources programs—such as job training, vocational education, higher education, welfare, and health care" (Fosler 1991: 299).

Given the recent history of cooperative federalism, and especially ongoing concerns about the relative weakness of states and localities in opposition to national power, perhaps the time is right to shift attention away from a command-and-control mode of federalism. And, despite the fact that education is traditionally a state and local concern, perhaps it is time for commentary to require, in regard to it, "a thoroughgoing *blending* of federal, state, and local responsibilities in the design and conduct of public policy" (Fosler 1991: 305, emphasis added). Of course, any proposal to blend public policy responsibilities is no doubt fraught with practical difficulties. But these are difficulties of ideals and practices worth understanding if the unique contributions of states and localities to human capital development can be tapped.

Indeed, in conjunction with their relative increase in autonomy associated with the New Federalism, states and localities have integrated an array of relevant programs in human resource development. States have proven to be better situated than the national government in constructing policy decisions attuned to their respective regional economies and labor markets (Fosler 1991: 306–07). Policy innovation by states and localities is a tender plant that needs to be nurtured, and any future growth in their autonomy, and sovereignty, has to be protected against the counterproductive forces of centralization. But they cannot hope to succeed without national support.

This is where commentary about a more inconstant dynamic for federalism comes into the picture. Competition among states and localities, and between them and the national government, should increase, as one commentator has put it, "the motivation . . . for each State to make the best use of its own internal resources, including its people." In addition, "initiatives fashioned locally are . . . more likely to motivate and win commitment than are programs that are federally imposed" (Fosler 1991: 309–10). Winning political and economic commitments could be a significant long-term bulwark against national power. So, to maximize both the social-gain rule and decentralization, different levels of government should entertain different levels and types of public services in much the same way as various markets provide goods and services (Dye 1990: 198; Fosler 1991: 310).

But there are problems. One is the political culture. Notwithstanding the rhetoric of electoral politics, the prudent view I want to endorse is that the very idea of "different levels and types of public services in different locations" is not easily accepted (Dye 1990: 198). The primary problem with such diversity, as I understand it, is that it may produce an unequal distribution of programs and services. That possibility contradicts welfare state imperatives for egalitarian distributions and also reinforces settled expectations "that states and localities should play a derivative role in policy areas that are crucial to national health and prosperity" (Fosler 1991: 298).

Another problem is structural. Here again I borrow from others: "education and the national economy are inextricably connected" (Boyer 1991: 171), and in human capital development there are things that only a national government can do well. Despite the central role that state and local governments, as well as the private sector, may have in the design and implementation of human capital investment (Fosler 1991: 310), only national political leadership and fiscal wherewithal are sufficient to implement a national agenda that ties together the fragmented and piecemeal efforts of the other three. And, if the national government is to provide the framework for an efficient intergovernmental system of capital development along with mechanisms that offset the inegalitarian consequences of competition, it has to be actively involved "in the design, funding, and execution of human capital policies" (Fosler 1991: 305).

What all this adds up to is that uncertainties regarding the consequences of balancing sovereignty interests make "mobilizing the federal system for [human capital] investment" a desirable option. But this mobilization would "require action along two parallel and mutually reinforcing tracks: *cooperation* to bring the interrelated features of the system into harmony, and *competition* to stimulate each governmental jurisdiction and region to develop its own potential" (Fosler 1991: 317).

Thus, Justice Thomas's originalism, properly amended, has started us on a path that bites deeply into the inconsistencies of federalism and Commerce Clause adjudication. What these inconsistencies hide is a neglected constitutional politics of cooperation and competition that has little to gain from disputes about the sufficiency of facts to determine whether the substantive-effects test is satisfied or not. And what this neglected politics needs is an agnostic look at the Constitution so that a politics of conflict over competition and cooperation can be pursued. To continue on this path, we loop back to an amended originalism for a conception of liberty that is inextricably intermingled with the Constitution as a text, sovereignty interests about power, and circumstantial fact considerations. My candidate for such a conception is "ordered liberty" (from *Palko v. Connecticut*).[12]

When Justice Benjamin N. Cardozo confronted the question when the prohibitions of the first eight Amendments to the Constitution should be taken to apply to the states, granted the force of the Due Process Clause of the Fourteenth Amendment, he denied the appropriateness of any formulaic answer. Instead, he advocated the principle that where to draw the lines depended upon consequentialist determinations of whether a supposed violation of the amendments constituted a hardship so severe that it traduced the social and moral welfare of the polity—the settled expectations regarding the objects of everyday life—or the "liberty and justice which lie at the base of all of our civil and political institutions."[13]

Justice Cardozo advanced this concept of ordered liberty to indicate that textual and nontextual determinations were to be melded together to specify why provisions of the amendments are, or are not, to be applied to the states as indispensable for protecting freedom in a constitutional polity. Regardless of how far, as a judge, Justice Cardozo was willing or able to go in his own meld, agnostics true to the tenets of politically sufficient commentary and the spirit of *McCulloch* should go very far indeed with it.

To draw lines around ordered liberty that partake in underdetermined considerations about abstractions like liberty and justice would yield consistently hesitant and intermittent conceptions of rights and powers. These conceptions might well be akin to the kinds of considerations about law and politics that revisionist commentary seeks as amended, of course, by politically sufficient commentary. And unlike adjudication or commentary in the grip of intellectual jurisprudence, agnostics cannot help but shuttle back and forth between conservation and criticism of society's customary ways of thinking about things like "liberty" and "justice." This agnostic shuttle may, at any point, come to a provisional and hesitant rest on the left or on the right of the political and legal continuum. It may also compromise positions on the left and the right to the extent of revealing aspects of politics and law that are neglected, or vaguely sensed, or rejected by customary commentary. But wherever it may rest temporarily, this kind of commentary—which I call commentary to a middle course—must declare the strengths and weaknesses of its recommended course of action. It is essential to say, in that regard, that commentary to a middle course, to be faithful to its own imperatives, must consider the strengths and weaknesses of the role played by the courts and judicial review in the subject under investigation.

The remaining chapters of this book provide specific examples of commentary to a middle course. I should say now that it would be a mistake to conclude from my general remarks about this commentary that it requires anyone—agnostic or otherwise—to abandon firmly held beliefs about what is practical or best for the polity. We rarely abandon our firmly held beliefs in any case. But if this commentary is persuasive it could challenge nonagnostics and agnostics alike to be more self-conscious about the strengths and weaknesses of their arguments on behalf of those beliefs. For those who choose to remain in the grip of the ideology of involvement and intellectual jurisprudence, this self-consciousness might yield (for better or worse) more subtle and sophisticated answers to the rightly decided question on behalf of those beliefs. For those who do engage agnosticism to some degree, this self-consciousness might make them more empathetic in their response to the beliefs they oppose. More important, it might compel teachers, critics, and their audiences to deliberately question the extent to which their beliefs and the beliefs of others rest on an avoidance of questions with underdetermined answers. In such cases nasty issues about controversies that we really do not understand or do not want to understand may have some space to appear. In bringing issues like this to the forefront, agnosticism encourages adherents, and others who have a mind to listen to them, to entertain second and third thoughts about whether commentary of all stripes may be woefully incomplete and premature. This is an optimistic scenario for the impact of agnosticism on commentary as civic education, and I will address it in the concluding chapter. Immediately at hand is an example of agnostic commentary about ordered liberty that seeks a middle course between criticism and conservation of federalism.

· 8 ·
A Middle Course on Reform

This chapter presents an amended originalism regarding ordered liberty. It depicts a *McCulloch*-like dynamic of rights and powers to orient commentary toward troublesome uncertainties attending efforts to reform federalism. This dynamic melds textual considerations about sovereignty and participant interests and plain political considerations about governmental responsiveness, articulation of the politics of interests, and budding issues of human capital development. Such commentary does not resolve the uncertainties it encounters. But that is not problematic in and of itself as long as we remember that agnosticism is not conceived as advice to lawyers and judges about how they rightly decide cases if they would just imitate commentary in their work. Rather, agnostic commentary is advice for critics, teachers, and students to pursue that Jeffersonian critical citizenship, whereby they experiment exuberantly (if hypothetically) with what is practical and best in law, politics, and policies.

By necessity experimentation depends upon conditional "if-then hypotheses" and generalities about the Constitution, its formalisms, and contingent fact considerations. Such experimentation in commentary is therefore far more vague and conjectural than a problem-solving orientation tolerates, but (as I argue below) that is a price worth paying if it can overcome the intellectual gridlock of commentary as usual. And it is a price more than worth paying if it leads as well to a more self-critical and forgiving regard for the unanticipated and unintended in the law, politics, and policies.

This chapter also brings things together, by way of politically sufficient commentary, much of what chapter 1 indicates agnostic commentary endorses in political science (and legal) literatures. These literatures have attempted to reshape the form and substance of commentary dealing with legal relationships and political arrangements. Accordingly, readers will find that this chapter's discussion of federalism and the environment intersects with new republicanism's efforts to encompass the diverse views that citizens and groups in a pluralistic society bring to debates about law, policies, and intellectual authority. This chapter's discussion also follows the new republicanism by using the underdeterminacy of legal materials to construct novel, even competing, visions of the present and the future.

This discussion of federalism and the environment also attends to two goals of the new constitutionalism in commentary. Firstly, it focuses equally on issues of power (and therefore sovereignty interests) as on (participant and audience) interests in civil liberties and rights of participation for constructing arguments about ordered liberty. Secondly, it depends upon social science–like considerations rather than abstract moral or political philosophy for its standards as to what is practical and best in legal and political policies.

But ultimately this commentary on federalism and the environment breaks with new republicanism and constitutionalism and uses intellectual means unique to agnosticism. Agnosticism's uniqueness arises from a decision to shuttle back and forth in a middle course between conservation and criticism of what is practical and best in law and policies. But deciding to do no more than shuttle back and forth in this way takes ideological self-discipline (as discussed in the first two chapters). For examples of why this is so, this chapter begins with two highly charged environmental law cases in 2001. These cases concern environmental law and policies related to the Commerce Clause and federalism, as considered in the previous chapter and elaborated upon here.

The first of these cases is *Solid Waste Agency of Northern Cook City v. United States Army Corps of Engineers.*[1] Here, the Supreme Court majority, in a five-to-four ruling, with glancing references to *Lopez* and *United States v. Morrison,* held that the Clean Water Act and the Commerce Clause do not extend to nonnavigable, isolated, intrastate waters. The second of these cases is *Whitman v. American Trucking Assns., Inc.*[2] Here, in a complicated ruling that generated three concurring opinions and a patchwork majority for specific elements of the case, the Court held, in part, that consideration of implementation costs are prohibited in the administration of the Clean Air Act. It also held that the Court of Appeals erred in its finding that Congress had unconstitutionally delegated legislative authority to the Environmental Protection Agency (EPA) by failing to provide the latter with determinate criteria for establishing environmental harms.

It may well prove difficult for nonagnostics to resist reading the opinions in these cases solely in terms of their doctrinal and formalistic significance for federalism, Commerce Clause adjudication, and the status of risk-assessment strategies in environmental policies. For other nonagnostics, these doctrinal and formalistic concerns will be put into the context of the persistent five-to-four division on the Rehnquist Court, complicated rival jurisprudence arguments, and predictions about how potential replacements for impending retirements on the Court will vote in future cases. And for those nonagnostics who remain furious about the Supreme Court's decision to end the electoral recount in Florida in the presidential race between George W. Bush and Vice President Al Gore, opinions of the Rehnquist Court will be read solely for evidence of their rank partisanship. (More of *Bush v. Gore* in the final chapter.)

Each of these readings is reasonable enough on its own terms. Moreover, there is no reason why an agnostic cannot acknowledge that each reading has intellectual and political strength, to say nothing of seductiveness. But a most important lesson an agnostic learns from adhering to the tenets of politically sufficient commentary is the self-discipline necessary to resist just one reading. An agnostic, following the new institutionalism, has the self-discipline to keep one eye open for how the law and politics can yield *multiple* contestable interpretations, and for how underdeterminate any single interpretation of law, politics, and policies can be. These multiple contestable interpretations provide the material for shuttling back and forth between them to construct what will become better or worse answers to the rightly decided question. More important, they provide the material to understand how and why better, or even "the best," answers should always be treated as subject to reconsideration.

Ordered Liberty and Environmental Policies

Environmental policies concerns air and water quality control, public land use, mining law and policy, forestry practices, wetlands and water quality, restructuring electric utility delivery, commercial fishing control, pesticide management and control, industrial and agricultural chemical/toxic waste cleanup, acid rain, and wildlife preservation. These and yet other problems form a labyrinth of ecological, political, economic, and social-psychological issues that characterize controversies over the environment. Except for the rank partisans and ideologues, the problems of the environment and the issues they raise force everyone—citizens, industry, labor, interest groups, legislators, regulators, and adjudicators—into a bewildering array of puzzles and dilemmas. How do we describe and evaluate the trade-offs between public goods and benefits, public harms and private interests? How do we produce the applicable questions in order to get adequate answers about the extent to which, or whether, persons and politics can control themselves, social processes, nature, and the future?

Fortunately, the controversies that have marked environmental politics and policies need not be addressed in any comprehensive way for my purpose here: to set forth an originalism about ordered liberty that is based on the Tenth Amendment, in tandem with the Ninth, and that will help clarify some implications of these questions. Instead, a broad overview of environmental action and policy is sufficient to provide circumstantial evidence for the role for these two amendments in the formulation of that originalism.

The first stage in environmental politics and policies began with the passage of the National Environmental Policy Act in 1970. In the three decades or so since then, the Environmental Protection Agency, some ten major environmental laws, and about four times as many statutes regulating pollution have succeeded uncommonly well at shaping political and legal attitudes and an ethos of industrial compliance. Notwithstanding prolonged and costly litigation, and the inevitable attempts to evade them, legislative mandates and their environmental enforcement standards have been accepted by all as part and parcel of doing business. The EPA and various environmental groups have also played a major part in the civic education of the polity to environmental issues, agenda setting, and accountability.

Arguably, a second stage in the legislation and administration of environmental policies began with the Reagan administration. Administration budget cuts reduced the personnel of environmental agencies at the same time that congressional policies, particularly in regard to air and water quality, increased the EPA's workload. Deregulation policies have multiplied significantly the number of state and local administrative agencies responsible for implementation programs. This multiplication of agencies had a twofold effect: it produced a backlog in the EPA's oversight workload, and it made for a corresponding backlog in federal decision-making.

The Reagan Administration's New Federalism, expressed as the need for efficiency in federal-state relations (and in the form of some political hostility to environmental protection policies), produced two presidential executive orders, 12291 and 12492 (1981). These orders required environmental agencies to submit to the Office of Management and Budget (OMB) analyses of proposed programs that demonstrated that the benefits of implementation outweighed costs. They also initiated a hierarchy of policy options that favored least costly implementation rules for regulatory targets and procedures.

By all accounts, the executive orders were more significant than the budget cuts or deregulation. The OMB reviews by themselves, many believe, constituted a kind of "secret channel" through which industry was able to influence regulatory legislation. It is also believed that EPA officials were sensitive to how the OMB might react to proposed regulations and altered them accordingly. Finally, even the fact that the OMB consists of economists has been a source of worry for those who believe that economists have lacked the expertise, the experience, or the interest to pursue institutional initiatives related to state and local government as primary agents or coregulators.

Still, on the other side of the ledger, the EPA's success in educating the public about efficiency, agenda setting, and accountability stood out. Under the leadership of William Ruckleshaus (1983–1984) and Lee Thomas (1984–1989), the EPA made it clear that the time had come to base future environmental strategies on assessments of the economic costs of policies relative to their supposed benefits in correcting for putative harms. Alongside these assessments, the EPA indicated that it had begun to formulate calculations of the rank-order of environmental risks in preparation for setting its implementation agenda. It also promised to be more responsive to public demands to take up local ecological threats such as garbage disposal and to attend to international threats such as sewage waste in the oceans, global warming, and depletion of the ozone layer by becoming more involved in forums concerned with the global environment (Landy, Roberts, and Thomas 1990: 251–58).[3]

The George H. W. Bush years added little more to the ledger. But the Clinton administration did advance some broad ideas about bureaucratic reform (more on that shortly). Also, early in 1999, it did offer budget recommendations based on increased environmental power-sharing, including an EPA bond fund that would subsidize loans to states to create parks, protect water quality, and clean up industrial waste sites without EPA mandates about site qualifications. In principle, a loan program should reduce federal-state tensions over the enforcement of environmental laws, and perhaps encourage advocates of deregulation to increase federal expenditures. Even so, institutional issues remain unresolved, and today virtually all parties to the controversy recognize that the theory and practice of environmental protection are in need of significant, if not radical, reform.

There are, as always, those who want more than institutional reform. Self-styled insurgent 1994 House Republicans wanted a policy revolution. Some would have dismantled the EPA entirely and terminated federal mandates and funding, and thus have left it to the states to implement environmental policies. Others, of a libertarian bent, would prefer a "common law" approach that left it primarily to market forces—not legislatures—to sort out environmental policies.[4] As for alleged harms arising from market inefficiencies and distortions of market forces due to the unequal distribution of resources—this is something the common law approach would leave for citizens and courts.

Perhaps somewhat closer to the mainstream than these parties, but still extreme, are some national environmental organizations and public interest groups that stand unalterably opposed to any changes to command-and-control environmental laws. They would see any alteration in the status quo as a capitulation to industry and private property interests. At the farthest extreme on the left are the various radical ecopolitical activists, members of Earth First!, various "greens," and self-proclaimed ecoterrorists.[5] They are radical rejectionists and view electoral politics, legislative enactments, and market forces as shams. For them, the real problems are, variously, capitalism, modern Western culture, the nation-state system, North/South politics, racism, the patriarchal and militaristic rape of ecosystems, or simply the unwillingness of humanity to cease interfering with the world of nature. These activists are advocates of revolutionary ideas such as anarchism, democratic socialism, neo-Marxism, various feminisms, or nativism.[6] But none of the constituencies at the left or right extreme is (as yet) a major factor in the public debate over environmental politics and policies. So the public debate is, for better or worse, over reform.

Here the differences of opinion are wide and deep, largely because parties to the debate disagree about how to integrate the three main factors for characterizing environmental problems. These are risk assessment, risk management, and sustainability. Risk assessments describe scientific judgments about harms to persons, society, and the ecology. Risk management describes the relative economic and social costs and benefits of implementation strategies. Sustainability is a revisionist version of rejectionist descriptions of the interrelationships between nature, society, and justice. And, it is fair to say, "when the subject moves beyond description to prescription, or from objective to means, even wider disagreement occurs" (Wells and Hamilton 1995: 112–13). This is true especially in regard to procedural issues of inter- and intragovernmental relations as well as intervention in the marketplace. What should remain the same about these relations and interventions? What should change? What is efficacious reform and how should it be brought about?

Those who advocate greater institutional reform, increasing the diversity of voices in environmental controversies, and expanding programs for the development and diffusion of environmental technologies and education have reason to give pessimistic answers to these questions. Juxtaposed to a record of compliance and successful civic education is an accumulation of policies that have triggered an intimidating list of (basically nonpartisan) worries. The EPA is said to have engendered overly complex enforcement rules and procedures and to have emerged, over time, with programs that lack programmatic clarity and coherence. It is also said to have failed at integrating interagency policies at the federal level and at intergovernmental integration of itself and state and local governments. On the political economy front, state and local politicians have been distressed by antagonisms between themselves and the EPA over the Superfund program, which is supposed to provide for cleaning up toxic sites, and over a dearth of criteria for assessing priorities and the prolonged litigation it has engendered.

Last, there are worries about the completeness of the EPA's role in civic education. The EPA is not given high marks for public education about the comparative harms of various public health dangers. Nor does it receive high marks for educating the polity to distinctions between real or potential harms and unsafe conditions. It is also criticized for promising, on behalf of various policies, ecological and/or social benefits that are vague and simplistic or otherwise at odds with complicated and ambiguous scientific findings and consequentialist considerations.

As if that were not enough, there is a widespread consensus that the EPA does not appreciate the possibility of diminishing returns from policies or make important end-point decisions about infeasible or costly compliance standards. Specifically, there is the perception that it has miseducated the public about, or failed to communicate to it adequately, the complexities of risk assessment, risk management, and concerns about environmental sustainability.[7] Here the worry is the experts'. Lawyers and economists, who currently hold a preeminent role in making decisions about the future of environmental laws, are thought to be, by intellectual training and professional inclination more sympathetic to risk assessment and management strategies than toward either sustainability or novel institutional reforms. Advocates of sustainability urge that greater weight be given to analyses of ecosystems, technology, and cultural values.

One explanation for these worries—the predicament of bureaucratic autonomy versus accountability—provides a framework within which to consider those troublesome uncertainties mentioned in the beginning of the chapter. The predicament is that to be free from undue political and economic influences, bureaucracies must be semiautonomous and independent of the public and other governmental bodies. Hence, EPA rules and procedures, programs, policies on governmental integration, and the rest of it. But semiautonomy tends to breed a lack of democratic accountability, as is manifest in public worries about inflexibility and defensive, if not self-serving, agenda building and policy formation by experts at odds with the public interest. Hence specific worries spread about whether bureaucracies are responding to the interests of their constituencies. Policy makers consistently confront this predicament of how to satisfy accountability without undermining autonomy.

One recent approach to this predicament was the Clinton administration's plan to "reinvent government." The aim of its "National Performance Review" of bureaucracies was to reorganize and downsize bureaucracies. The hoped-for result was to create more room for economic and political "market" forces, including opportunities for citizens to object to policies, and for policy processes that are more friendly to bottom-up entrepreneurial policy-making by these local voices and bureaucrats. This plan for reform, alongside a decentralized federalism, is what I want to use to push ideas about reform to their practical outer limits of concurrent powers, a culture of rights for participatory politics, and shared responsibilities.

Actually, constitutional adjudication and jurisprudence do suggest a few insertion points for what ordered liberty might require in regard to these things. For example, in regard to powers, there is a faint but renewed interest in Tenth Amendment adjudication. In response to a challenge to a federal regulation on waste policy, the Court located a "core of sovereignty retained by the States under the Tenth Amendment," notwithstanding the Commerce and Supremacy Clauses.[8]

At one level this ruling only reconfirms that the amendment is a truism because it was used as a rule for interpreting the Constitution as a document of dual sovereignty and enumerated powers. That is, the Tenth Amendment is read to direct the Court to ask what other aspects of the Constitution, or its theory of dual sovereignty, protect state sovereignty. The practical consequence of this rule of construction is that dual sovereignty generally, and for environmental politics and policies specifically, absolutely prohibits Congress from commanding states to legislate or administer on its own behalf. However, the state sovereignty that is protected by this rule does not prohibit Congress or its administrative agencies, under the Commerce and Supremacy Clauses, from exercising its control by offering states virtual Hobson's choices or hard-to-resist financial incentives to get its way. Thus, a congressional prohibition against directing the creation of state laws or against forcing states to administer federal policies is but a minimal check on the politics of command and control and a slight contribution to the idea of shared responsibilities. But this prohibition does substantiate that the Tenth Amendment requires reading the Constitution in terms of sovereignty interests in concurrent powers. If the goal of commentary is to address the bureaucratic predicament and to encourage democratic partnership beyond what is afforded by prohibitions against outright commands and mere acquiescence to federal legislative and bureaucratic pressure then a more expansive reading of the Tenth is required.

(Intellectual) jurisprudence does hint at a way to expand the Tenth Amendment by linking it to the Ninth Amendment. The Ninth Amendment says, "[T]he enumeration in the Constitution, of certain rights, shall not be construed to deny or disparage others retained by the people." Scholars interpret these words in exasperatingly different ways, so prudence dictates being cautious with them. That said, if the Ninth is also read as a rule of interpretation, then a relatively cautious originalist reading of it is that the Framers meant it to be understood to permit claims about citizens' rights that are not enumerated in the text (Tribe and Dorf 1991: 54).

A rule of construction cannot indicate the source and substance of these unenumerated rights. For the sake of a properly amended originalism about democratization, one might hypothesize that the Framers intended the Tenth to prohibit the evisceration of state power. And, correspondingly, a Tenth Amendment–driven theory of dual sovereignty requires Ninth Amendment rights that protect citizens' participant interests in state and local politics that help to preserve state power. These Ninth Amendment rights might include guarantees of equal participation in policy agenda formation, bargaining, negotiation, and decision making, as well as in political communication related directly to this participation.

The theory behind these rights is that if participation is facilitated by state and local policies, then the costs of participation by interested citizens might thereby be decreased and greater numbers of citizens might have a stronger interest in collective action. They might also have a greater interest in state, local, and bureaucratic processes, as well as in processes of conflict and conflict resolution that are efficacious competitors to the politics and law of command and control. In this scenario, Ninth Amendment participation rights help energize Tenth Amendment sovereignty interests.

Granted the centralization of political and fiscal power in the polity, the institutional manifestations of this constitutional law would require a redrawing of the lines of command and control. The federal government might coordinate efforts by states and localities to set up priorities, and it might sustain those efforts by providing pertinent risk assessment, management, and sustainability information to them as well as to industry and interest groups. It might also fund states and their localities outright, or with matching or block grants, or by tax incentives and bond initiatives. Certainly some problems would require national (and international) aspirations and goals. But for other problems, decentralized authorities would have the power and responsibility to determine issues like risk assessment, management, and sustainability choices—and the means of pursuing them.

Another task the central government might take on is to provide best-estimate environmental benchmarks for specific environmental problems, based on administrative agency findings and data accumulated via federal legislation. It might also collect scientific and management data on successes and failures among state and local efforts to manage those problems (Kirz 1995: 106–07, 110) and provide expertise to help states and localities evaluate present and future policy choices.

But (again according to this scenario) states and localities would be free to rank their environmental problems according to their best judgment of participant and sovereignty interests in various industries and environmental issues. The most urgent problems would thereby be pursued, and compliance with benchmarks on other less urgent problems delayed. States and localities would feel encouraged to experiment with mechanisms for increasing citizen participation in addressing policy problems and solutions through funding allowances and allowances for delays. For example, states and localities might predicate that some problems are best left to independent experiments, or, concurrent with other states, merge market-based and voluntary compliance strategies with common law oversight.

Rather than devices of command and control, states and localities might try some marketplace mechanisms so that companies that exceeded environmental standards would gain greater implementation flexibility. Or they might imitate the Compliance Audit Program of the EPA and exempt self-reported violations from fines or reduce the penalties they incur. Or again, they might include negotiated settlements between competing constituencies to make risk-management choices that differentiate between imminent problems and those that appear to be less urgent or at least less distinct, or that are the focus of competing interests that are less susceptible to balancing. Still again, they might encourage environmental groups, industry, workers, and citizens to form committees to formulate agendas and policies. Or, finally, there might be review panels, made up of all relevant experts and representatives (of, for instance, governments, small business, conservation organizations, labor unions, institutions of higher learning, etc.) to oversee policy programs.[9]

Adjudicating Environmental Politics and Policies

Logically, this democratized policy-making promises *McCulloch*-like persistent conflict between and among governments, as well as between bureaucracies and interests, which moves beyond the usual conflict over governmental intervention or nonintervention. It also promises conflicts that will branch out in various and unpredictable directions in regard to semi-autonomy, accountability, rights, and powers as a consequence of the multiplicity of factors that attend various state and local policy formation and implementation.

Current state or federal law cannot be expected to settle very much about these conflicts. Initially, the law that emerges from these bottom-up environmental processes will come from state- and local-level common law actions. These actions might consist in procedural complaints by citizens, inspired by the Ninth Amendment, about inadequate access to the policy-making process. They might also consist in claims by citizens, inspired by the Tenth Amendment, that federal actions impinge on their participatory and sovereignty interests in shared responsibilities. Whatever shape they take, it will also fall to these common law actions to determine substantive issues such as what count as the liability, negligence, and compliance of firms and challenges to scientific, economic, and ecological policy judgments.

These actions would necessarily be steeped in circumstantial fact considerations. Their adjudication is easier to write about than to accomplish because judges would have to review decisions about risk assessment, management, and sustainability that have a number of dimensions, and that do not necessarily fit with one another. Consider just six difficulties that judicial review would need to grapple with. One: review would have to distinguish between scientific and nonscientific criteria for estimating risks to populations or natural resources. Two: review would have to evaluate statements of what counts as a reasonable range of scientific uncertainties about the impact of risks and to what extent it is feasible to rely on scientific findings to estimate risks to specific populations or natural resources. Three: review would have to oversee calculations of the costs of implementation strategies that integrate scientific risk assessments with economic and sustainability assessments of the effectiveness of proposed risk reduction strategies. Four: review would have to decide whether policy makers have considered a reasonable range of alternative strategies that account for variation in risk correlated to geographical regions. Five: review would have to analyze performance and other market-based mechanisms to gauge the maximum in achievable results of alternative strategies. Six: review would have to analyze the potential effects of policies on small businesses, net employment, and financial burdens due to policy compliance.

Local and national organizations and public interest groups, including those on the extreme, would be encouraged by democratization to litigate one or another dimension of risk assessment, management, or sustainability that they found missing in these bottom-up processes. Complicating matters even further, adjudication would not simply revolve around expert witness, about which judges have begun to teach themselves. It would also concern newly emerging civil rights claims about the impact of environmental policies, such as those related to waste disposal facilities near minority and poor populations. In sum, decentralization would require common law-like judges to assess the merits of competing findings of procedure and fact, opinions about harms, and rights claims, in contexts where there is no scientific, economic, or political consensus. Such assessments "are admittedly in major respects unfamiliar terrain for judicial discourse, and as a consequence evaluative guideposts are thinly scattered" (Edley 1990: 199).

Consequently, common law-like judges would necessarily exercise very broad discretion as they distinguished between expert and spurious opinions, and where scientific, technical, and social evidence is entangled in a myriad of (sometimes hidden) partisan and interest-group accommodations. State and federal appellate adjudication would be no less discretionary. Review of trial court results surely would have to tussle with more or less familiar issues of fairness within the context of Due Process, Equal Protection, and Taking Cause challenges. But these challenges would have to be reconfigured in light of novel Tenth and Ninth Amendment law protecting state sovereignty and participation interests.

Here again there are vague intimations in traditional administrative law that help thinking about what this adjudication might be about. Judicial discretion has arisen there because regulatory legislation often does not articulate precise goals. Consequently, administrative law has evolved to some degree into "a surrogate political process to ensure the fair representation of a wide range of affected interests in the process of administrative decision" (Stewart 1975: 1670). One scholar has called this partial transformation of administrative law an "interest-representation model" of adjudication (Stewart 1975: 1722).

As a surrogate process for correcting flawed efforts at bottom-up policy making, interest representation adjudication would oversee the balance between bureaucratic autonomy and accountability. It would also review claims about preferential treatment of powerful organized interests, the failure to address relevant interests differentially affected by possible policy alternatives, and other such matters related to fair procedures for representation and results (Stewart 1975: 1734, 1758–59).

This adjudication might proceed as current desegregation law does: it would be designed to be deferential to political processes by providing only general guideposts for policy makers rather than dictating solutions. Judges would review policy decisions for their fact-finding integrity, the extent to which they adequately represented all relevant parties to the dispute, the extent to which a good faith effort was made to meet benchmark criteria, and issues of federalism. Then they would determine whether policy makers considered all the available policy options and have an explanation for the one they select.[10] But policy makers would not be told how to balance policy options, and adjudication would leave them free to balance competing interests as they saw fit.

However, judges, inspired by the Ninth and Tenth Amendments, would, in their surrogate roles, inquire into whether there was "too much, not enough, or flawed politics" in policy making or the marketplace (Edley 1990: 192). When need be judges would remand to regulators and negotiators the responsibility to be "more ambitious [in pursuing] the goal of sound [democratized] governance" (Edley 1990: 170–71). Here the roles of the amendments would need to be circumscribed by two principles. One principle is diversity: judges would need to recognize that there is a multiplicity of ways to further the processes of interest group competition, balancing, and accommodation as the foundation of citizen rights and state power. The companion principle is that courts, in and of themselves, "can almost never be effective producers of significant social reform" (Rosenberg 1991: 338). What these two principles add up to is that judges would need to foster the perpetuation of a tug-of-war between the shifty and inexact results in the adjudication of ordered liberty and the results of democratized politics. In this tug-of-war, what ultimately counts as ordered liberty would necessarily have to emerge from the Court's shuttle between its conservation and its criticism of itself as a guidepost to rights and powers.

As imprecise as this version of democratization is, is it sufficient to raise those promised troublesome uncertainties about whether it is practical and is best?"[11] These uncertainties are relatively plain ones, and it should be apparent that they apply to any commentary about reform, independent of partisan politics. Their significance lies, for agnostics and nonagnostics alike, in the warning signals they should send up about the need to trim the sails of expectation when pursuing experimentation in commentary.

Troublesome Uncertainties

Agnosticism dictates that tests of what is practical and best focus on neglected politics and policies. Located in the inevitable gulf between the potential and the actual that opens out of existing facets of law and policies, neglected politics and policies demand attention because they undercut gestures toward problem solving and the desire for the rightly decided that might lurk in commentary. One such test relates to common facets of power accounted for by "the dilemma of democratization."[12] This dilemma arises because, although it may be deemed necessary to discontinue command-and-control management, delegating authority and discretion to state and local governments, administrative agencies, and marketplace forces can be no less uncertain politically, economically, and legally.

Politically, delegation can be problematic if no allowance is made for how congressional action would only legislate aspirations and goals via general or vague mandates. Such give is necessary for democratization, yet it could make it that much more difficult for everyone involved to evaluate long-term benchmarks for compliance. Decentralization of bureaucracies could be problematic if it resulted in short-term discontinuities in patterns of implementation and enforcement. In such situations there could be potentially disastrous longer-term environmental consequences, and accountability would be difficult to assess. At the same time, delegation of authority and responsibility would become problematic because it would encourage bureaucrats and policy makers to avoid making difficult decisions. In this situation everyone involved in policy making would be shielded from blame when decisions were not made, or when mistakes were made, or when the inevitable unintended results occurred.

Democratization can also be problematic if it neglects the paradox of collective action. If more citizens are not induced to participate, they remain free riders, enjoying collective goods without participating in their production; or if those who participate are basically the resource-rich, democratization will be no more than the functional equivalent of an entitlement program for the same resource-rich. Even worse, democratization could aggravate tendencies of local oligarchies of power and influence to control policies.

Democratization can also be problematic if it neglects the extent to which international environmental problems and the difficulty bringing them under organizational control undermine the very idea that environmental policies ought to be nation-centered at all. The emphasis in democratization of sovereignty and participant interests may be anachronistic in an increasingly integrated world economy and politics.

Second, on the political economy front, modest block grants could be problematic if they are too small to redress imbalances of political and economic power, such as the unequal distribution of resources between states and among localities that force governments to do less than is necessary and desirable. Modest block grants also would have little impact on the unequal distribution of power between industry and public interest groups, leaving governments more vulnerable to pressures from industry to shape policies their way.[13] If this happened, then democratization would increase the extent to which risk assessment and management were driven by cost considerations. At another level, to the extent that expertise is essential to sound policy-making, the fragmentation and loose coordination associated with democratization could result in qualitatively inferior, though popular, policies.

Third, decentralization and democratization could affect the role of courts in problematic ways. Vague public policy mandates and common law adjudication would give judges broad discretion to adjudicate conflicts between constituencies. Scientific and economic risk assessments of harms, technical cost-benefit calculations, and peer review oversight of ordered liberty would undoubtedly trigger even more litigation than already occurs. As indicated above, in this litigation expert witness would not by itself suffice; the lack of consensus, the difficulty distinguishing between expert and spurious opinions, the subtle influence of partisan groups on findings—all would add to the judges' difficulties in making their assessments of harms. But there is even more: such litigation would also require judges to think about the Ninth and Tenth Amendments in ways that are foreign to precedent and jurisprudence, and as a result, uniformity and predictability in the law would be undermined by ordered liberty.

There is, in addition, some empirical evidence that "where rules are imprecise or nonexistent, the courts most often have imposed even tougher requirements than might have been imposed by administrators," and the costs for these requirements fall to states and localities (Anton 1989: 200). To the extent that is true, judicial intervention could well reduce the flexibility that decentralization and democratization are supposed to encourage.

If all this is not sufficient to raise red flags, common law-like adjudication of environmental issues could be problematic to the extent that judicial education and recruitment, lack of judicial craft or competence, and the role of courts in society come into play. Given how judges are socialized and recruited, there is little reason to believe that judges would be sympathetic, at least in the short term, to ordered liberty adjudication. Moreover, it would require so much of them intellectually and in terms of time, that there have to be doubts about whether judges have the resources to do the job. Lastly, ordered liberty adjudication would strain the outer boundaries of what is conventionally understood to be the judicial capacity to ascertain social facts and consequentialist considerations. To the extent all of this is valid, ordered liberty appears impractical compared to the relative certainty and uniformity of conventional legislative, bureaucratic, and judicial expertise and command, regardless of their social policy costs.

Appellate law is even more problematic. The Rehnquist Court's 1995 tussle with the litigation of environmental harms and the Endangered Species Act in *Babbitt v. Sweet Home Chapter of Communities for a Great Oregon* does not provide a promising scenario for Supreme Court adjudication of challenges over environmental decisions.[14] All of the *Babbitt* opinions center on conventional statutory interpretations of congressional intentions and legislative purposes and on competing constructions of words such as "harass" and "incidental harms" to describe and evaluate what constitutes habitat modification. This is anecdotal evidence of the Court's disinclination to tackle the circumstantial fact considerations that would be central for evaluating risk-assessment and sustainability strategies.[15] On the other hand, a Supreme Court inclined to tackle these considerations (a heroic assumption) could undermine democratization by reinventing modes of judicial command and control.

Finally, even if Justices found an amended originalism efficacious (an even more heroic assumption), and they did not reinvent judicial command

and control, then they would still have to reconcile virgin Ninth and Tenth Amendment adjudication with almost fifty years of adjudication demonstrating that dual sovereignty is antithetical to protecting due process and the equal protection of citizens. From this vantage point, ordered liberty might seem to suffer from the taint of intellectual jurisprudence. This only goes to show that even agnostics find it hard to resist its grip!

But, as Aristotle says in the midst of uncertainties, "enough of this." A nonagnostic can find sufficient reason here to decide that this dynamic of power and rights is neither practical nor best. But agnostics should not come to that conclusion so quickly. Rather, they should take a middle course and treat these uncertainties as opportunities to shuttle back and forth between conservation and criticism of claims about what is practical and best. In doing so, they would be acknowledging that there is often a troublesome trade-off between advocacy of a political or legal process for achieving results and the best or most practicable substantive results, however those results are conceived. Therefore, agnostics should prepare themselves to try to analyze second- and third-best processes and results as well.

Pursuit of these alternative solutions may well take commentary to places at odds with our own partisan predilections. Pursuit will certainly require practice at the arts of intellectual strategy and accommodation, and this too may not appeal to all of our partisan predilections. But it is good for agnostic scholarship. Those who are willing to challenge themselves to practice these arts will have to learn either to modify their partisanship or to sustain it amidst uncertainties.[16] Either way, agnostics are likely to be at a persuasive disadvantage against those who argue with the certainty of conviction that comes from being committed to problem solving and the rightly decided opinion. But agnostics should not find that too high a cost to pay.

However, should agnostics pay the cost of what skepticism requires when it comes to their strongest and most stable moral convictions? There is a point of view that suggests not. Few persons want to think of themselves as compromising their fundamental moral convictions. So agnostics might suffer cognitive dissonance arising from the desire to be consistent and to hold on both to agnosticism and to their political morality. This is a "natural reaction" to this kind of conflict. Inconsistent beliefs make most persons anxious, and anxiety has to be relieved, one way or another. Even agnostics, so the reasoning goes, despite their relatively higher tolerance for inconsistency, will need such relief. Hence it seems logical to conclude that either agnosticism or political morality will have to give way. In the next chapter I argue against this logic by comparing the intellectual jurisprudence of

Ronald Dworkin to agnostic jurisprudence. The primary purpose of this comparison is to show why an agnostic habit of mind that thinks along the lines of ordered liberty should be able to tolerate this cognitive dissonance to a degree sufficient for agnosticism and the strongest moral convictions to coexist.

·9·
Ordered Liberty and Political Morality

Ronald Dworkin is one of a handful of teachers who are competent to write for elite audiences inside and outside law school. His scholarly publications and his essays in the *New York Review of Books* make him one of the most widely read advocates for abstract principles of political morality as the linchpins for rightly decided questions and answers. Equally significant here, for decades Dworkin has been an implacable foe of the legal pragmatism that informs the interpretive strategies of agnosticism. It is Dworkin's hostility toward pragmatism that makes his particular version of civic education about political morality and the law an especially good occasion for addressing whether agnosticism and morality, generally speaking, can coexist.

Dworkin and Political Morality

Let us begin with my understanding of the four guiding principles of Dworkin's jurisprudence that distinguish it sharply from agnostic skepticism. First, his jurisprudence is fully committed to the idea that philosophical and/or theoretical abstractions about political morality are primary and essential for reading the Constitution and its precedents. Based on some of his later writing,[1] I think the difference between philosophical and theoretical abstractions for Dworkin is mostly a matter of degree, not kind (Dworkin 1996: 124–25). If so, then the idea he is trying to convey is that principles of political morality are general ideals, standards, or maxims that are independent of and conceptually superior to strategic policy considerations. Second, and following from the first, Dworkin's jurisprudence eloquently defends the necessity of the messages of solace in unity and integration, specifically regarding equality and minority interests, that taking rights seriously carries with it. Third, it insists that even when there may be no single determinate legal reason for deciding a case, there are abstract moral reasons embedded in constitutional principles that provide grounds for saying which among conflicting legal reasons is the most correct one. To be sure, Dworkin readily admits that the existence of multiple legal answers to the rightly decided question in many hard cases makes what consistency requires in constitutional interpretation both "uncertain and controversial" (Dworkin 1986: 163).

Nonetheless, he denies that uncertainty and controversiality require the kind of conclusions we have read about here in relation to underdeterminacy and ordered liberty. Indeed, Dworkin has been most emphatic throughout in his insistence that given the competition about what the Constitution requires and the varied principled answers to the rightly decided question, the rule of law demands abstract and principled reasons for choosing between them. Otherwise, he says, there can be no genuine distinction between legal principles and mere political reasoning and consequentialist policy considerations.

Finally, Dworkin's jurisprudence is avowedly antagonistic to legal pragmatism. Apart from his philosophical objections to it, which are of no concern to us here, Dworkin's central objection to pragmatism is that it lacks any good way to warrant "genuine, nonstrategic legal rights" for individuals and minorities that "trump those consequentialist considerations that always threaten to produce inconsistent outcomes" (Dworkin 1986: 160).

Dworkin's candidate for a proper warrant for rights is "integrity," a term he uses to mark a morally defensible distribution of economic and political goods that treats like cases alike, indicating an "equality of concern," free from rank political prejudice. He acknowledges that there are other equally sound candidates for legitimate warrants. What makes them legitimate is that they can be defended, at some level of generality, as abstract moral criteria, independent of strategic considerations, that are located in the Constitution and its doctrinal history. For Dworkin, if these warrants are not at work in the law, then judges will impose their own policy predilections on the text and opinions (Dworkin 1986: 160–68; Dworkin 1996: 10–11).

It follows from this that pragmatism must be fatally flawed in that it provides no such *independent* criteria for legal judgments, and thus no reason for judges to constrain themselves and to represent justice consistently. Skeptics, admittedly, are unconcerned with protecting judges from their missteps. So, for the sake of argument, let us say that, in commentary, judgments about the law cannot be just in any strong sense of that term if they are not constrained by independent ideals of political morality. But also for the sake of argument, let us lay aside the conclusion entailed by Dworkin's philosophizing that agnosticism's pragmatism is fatally flawed. Then, taken together, Dworkin's four principles emerge as core pressure points against an agnosticism that melds principles and circumstantial fact considerations.

The aggregate pressure these principles produce against agnosticism leads to this hypothesis: If, in hard cases, abstractions readily identifiable with political morality are not maintained as primary and essential for reasoning about the Constitution and its precedents, then something like the amended originalism of the previous chapter can be dismissed as a mere polemic for personal policy predilections about democratization. It would be futile for me to try to persuade anyone that this hypothesis is wrongheaded or that it cannot be substantiated in one case study or another. Instead, I offer as an exemplar just one case study of law's efficaciousness that confirms both Dworkin's and an agnostic's sense of how principles of political morality operate in the law. That is enough to suggest that agnosticism and political morality can coexist, and to cast doubt upon the hypothesis at issue. Consider, then, an agnostic look at how the seminal case of *Planned Parenthood of Southeastern Pennsylvania v. Casey* (1992) treated precedent,[2] and then Dworkin's philosophizing about it.

An Agnostic *Casey*

The State of Pennsylvania was at the forefront in passing restrictive abortion laws. Its resistance to *Roe v. Wade*,[3] which had decriminalized abortion and established the aggressively litigated trimester schema for regulating abortions, included 1988–1989 amendments to its Abortion Control Act. These amendments (Pennsylvania Abortion Control Act, 1982, amended in 1988–89, 18 Pa. Cons. Stat. §§3203–3220, 1990) required that a woman receive specific information (an explanation of abortion procedures and risks along with alternatives to abortion) and sign an informed consent form twenty-four hours before an abortion was performed; a minor secure the informed consent of a parent or a judicial bypass if the minor did not wish to or could not obtain that consent; a married woman sign a statement indicating that her spouse was notified of her intention to have an abortion; and certain reporting requirements be met by facilities providing abortion services.

The district court, in defense of *Roe*, struck all the provisions as unconstitutional. But the circuit court reversed the district court's findings on all but the spousal notification provision, applying the "undue burden" test (previously recommended by Justice Sandra Day O'Connor), in contrast to the trimester schema, as the proper standard of *Roe* legitimacy. Both sides in oral argument before the Supreme Court were intent on launching an all-or-nothing strategy. "Driving the strategy," wrote the *New York Times* legal correspondent Linda Greenhouse, "was a judgment that there is in fact no middle course worth fighting for in the abortion battle, and consequently that the most serious risk in the Pennsylvania case [lay] in the Supreme Court's coming to rest there."[4] Walter Dellinger, later to become solicitor general under President William J. Clinton, filed an amicus brief in support of *Roe* for a number of members of Congress. He represented the sentiment against a middle-of-the-road decision as the worst possible outcome. The people at risk are vulnerable women, the young, and the poor. Their rights wouldn't be protected politically unless suburban Republican women found themselves at risk, too. Only if it is clear that no one has rights will there be a political groundswell to restore those rights."[5]

This reaction typifies not only abortion politics and litigation, but our judicial system that encourages litigants in any contest "to fight it out [in the] reasonable hope that they will get their way without compromise" (Wolfe 1991: 93). But a five-to-four decision,[6] announced by Justices O'Connor, Anthony M. Kennedy, and David H. Souter, made that compromise. Their joint opinion sustained *Roe* but replaced the trimester schema with an "undue burden" test as the measure, under the Due Process Clause, of the legitimacy of abortion regulations. They sustained the circuit court's ruling, but struck the spousal notification provision.

It is no surprise that the initial reaction by the press to *Casey* was to say that it was "startling," "confounding," and "surprising." Both sides of the abortion controversy, reflecting those sentiments, and the sentiment against a middle course, were left "scrambling over each other to concede defeat" in the face of the new law (*Newsweek,* July 13, 1992).[7] *Casey* is a surprising opinion, and it is a defeat for those who think about litigation and adjudication in absolute or abstract terms. To understand why this is so, consider the jurisprudence of *Casey*'s defense of *Roe,* which melds principled concerns about due process with contingent social fact considerations.

The *Casey* Court cited Benjamin Cardozo's *The Nature of the Judicial Process* (1974)[8] to warrant the claim that "reasoned judgments" about the "tradition" of due process and the Fourteenth Amendment require, most importantly, "prudential and pragmatic considerations" in deciding whether to reaffirm or overrule a precedent.[9] These considerations about judicial politics are specified in a complex test of precedent that requires four inquiries: (1) whether the central rule has proved to be legally efficacious over time; (2) whether an alternative conception of state power can be asserted without violating citizens' settled social expectations associated with the central rule; (3) whether society has come to reject the central rule because of the evolution of (in this case, abortion) law since the controlling precedent; and (4) whether social fact considerations that underpin a precedent have so changed that its central rule is either irrelevant or cannot be justified as a means of dealing with the issues it addresses.[10]

This test is a welcome one from an agnostic's perspective because it situates the virtues of the principles of precedent—for example, consistency and uniformity in the law, maintenance of perceptions of judicial legitimacy, and abstract principles of justice—within that complex of underdeterminate judicial process considerations discussed earlier. Adopting Cardozo's conception of precedent means emphasizing the social value of the rule of law rather than solace in formulaic appeals to legal rights and powers. Remarkably, this emphasis is very clearly demonstrated by *Casey*'s application, in defense of *Roe*, of *West Coast Hotel v. Parrish* and *Brown v. Board of Education*.[11]

West Coast Hotel and *Brown* are cited in *Casey* to warrant the principle that an overruled precedent not only indicates that one doctrinal claim has replaced another. It also indicates that the Supreme Court would be compelled to overturn a precedent when it has found social, cultural, and economic "facts that the country could understand, or had come to understand already, but which the Court of an earlier day had not been able to perceive."[12] The *Casey* Court denied that facts of this kind, which were deemed to be at work in *West Coast Hotel* and *Brown*,[13] are at work in *Casey*. This finding is central to the Court's further findings that (1) *Roe*'s central rule decriminalizing abortion has proved to be legally efficacious over time; (2) an alternative conception of state power would unsettle settled expectations; and (3) *Roe* remains relevant as a means of dealing with the issues it addressed.

But some will reasonably argue that the finding that *Roe* is still efficacious is inconsistent with how *Casey* characterizes *Roe*'s central rule and pushes aside the trimester schema for the undue burden test. In *Casey*, *Roe*'s central rule is characterized as follows: (1) A woman has a right to an abortion before viability free from undue state interference; (2) a state has the authority to restrict abortion after viability (contingent on exceptions so as to protect a woman's life and health); and (3) a state has the authority, limited by the undue burden test, to protect the health of a woman and the life of the fetus from the onset of pregnancy. Thinking formalistically, it is not at all counterintuitive to assert that, in regard to first-trimester regulations, the first and third characterizations, depending as they do on the undue burden test, contradict Justice Blackmun's view (as author of *Roe*) that first-trimester regulations are subject to the more prohibitive strict scrutiny test.

The line of reasoning that follows from this intuition is that to insinuate the undue burden test into abortion law is to indicate that *Roe*'s central rule has not proved to be legally efficacious as a means of dealing with the issues it addressed. It would also follow that *Casey* has introduced an alternative conception of state power that potentially unsettles settled expectations about the decriminalization of abortion. This line of reasoning is itself internally consistent. Yet once we refuse to think just formulaically about the rule of law, there is an alternative point of view that perhaps is less neglectful of politics and policies. And this point of view finds that there is no clash between *Roe* and *Casey*'s characterization of its central rule.

We note the presence of political considerations when, in *Casey*, Blackmun admits that even strict scrutiny of regulations requires "expert testimony, empirical studies, and common sense" to draw lines between *Roe* rights and legitimate state "humanitarian or pragmatic concerns."[14] Substantively, this admission of the necessary role that contingent social fact considerations play in abortion adjudication leads Blackmun to contend that first-trimester regulations requiring a woman to make thoughtful and informed decisions about abortion are legitimate, but that a regulation that seeks to persuade a woman to choose childbirth over an abortion is not.[15]

Now, simply on an intuitive level, and taking into account the complex bundle of consequentialist and social fact considerations that go into adjudication, can one predict that, given *Roe*, an advocate of the undue burden test necessarily will disagree with Blackmun that a first-trimester regulation about informed decisions is legitimate because it does not interfere with choice making? I think not. Taking that same bundle of factors into account, it is vastly harder to predict what an advocate of the undue burden test would say about the status of a regulation seeking *to persuade* a woman to choose childbirth over an abortion. Blackmun says that this regulation fails the strict scrutiny test. But it is certainly possible that this an advocate of the undue burden test, given the factors involved in the judicial process and legal reasoning, might just as well disagree as agree with the advocate of strict scrutiny that the second regulation is illegitimate.

The point is that from this perspective what is pertinent is not the legal test per se, but how social fact considerations are interpreted from within a given conception of the judicial process and legal reasoning. Thus, despite his preference for strict scrutiny of first-stage regulations, Blackmun's own words provide the basis for saying that the undue burden test does not represent a break with the central rule of *Roe* as even he conceived of it. He acknowledges that the central rule requires "expert testimony, empirical studies, and common sense" to draw lines between permissible and impermissible regulations. In other words, when Blackmun attempts to draw a bold line between strict scrutiny and the undue burden test, and yet admits the inevitability of social fact considerations, he is unwittingly admitting the plausibility of line drawing under the undue burden test.

When we free ourselves from thinking formalistically and formulaically we see more clearly why, as a matter of substantive law, the fundamental *legal* right of *Roe* is no more than the "ultimate decision [to abort], [and] not a right to be insulated from all others in doing so."[16] We also see that regardless of whether one advocates strict scrutiny or the undue burden test, under the Due Process Clause it is inescapable that social fact considerations are crucial linchpins to determine whether health, safety, and welfare regulations square with the *Roe* right. Those very considerations entail recognition of the fact that "not every law which makes a right more difficult to exercise is, ipso facto, an infringement of that right."[17]

At bottom, then, whatever the preferred test, commentators must distinguish between what it means to restrain someone and to interfere with a choice to do something. These distinctions are never clear ones under any circumstances, and they are proportionally even more vexatious when factors such as class, race, personal experiences, and moral convictions have to be considered. What *is* clear is the need for nonformulaic determinations about the liberty to choose based on the premise, quoted above, that not every constraint on a right constitutes, by definition, its infringement.

It is worth repeating: the idea that strict scrutiny and the undue burden tests of regulatory power necessarily represent alternative conceptions of state power and sovereignty interests should be put to rest as a political misunderstanding arising from formalistic thinking about adjudication. If one avoids this misunderstanding then one sees clearly the justifiability of the *Casey* Court's view that the undue burden test coheres with the conclusion that *Roe*'s central rule decriminalizing abortion has proved to be legally efficacious over time. The *Casey* Court's view is not a new conception of state power that would unsettle settled expectations, but a way to signal that the Court is today willing to remand to states more autonomy over abortion regulations than it had in the past. In that sense *Roe* remains relevant as a means of dealing with the issues it addressed, since the extent of regulatory power was precisely the issue the trimester schema was meant to address.

But it is then also justifiable to argue, as the joint opinion does,[18] that the evolution of abortion law since *Roe,* which had legitimized first-trimester regulations, has made the trimester schema and strict scrutiny a misleading way to think about abortion regulations, and to argue that the undue burden test better signals the kind of contingent social fact considerations that must come into play in determining whether informed consent provisions and all the rest are a substantial obstacle to the liberty to choose.

Moreover, unlike the strict scrutiny test, which is ordinarily meant to signal some considerable degree of certainty about the extent to which governmental power ought to be limited (even if in practice, as Blackmun's remarks reveal, that signal is sometimes misleading), the undue burden test emphatically signals underdeterminacy. Advocates of that test should, if theory and practice are to coincide, readily acknowledge that "disagreement is inevitable [and to be expected] in the application of any legal standard which must accommodate life's complexity."[19] It is equally inevitable that these disagreements are going to generate the charge, on and off the Court, that any adjudication as heavily dependent as *Casey* is on evaluating the social value of the rule of law is inconsistent with precedent and incongruent with the social fact considerations that abortion is about.

Chief Justice Rehnquist and Justice Scalia are a case in point: both wrote dissents to the effect that to abandon *Roe,* and to leave abortion regulations primarily up to the states, would not illegitimately unsettle settled expectations. This clash between the joint opinion and dissents over the requisite criteria for sustaining a precedent is significant. Here is what it is about.

The *Casey* Court's factual contention for sustaining *Roe,* and for not allowing states to have final discretion over the abortion controversy, is that "for two decades of economic and social developments people have organized intimate relationships and made choices that define their views of themselves and their places in society, in reliance on the availability of abortion in the event that contraception should fail." These developments appear to require the conclusion, according to the Court, that any alternative to *Roe's* conception of state power would undermine those intimate relationships, those habits of life, which the Due Process Clause, and precedent, are meant to protect. It would, in fact, thereby deny "the ability of women to participate equally in the economic and social life of the Nation."[20]

The dissents' rejoinder is that the Court's position is incongruent: it is just as reasonable to attribute the economic status of women and their present place in society to their educational accomplishments or society's recognition of their capacity to fulfill roles heretofore thought appropriate only to men, as it is to attribute their achievements to their ability to control their reproductive lives. The dissents also rejoin that the *Casey* Court's fact claims are selective ones; alternative facts are consistent with alternative conclusions, and *Casey*'s test for precedents cannot avoid the inconsistency attendant on the selection of facts. Hence, the rule of law that arises from it is necessarily "undeveloped and totally conclusory"[21]—a sure indicator that the test is an unprincipled contrivance in the service of the majority's policy preferences for sustaining *Roe*.

This clash is being expressed via two competing rhetorics: utility and analyticity. The *Casey* Court uses the former to make it appear that what the rule of law requires ultimately depends on its passing the test of social efficacy. The dissents employ the latter to make it appear that social efficacy ultimately depends on the rule of law that passes the tests of logic, congruence, and consistency. These are two equally sound competing rhetorics for expressing what the rule of law requires, but there is no matter of right or wrong here. Reasons and arguments can be crafted in a better or worse fashion about what is required. But there are no *criteria* that will settle the question whether the joint opinion or the dissents have the better argument when it comes to fulfilling the goals of legal stability and predictability, judicial prudence and legitimacy, fairness, and the proper distribution of political power between courts and representative bodies. An impasse is present, and the differences about what precedent requires are irreconcilable.

There are those who interpret the rhetorics of utility and analyticity and the impasse between them as a sincere difference of legal opinions about what the rule of law requires. By this interpretation, the impasse is rightly decided by the final say of adjudication. The lesson taught here is that litigators, adjudicators, and citizens have a duty to acknowledge the finality of judicial authority and therefore ought to abandon the divisive politics in question as a constitutional wrong. Others interpret the rule of law reading as a mere subterfuge that hides the clash of personal policy predilections and partisan politics that actually produces the impasse. The lesson taught by this interpretation is that the law is about winning and losing, and that lesson encourages persistence in disunity and even divisive politics in the hope of triumph at some later date.

Both lessons are taught so that the other one is made to appear wrong and that there is no middle course: choose the rule of law or instrumentalism, or choose obedience or protest. It cannot be denied that these are practical lessons to learn. Yet they are insufficient because they both make it too easy to ignore the utility-analyticity impasse and thereby to sidestep a confrontation with any of its deeper legal and political implications. The impasse's implications, however, must be pursued, and what follows now is an attempt to identify them.

Despite a perfectly understandable hope to transcend it, underdeterminacy will emerge. Ambiguous, confused, contradictory, and tendentious values and interests are at the root of all politics, not just the politics of abortion, and they cannot be easily prevented or discounted. To make the clash between utility and analyticity out as a dichotomy between the rule of law and rank partisan predilections is to illustrate yet again that habit of mind that cannot abide relativism. But if abortion values and interests are given their due, not pushed out of sight, then it begins to appear that there is no Archimedean point from which to view the impasse. If there is no such point, and if one is not an absolutist when it comes to abortion values and interests, and if one is not committed to the law and politics of abstraction, then the deeper legal and political implication of the impasse is clear: abortion values and interests confirm the codependency of both the rule of law and instrumental interpretations of it. Both are important responses to the controversy, and both must be pursued simultaneously. To put it another way: the relativism behind the impasse provides the material that calls out for a *Casey*-like middle course to the abortion controversy. It calls out as well for continued and unpredictable conflict between the rule of law and rank instrumentalism, despite imprudent impositions, by courts or legislatures, of political and moral aspirations that would truncate that conflict.

One cannot help but note the coincidence between the *Casey* decision and the ambivalent attitudes and values of most citizens as contrasted to the attitudes and values of abortion activists and litigators on both sides. By means of its merger of rights and powers, *Casey* clears out a neutral political space within which the ambiguous, confused, contradictory, and tendentious politics can be played out in national and state legislative and protest politics. To use the words "neutral political space" is to flirt with danger; by using them I do not mean the state is a mere umpire in the politics of abortion; nor do I mean that political resources are evenly distributed between conflicting parties. "Neutral political space" means that political conflict cannot help but be constrained by the Court's requirement that governments confront the politics of abortion only within contexts that render ineffective any attempt to burden a woman's "own conception of her spiritual imperatives and her place in society."[22]

As a statement of the rule of law, *Casey* roots this principle of moral and social neutrality in a legal analogy between due process and the First Amendment, via *West Virginia State Bd. of Education v. Barnette*[23] and *Texas v. Johnson.*[24] What these First Amendment cases establish is the political theoretical principle that when opposing sides on a liberty issue find each other's personal sentiments and values morally and philosophically offensive,[25] the obligation of the state is to protect the liberty of all citizens by not imposing one view or another on them.[26]

It is essential to recognize that this principle of neutrality requires the decriminalization of abortion: it does not require persons to give up a specific kind of divisive politics or to abandon personal policy predilections about the desirability of specific regulations. Rather, the undue burden test sets the tracks for future political conflict to run on. Implicitly it implies a point of view that intellectual jurisprudence cannot abide: that it is imprudent to look to courts to rightly decide a conflict in an uncompromising fashion.

Journalists and scholars were quick to predict an intensification of the abortion conflict, a relatively safe prediction to make because pre-*Casey,* there were no signs that abortion was abating as one of the hot spots of national and state electoral contests. And, in fact, over the decade, as we know, abortion rhetoric and legislative tactics generally have become increasingly more hyperbolic and nasty. The states are the main site for legislative action, and subsequent to Congress's frustrated effort to secure some measure of a national advantage for the pro-choice side with a Freedom of Choice Act, they remain wide-open for ongoing, often nasty, localized fights over familial notification, waiting periods, mandatory (pre-abortion) medical education, funding, fetal protection provisions, and the likes of partial-birth abortion procedures. Indeed, it seems that nothing short of banning abortions would have stopped shootings and other violence at abortion clinics, or have prevented the stalking of abortion providers and picketing of them at clinics or at their homes.

But, and more to the point, what predictions about *Casey* and its intensification of the conflict failed to note is that, altogether independently of Court action, the politics of abortion is so intrinsically intense that it has diffused itself into other related conflicts. For example, consider this list of conflicts: in medicine (e.g., fights over whether to permit RU 486, the so-called morning-after pill, into the country); over fetal protection (e.g., debates over criminal penalties for homicide when a pregnant woman is murdered); over social harms (e.g., disagreements about whether to apply alcohol/drug and child abuse laws against pregnant women who are drug abusers and debates about restructuring welfare reform and the status of government subsidies for children born out of wedlock); in graduate education (e.g., whether accreditation agencies should mandate training in abortion procedures in programs specializing in gynecology/obstetrics regardless of the religious or philosophical mission of institutions); in torts (e.g., the status of malpractice suits: for emotional trauma after abortions, standards of care, failure to inform patients of the availability of abortions out of state, postabortion cancers ostensibly linked to abortions, and postabortion complications related to infection, hemorrhaging, or tissue/organ damage); over physician-assisted suicide (e.g., the rights of mentally competent and terminally ill persons, in consultation with a physician, to terminate life); and over international/human rights politics (e.g., the mandate of governments to assure couples and individuals reproductive rights and respect for the sovereign responsibilities of governments to protect various religious, cultural, philosophical, and ethical values).

The hard practical truth is that abortion and all the collateral conflicts attendant on it are so complex and disorderly that there is any number of ultimately consequentialist accommodations that have to be struck. Abortion is the tip of an iceberg of unsettled and unsettling issues about self, society, and public goods. And there is no prudent way to lay down abstract generalizations about what these accommodations should look like without underestimating what conflict will make of them after it has had its chance to work them out.[27] This is undoubtedly the case for all hard questions, and whether such conflicts are encouraged or discouraged provides a litmus test of any public constitutional theory about them. The diffusion of conflict over abortion is significant in that it brings to the surface the hard policy choices (perhaps dilemmas) that swell directly or indirectly out from it. A cursory review of these policy choices—and the ever rising stakes in them—ought to be sufficient to make anyone want to know whether aspirations of real substance and significance beyond the most hypothetical kind—moral, constitutional, or otherwise—motivate persons when they engage in these conflicts. At the very least, from a practical standpoint, they are in and of themselves interpretable as evidence of fragmentation and disunity in the polity. Whether some, much, or all of this fragmentation and disunity should be characterized as a sign of a healthy or a dysfunctional polity is always disputable, and it should be disputed. What cannot be disputed is that *Casey* tacitly flirts with the adjudication that encourages strategies of confrontation, compromise, and negotiation that a jurisprudence of an amended Ninth and Tenth Amendment originalism is meant to encourage.

Dworkin on *Casey*

In contrast to the above analysis, which stresses social fact and consequentialist considerations and the underdeterminacy of the conflicts between the joint opinion and the dissents, Dworkin interprets *Casey* as a paradigm of "disciplined . . . moral reading of constitutional *integrity*" (Dworkin 1996: 10, original emphasis). In an article originally published in the *New York Review* (1992) and then republished in *Freedom's Law* (1996), Dworkin attributes two virtues to *Casey*. One is that the *Casey* Court reads the Constitution "as a charter of principle . . . in light of general principles they [Justices] can responsibly assign to the text of the abstract clauses of the Constitution." The second is it that it treats precedents in terms of "the overall goal of principled integrity" (Dworkin 1996: 124–25).

In regard to its reading of the Due Process Clause, Dworkin quotes with approval the Court's ordered liberty assertion that personal liberty includes the right "to define one's own concept of existence, of the meaning of the universe, and of the mystery of life" (Dworkin 1996: 120). Dworkin finds this conception of personal autonomy praiseworthy because it recognizes that the Due Process Clause must be understood to include fundamental unenumerated rights. Dworkin agrees with the Court that judges can reasonably disagree about what fundamental rights are. Perhaps that explains why he finds nothing to say about the shift from the trimester schema to the undue burden test. He does praise the test as a way to stop a state from "dictating to its citizens which decision they must ultimately make" (Dworkin 1996: 121), and he does acknowledge that drawing lines for limits on state power is difficult.[28]

As for precedents, Dworkin applauds *Casey*'s defense of *Roe,* but not because of the Court's social fact considerations, which he dismisses as "odd" and a weak justification for precedent (Dworkin 1996: 124). Instead, he argues that the core defense of *Roe* was the criterion of conscientious consistency "with more general principles the law and community had come to adopt, both about the moral responsibility of government and about the psychological and social meaning of discrimination" (Dworkin 1992: 125).

It is Dworkin's conclusion that *Casey* was rightly decided, and that no other conclusion is possible because there have been no counterbalancing abstract principles since *Roe* that challenge its principle of autonomy.

Thus, for Dworkin, there is no need to analyze the differences between the joint opinion and dissents. On the contrary, Dworkin casts the differences between them as merely a contrast between jurists who have a principled view of the Constitution and those, like the dissenters, who do not have such a view. Therefore Dworkin's ultimate commendation for *Casey*, and the reason that he thinks it was such a surprise, is that some of the Justices who might have been expected to do otherwise validated moral reasoning as the linchpin of legal reasoning. Thus it may be "one of the most important Court decisions of this [twentieth] century" (Dworkin 1996: 117).

Agnosticism and Political Morality

It is tempting to declare that the reason Dworkin finds *Casey*'s fourfold test of precedent to be driven by abstract principles rather than an efficacious meld of principle and social fact considerations, as agnostic commentary finds them there, explicit in the law, is his hostility to pragmatism. But that temptation is to be resisted because it is one with intellectual jurisprudence. An alternative way to deal with the differences between Dworkin's analysis and mine is to attribute them to those competing rhetorics of utility and analyticity and the competing rhetorics of agnosticism and moral philosophy.

My analysis of *Casey* follows the rhetoric of utility and social fact considerations, whereas Dworkin's analysis follows the rhetoric of analyticity and logical considerations. Hence I argue that the joint opinion is characteristically the rhetoric of utility, whereas Dworkin contends that it is the rhetoric of analyticity. From the rhetoric of intellectual jurisprudence, Dworkin insists that *Casey* is rightly decided, and he dismisses the dissents. From the rhetoric of agnosticism, I insist that both the joint opinion and the dissents have reasonable positions.[29]

An impasse is present, and the differences between us about what commentary requires are irreconcilable. One of the implications to be drawn from *this* impasse is that there is no Archimedean point from which to address the question whether agnosticism and morality can coexist. By the rhetoric of analyticity and the rightly decided, to think along the lines of ordered liberty requires that agnosticism give way to political morality. But by the rhetoric of utility and agnosticism, ordered liberty is a way of maintaining, all the way down, tensions between itself and principles of political morality.

The fundamental difference between the rhetoric of analyticity and the rhetoric of utility is that only the former requires neglecting the possibility that the other rhetoric has any merits. Agnostic rhetoric precludes any such formulaic way to determine what is required by way of agnosticism and political morality. It advises that there is no other recourse than to consult the Constitution, precedent, and consequentialist social fact considerations to learn how to reconcile agnosticism and political morality.

This advice is at odds with intellectual jurisprudence and the ideology of involvement because it encourages us to experiment skeptically with moral principles and consequentialist considerations in inexact ways. This experimentation is unpredictable and risky. Its skepticism and relativism about morality could equally well be put into service to maintain the status quo as to encourage democratic reform, to lower or to raise political aspirations, to encourage or discourage egalitarian values, and to encourage confidence in the nation we have been or rather the nation we are becoming.

The point of saying this is not to deny the possibility or even the plausibility of commentary that demonstrates the "correctness" or propriety of specific legal, or political commitments. Quite to the contrary, since such demonstrations are what intellectual jurisprudence is all about. Rather, the point is that faithfully executed experimentation in commentary will always demonstrate the relative weaknesses of such demonstrations. Accordingly, in agnostic commentary it is appropriate to advocate the "correctness" or propriety of specific legal, or political commitments, as long as that advocacy is suitably qualified by the tentativeness and suspicion that skepticism and relativism require.[30] This kind of advocacy acts as a check against premature judgments and an unjustifiable confidence in itself.

But there is a "charge of callousness" to consider against agnostic commentary: commentators are, by and large, among those who are least likely to be at the center of political combat or to suffer the flesh-and-blood consequences of mistakes in public policies or their unintended results. Why then should they, or more to the point, others, tolerate such skepticism and relativism?

This is a hard question to answer. It is better answered after we have seen more of what commentary to a middle course achieves. For now it is enough to say, as Prospero did about Caliban in Shakespeare's *The Tempest*, "This thing of darkness I acknowledge mine."[31] The significance of this acknowledgment should not be underestimated. Like Shakespeare's Prospero, those who choose to be agnostics must be willing to concede that there is a troubling disconnection between the logic of reason—academic, legal, political, and moral arguments—on the one hand, and, on the other, the passions of everyday life, which are indifferent to actual moral and political injustice. Those who have thought and felt deeply about catastrophic events such as the attacks on the World Trade Center and the Pentagon on September 11, 2001, or the ongoing conflict in the Middle East, or the scourge of AIDS in Africa, and who live relatively free from the effects of these events, might have already experienced this disconnection. For them and for agnostics, the gap may sometimes feel unfathomable. But agnostics, like Prospero, should try to make sense of this disturbing disconnection by struggling to see and to understand what they might otherwise have neglected.

What lies ahead is the final part of this book, where I consider two case studies that illustrate an agnostic commitment to relativistic and skeptical advocacy about the law, politics, and moral commitments. The second study in particular sets up my final remarks about agnostic struggles by tolerating skepticism and relativism in constitutional and legal commentary as civic education.

PART · III ·

· 10 ·
Deeper Skepticism

We have reached the last part of this book. Before proceeding with it, it is useful to reiterate some of the primary elements of commentary to a middle course. We have learned that in order to distance itself from the ideology of involvement and to put a brake on intellectual jurisprudence, agnostic commentary experiments with the underdeterminacy behind the law's formalisms, abstract principles of political morality, and characterizations of facets of political power. This underdeterminacy makes possible skepticism about the political sufficiency of legal formalisms, abstractions, and characterizations of power and, hence, about their capacity to provide determinate rightly decided answers to policy questions.

Yet agnosticism does not entail rejecting the utility of these formalisms, abstractions, and characterizations altogether. Instead, it activates them in order to seek out neglected politics and policies. In this search, agnostics commit themselves to a social-scientific spirit that manifests itself in a good faith effort to test policy predilections and deeply held principles of political morality against the results of their commentary about ordered liberty. As I have configured that test, this commentary mixes formalisms and principles of political morality with consequentialist social fact considerations, often in a shifty and relativistic way, to develop policy scenarios about vaguely sensed yet exigent practical matters.

In this chapter I want to underscore and elaborate the point that this test recommends the construction of second- and third-best practical alternatives to these scenarios. The virtue of constructing these alternative scenarios is that they encourage intellectual modesty in addressing issues of neglected politics and policies. Given the grip of intellectual jurisprudence, and the tendency of all of us to disclose problems in the work of others that we fail to see in our own, these scenarios impel agnostics to remain open to the underdeterminacy of the materials with which they work and to the unpredictability of political and legal events.

The inspiration for agnostic constructions of second- and third-best scenarios arises from one of two points that political scientist Ronald Kahn (1994, 1999) in particular has made in his cutting edge work on the role of social facts within opinions and in commentary. The first point is that scholars ought to be especially attentive to the extent to which, in both instances, social fact considerations originate in distinct and more often than not competing viewpoints or theoretical frameworks about the political system, power, and rights. The second is that new institutionalists ought to use social fact considerations and the best social science evidence possible to recharacterize the law's formalisms and conceptions of the role of courts in American politics for the purpose of defending the interests of minorities and disadvantaged groups (such as the poor).

This chapter's considerations of second- and third-best scenarios are a decidedly agnostic response to the first point. If social fact considerations in legal opinions and commentary are shaped by distinct pragmatic, contextual, and historical concerns, then agnostics should use social fact considerations and the best social science evidence possible to inform their own recommendations about criticism and conservation of law, politics, and policies. But whatever sympathies agnostics may have with the second point about using social fact considerations to advance specific group interests should be pushed aside by agnosticism's shuttle back and forth between conservation and criticism of the law. The best that agnostics can do in this regard is to construct a range of scenarios addressing the relative strengths and weaknesses of policies that defend the interests of minorities and disadvantaged groups.

This chapter's considerations are also a decidedly agnostic response to two similar points made by advocates of feminist, critical race, and sexual difference scholarship. First, these scholars contend that formalist and social fact considerations in scholarship have systematically truncated, marginalized, or ignored entirely discriminated and oppressed groups' reasons and emotive responses to law, politics, and policies. Second, these scholars advance justifications for revisionist or rejectionist agendas that seek to remedy or to protest scholarship and politics as usual. Here again the best that agnostics can do is to construct a range of scenarios that address the relative strengths and weaknesses of what it means to include the excluded in commentary, as well as the strengths and weaknesses of revisionist and rejectionist agendas. It is within this context that we turn to issues of pornography.

Freedom of Speech Revisited

In discussing pornography, the Internet, and freedom of speech, chapter 5 proposed that solace in the law's formalisms or in facets of political power is unmerited unless the commentary in which it is offered broaches circumstantial and consequentialist facts, along with partisan and ideological considerations, that reveal both the strengths and the weaknesses of law and power. Those remarks laid the groundwork for commentary about ordered liberty. Now I revisit the pornography controversy to pursue an ordered liberty approach to alternative scenarios about content-based regulations, the First Amendment, and the role that applied social-scientific knowledge plays in developing the understanding and management of risks to persons and society. This commentary reconfirms a profound skepticism regarding the mutually exclusive legal formalisms and political abstractions that dominate the pornography controversy; it also suggests for this controversy an equally profound skepticism about the positive role agnostic commentary can play in pointing the way toward preserving the polity's utmost aspirations.

This commentary is, then, totally at odds with the point of view of interest groups, litigators, adjudicators, and academics in the pornography controversy who have succeeded in shaping the legal and political policy debate as an either/or battle between forces of right and wrong. It is also at odds with the law of the land: since the Supreme Court's summary affirmation of *American Booksellers Ass'n v. Hudnut* (1985),[1] which had invalidated an Indianapolis antipornography ordinance, it has been pretty much settled that "a particular phase of the legal anti-pornography campaign is dead in the water" (Frug 1992: 145). The majority of the interpretive community satisfies itself with the conviction that since *Booksellers* confirms the First Amendment formalism that content-based regulations are impermissible, it is rightly decided. A minority believes that it is wrongly decided because *Booksellers* violates one of two principles that ought to be part of First Amendment formalisms: (1) the community has the right to prohibit moral harms to persons and degradation of the moral order, and (2) the expressive activities of the powerful ought to be unprotected if they subordinate the weaker and perpetuate social abuse and inequality.

Booksellers is thought to mark a unique phase in the struggle with pornography. Every other step along the path of regulating sexually explicit materials, including the controversy over the Internet, has been motivated by the first principle. This time, attempts were made by radical feminists to regulate pornography expressly for its putative political, sexual, and psychological as well as social consequences. Because the consensus is that since *Booksellers* rejects both principles, this unique phase is, and should be, over, and it may well seem that commentary on it is and should be pretty much dead in the water too.

But the controversy over *Booksellers* needs to be revived in commentary to show how formulaic applications of civil liberty principles, such as the prohibitions against content-based regulations and the obligation to redress subordination and inequality, stand in the way of a deeper appreciation of what the controversy over sexually explicit materials might be all about. Specifically, I want to address one of the most interesting and notoriously difficult policy problems connected with antipornography ordinances: What is the legitimate role of the courts and governments when it comes to acknowledging the extent to which pornography helps to shape a social environment that subordinates women? It is my contention that this controversy over sovereignty interests, free speech, and censorship is not apprehended in the conflict between the mutually exclusive principles of free speech and equality. These principles so distort our view of the nature of pornography's harms and our assessment of their governability that no unqualified solace ought to be sought in them. Instead, greater, not to say central, attention ought to be given to consequentialist considerations and a regulatory power that follows a middle course. Such attention would uncover indications of the extent to which the political culture triumphs over if not mocks our satisfaction in or condemnation of *Booksellers,* and show that, even if a particular phase of the campaign is dead, more commentary is in order.

It is worth repeating that this commentary raises, without coming close to resolving, difficult political questions about what to say when solace in the law is unmerited and when legislative and judicial politics offer little hope of doing better. Raising such problems without pointing the way toward resolving them puts us again where we may not want to be, but it does place us where we might be better off when it comes to a politically more credible grasp of the controversy over pornography's harms.

The facts of the controversy are basically these: In 1985, the city of Indianapolis instituted a code that would have permitted private civil suits to recover damages engendered by pornographic materials that "graphically" depict

> the sexually explicit subordination of women . . . whether in pictures or in words, that . . . present [women] as sexual objects who . . . enjoy pain or humiliation, or experience sexual pleasure in being raped, or . . . [are] tied up or cut up or mutilated or bruised or physically hurt, or are dismembered or truncated or fragmented or severed into body parts, or are being penetrated by objects or animals, or are presented in scenarios of degradation, injury, abasement, torture, [or are] shown as filthy or inferior, bleeding, bruised, or hurt in a context that makes these conditions sexual, or are presented as sexual objects for domination, conquest, violation, exploitation, possession, or use through postures or positions of servility or submission or display.—Indianapolis, Ind., Code § 16–3[q] (1985)

Booksellers found that whatever validity there may be to claims that pornographic words and images contribute to the subordination of women, it does not gainsay the First Amendment principle that prohibits content-based regulations. By that principle, governments are prohibited from declaring a preference for one expressive viewpoint contrasted with another, or silencing one at the expense of the other. Radical feminists attack this principle as exemplifying the inadequacy of conventional constitutional reasoning to encompass the exigent public policy problems that concern women. That attack is nowhere more exhaustively articulated than in *Only Words* (1993) by Catharine MacKinnon, law professor and coarchitect, with Andrea Dworkin, of the idea of "radical" antipornography ordinances.[2]

MacKinnon's attack against *Booksellers* is multifaceted, but there is no need to encompass it all to capture the role mutually exclusive principles (unconsciously) play in it. Accordingly, our jumping-off point is MacKinnon's observation that *Booksellers* is rooted in the marketplace formalism. MacKinnon's objection to this formalism is that, explicitly and implicitly, it has become so deeply rooted and time-honored in thinking about free expression that it is virtually axiomatic to conclude that the public interest is rarely, if ever, served by governmental interference in communication. MacKinnon is not saying that such conclusions have no good reasons, legal or commonsensical, or that they are necessarily misplaced. She acknowledges, for example, that it is reasonable to fear that regulating some forms of expression puts the polity on a slippery slope to ever increasing governmental censorship. But she also is concerned about situations where, for example, the marketplace formalism is "adhered to with a fundamentalist zeal even when it serves to protect lies, silence dissent . . . intrude on associations and retard change" (MacKinnon 1993: 76–77).

To MacKinnon, one of the most important lies perpetuated by the marketplace formalism is that pornographers are publishers of ideas and images like all other publishers, and hence they must be free (i.e., have the right) to distribute their "ideas" to readers lest the polity be threatened by governmental censorship. This axiomatic formalization, from the antipornography perspective, conceals the environment of sexual inequality to which pornography contributes with words and images that depict and are the functional equivalent of relationships wherein women are humiliated, violated, and degraded for the sexual arousal and satisfaction of (primarily) men (MacKinnon 1993: 17, 25). In other words, where pornography is concerned, axiomatic concerns about freedom and censorship end up perpetuating cultural fragmentation and disunity—the sexual, social, psychological, political, and economic inequality that pornography exploits. They also silence dissent against pornography's harms by making them appear, in comparison to the law's formalistic precision, to be merely "abstractions" and to have only rhetorical or propagandistic validity (MacKinnon 1993: 40).

Those in the minority thus think and feel that "being offended" is the closest most of the rest of us come to grasping the effect of pornography (MacKinnon 1993: 59). As for the law, obscenity formalisms—which, you might recall from the earlier discussion of the Internet, legitimate regulations of sexual materials that appeal to prurient interests, depict or describe sexual conduct in a patently offensive way (as specified by state law), and lack serious literary, artistic, political or scientific value—are deemed to be woefully inadequate, in part because they are undermined by the social reality they are meant to police. For one thing, juries find it difficult to determine what is sexually offensive in a polity that experiences and tolerates an explosive diffusion of all kinds of pornography, so that ever wider community standards are de facto set for what is patently offensive. For another, more violent and repulsive pornography is also increasingly more prevalent, making it harder for juries to identify sexual materials as appealing to merely prurient interests. For yet a third, because it is commonplace to think that most words and images have at least some degree of literary, artistic, political or scientific value (MacKinnon 1993: 87–90), most sexually explicit materials are deemed to be covered by free expression formalisms.

This line of thinking concludes that the law in general, and *Booksellers* in particular, does no more than nourish lies, silence, and inequality. Hence, those effects can be undone only if the marketplace abstraction, and its associated obscenity formalisms, are set aside so the truths about pornography as a form of sexual abuse and aggression are given a central place. MacKinnon's candidate for this exchange is "equality rights," and although it may be the case that not all in the minority share her views about these rights, this is the formalism that lies behind antipornography ordinances. "Equality rights" reads the First Amendment as a charter for legal intervention and social change and mandates that "expressive means of practicing inequality" create a compelling state interest for remedies that secure free expression for all (MacKinnon 1993: 73, 106–07). Government intervention is, then, less a risk than a public policy imperative to provide opportunities for any persons "hurt through pornography to prove its role in their abuse, recover for the deprivation of their civil rights, and to stop [that hurt] from continuing" (MacKinnon 1993: 92). "Equality rights" must displace existing free expression formalisms because only the former is alive to the extent to which expressions may convey images and meanings that have the tendency "to violate someone, to subordinate someone, to abuse someone, to rape someone" (MacKinnon 1994: 71).

Civil remedies, like antipornography ordinances, are, in this view, meant to secure that guarantee of equality that the First Amendment (as understood by radicals) provides. They do so by redressing (ostensibly) the imbalance of sexual and state power so that "women's silence can no longer be the context in which pornography and speech are analyzed" (MacKinnon 1993: 9). In other words, civil remedies give "once abused women [the opportunity to be] heard" and thus bring to an end the lie that pornography is solely words and images. Once that lie is exposed, regulatory power is no longer hemmed in by the marketplace abstraction and obscenity formalisms. Then "the operative definition of censorship accordingly shifts from government silencing what powerless people have to say, to powerful people violating powerless people into silence and hiding behind state power to do it" (MacKinnon 1993: 10).

MacKinnon knows that an idea like "equality rights" is contentious. She also knows that what impels it—the business about pornography's harms to women—is even more so. Indeed, she readily acknowledges that it is difficult to explain how pornography constitutes the harms the minority says it does (MacKinnon 1993: 40). It is at points like this where social-scientific knowledge is called on to play a crucial, albeit unclear, role in controversies. In the given case, there are statistical studies to cite about pornography's harms, but, as is only to be expected, various methodological questions have been raised about them (Easton 1994). Making the waters even muddier is the phenomenology of sexual victimhood based very pointedly on an idea of aggression and subordination that itself drives the search for statistical data supporting harms.

Sexual victimization phenomenology is to be apprehended in terms that describe the relationship of words and abuse, terms that in effect strive to conflate them. Thus, we are asked to be concerned

> with the positioning of sex words in sexual abuse, in abuse as sex, [for] words of sexual abuse are integral [to] acts of sexual abuse . . . such that to utter them is to let loose in the body that feeling of doing it, and sex is done largely for the purpose of creating that feeling. The more pornography invades the sexuality of a population, the more widespread this dynamic becomes. It is not so much that the sexual terms reference a reality as that they reaccess and restimulate body memory of it for both aggressor and victim. The aggressor gets an erection: the victim screams and struggles and bleeds and blisters and becomes five years old.—MacKinnon (1993: 58)

Although a phenomenology of perpetrators and victims may be as decidedly polemical as it is difficult to reference, its implications are not so unclear. It challenges axiomatic reasoning about regulatory power. It proposes that formalisms that fail to treat words and images "as the institutions and practices they constitute, rather than as expressions of ideas they embody or further" (MacKinnon 1993: 12–13) cannot but fail to capture how the pornography industry is about making money by selling false portrayals of female sexuality for the pleasure of men. Economics and sexual hierarchy intersect in what is done with, and through, words and images. Consequently, to stop "what pornography does, in the real world, [and] not only in the mind" (MacKinnon 1993: 12–15), requires legal and political reasoning that recognizes how material conditions and relationships are organized to further subordination.

This centering of female fears about victimhood on the organization of material conditions and relationships, both economic and social, most certainly puts the minority at a rhetorical disadvantage when it comes to any practical possibility of persuading others, as they want to do, that *Booksellers* is wrongly decided. This is especially so since arguments about "victimhood" are increasingly unpopular in the political and academic culture. Nevertheless, for the sake of the minority position, MacKinnon gives it a try, indicating that "equality rights" and the material conditions of female fears about subordination ought not to be treated as altogether foreign to the more progressive, yet ultimately inadequate, conceptions of words, institutions, and practices that have already been accepted.She begins by linking sexual utterances to "the inequality context" of sexual harassment: "Words unproblematically treated as acts in the inequality context include 'you're fired,' 'help wanted—male,' 'sleep with me and I'll give you an A,' 'fuck me or you're fired,' 'walk more femininely, dress more femininely, wear make-up, have your hair styled and wear jewelry,' and 'it was essential that the understudy to my Administrative Assistant be a man'" (MacKinnon 1993: 14).

This linkage is meant to connect the familiar notion—the environment of sexual harassment—with the unfamiliar idea that "pornography makes the world a pornographic place through its making and use, establishing what women are said to exist as, are seen as, are treated as, constructing the social environment of what a woman is and can be in terms of what can be done to her, and what a man is in terms of doing it" (MacKinnon 1993: 25). But even MacKinnon admits that it is difficult to know for certain just how the environment of harms is shaped by the production and use of pornography (MacKinnon 1994: 68; MacKinnon 1993: 58).[3] So, ultimately nothing less than "something of a leap of [imaginative] faith [is required] in a society saturated with pornography" (MacKinnon 1993: 7) to see its harms and to identify "the woman's status as that of victim and then [to] privilege that status by claiming that it gives access to understanding about oppression that others [i.e., males] cannot have" (Bartlett 1991: 385).

This call for a leap of faith is proof that for the minority there is no compromise (or middle course) between principles that take seriously the capacity of pornography to structure and perpetuate domination and inequality and reasoning that takes seriously axioms about free expression and censorship. And the majority agrees.

To see why, consider this amalgam of ideas constructed from the popular writing of Floyd Abrams (1994), the prominent First Amendment litigator, and Ronald Dworkin (1993). This amalgam, it is relatively safe to say, expresses the basic opinions of the majority in the interpretive community. It is also relatively safe to say that most of the majority that finds *Booksellers* to be rightly decided find at least some forms of pornography to be really deplorable. More likely than not they suspect that some forms of expression are, in some contexts, also forms of action that ought to be regulated, say in regard to child pornography or the Communications Decency Act. And some number of them gesture toward the phenomenology of victimhood, at least to the extent that they refer to the possibility that target groups may endure some forms of expression which are abusive, aggressive, and untrue.

But that is as far as the majority is willing to go. Ultimately, the majority view is that the phenomenology of harms—which are the heart of the matter for the minority—is reducible to those mentioned above. And even for those who find some asserted relationships warranted (e.g., between violent pornography and abusive crimes), First Amendment formalisms proscribing content-based regulations are robust enough to outweigh them (Dworkin 1993: 38) because of the connections among free speech, human dignity, and democracy.

The weight of principle is increased for some (not Dworkin) by ancillary consequentialist considerations. Liberal democrats have a "profound distrust of the government telling us what we can say, what we can think, how we can express our views" (Abrams 1994: 57, 81). This distrust manifests itself in the majority's virtually total suspicion regarding any defense of governmental intervention, for it sees in such defenses merely a facade for the ever present desire of those in control of regulatory power to restrict or to silence unpopular or disfavored points of view (Dworkin 1993: 38; Abrams 1994: 81).

Ancillary consequentialist objections to content-based regulations warrant another axiom of fact and law: those who argue that some forms of expression ought to be regulated bear the burden of proof showing very direct and immediate harms to persons to justify intervention. Even then, supposing such harms can be shown to be there, obscenity formalisms set another burden of proof: Any such harms must be related to expression that lacks that shred of literary, artistic, political, and scientific value that puts it under the protective cover of the First Amendment. No wonder that, juxtaposed to this way of thinking, the phenomenology of subordination, difficult to reference to begin with, is said to amount to no more than speculation, exaggeration, dubious social science, and worse, intentional deception (Abrams 1994: 57; Dworkin 1993: 38, 40).

From the point of view of the majority, "equality rights" do not fare much better. They are also difficult to reference: in part because the principles and formalisms of First Amendment adjudication are so deeply embedded in our culture as reliable sources of (presumably) good law (Abrams 1994: 57), and partly because anything else is so counterintuitive that it appears to be inescapably "bad" (Dworkin 1993: 40). A "traditional understanding of [liberty and] equality" is what the majority finds sensible (Dworkin 1993: 42), and that tradition requires persons equally situated to be treated equally. Thus, the desire, the felt need, to make pornographers as pornographers more accountable than others for their expression, or to penalize them in order to equalize competition between the truth and pornographic lies about women, cannot compete with the conventional ethos of equality. Even if the truth never triumphs, that does not mean that somehow or other "freedom of speech has failed" (Gunther 1991: 1130) or that a desire and a felt need to go beyond tradition justify sovereignty interests in governmental regulations.

As for demands that the First Amendment be understood as a charter for legal intervention and social change—that the First Amendment ought to sanction the suppression of one form of expression in order to clear the way for another—the position of the majority is easily summarized. In principle, "freedom and expression and equality [already] flow together" (Abrams 1994: 56) when governments are prohibited from imposing officially sanctioned versions of the truth on citizens and interfering with the process that starts with free "private choices, tastes, opinions." And it ends with the shaping of the social, cultural, and moral environment of the polity (Dworkin 1993: 41). Thus social change is implicit in First Amendment freedoms, and whatever pornography's harms may be, support for antipornography ordinances is deemed to be a "frontal attack on the First Amendment" (Abrams 1994: 57) that undermines liberty and equality as traditionally understood. And, again, whatever those harms may be, they are best dealt with by means of public education (Abrams 1994: 57), "the disgust, outrage, and ridicule of other people" (Dworkin 1993: 41), and legislation compatible with obscenity formalisms. There is no compromise, and there ought to be no middle course. The effort to proceed as if there were a middle course or anything to compromise is, to appropriate the words of the majority, something "to be feared rather than celebrated, a mocking [politically] 'correct' euphemism for tyranny and the despotism of the thought-police" (Dworkin 1993: 41–42) that leads down the road to "McCarthyism" (Abrams 1994: 42).

Beyond Solace in Mutually Exclusive Legal Formalisms

The strategy of the two sides is clear: to depend on mutually exclusive formalisms and political principles to persuade others that even minimal concessions to or compromises with the opposing side are untenable. In the present controversy, the skeptical challenge to conventional commentary (if that description can be applied to MacKinnon's words) begins by giving more attention than usual to some relatively straightforward and otherwise well-known political and social judgments about pornography's harms. These judgments are at odds with the way those harms are characterized in the context of mutually exclusive formalisms.

Here, what needs to be seen is how those formalisms simplify or reduce pornography's harms to legal images that make it appear that their legal significance is quite certain and virtually unchallengable. So, even granting difficulties about knowing exactly how it is that pornography harms women, the phenomenology of victimhood (taken on its own terms) leads by virtual necessity to the conclusion that the proliferation of pornography is a social phenomenon that puts women at risk of violent and nonviolent, overt and implicit sexual subordination and abuse. The phenomenology of victimhood has been subjected to considerable (and perhaps too readily accepted) criticisms. Perhaps it is less well recognized that First Amendment abstractions and formalisms lead to equally formulaic conclusions that the rights of free expression are "the inevitable rule" (Abrams 1994: 81; Dworkin 1993: 41), and that the proliferation of pornography is a social problem basically beyond the legitimate reach of the law.

There is, in any case, an alternative to these formulaic approaches that follows from the premise that pornography is one "of the most complicated cultural events of our time, an event whose meanings are still quite indeterminate" (Frug 1992: 153). This formulation encourages us to see that sexual materials give rise to manifold and complex questions—about sexuality and sexual intimacy, sexual morality, the meaning and significance of sexual fantasy, and connections between sexual expression and self-identity—that do not have any obvious fit with a "cause and effect" way of thinking about the harms, or for that matter the benefits, of pornography. The question that arises, then, is, What follows from taking an underdetermined and noncausal view of pornography's harms?

Perhaps not much. The amicus curiae brief against the Indianapolis ordinance presented by the Feminist Anti-Censorship Task Force (1988) does a more than credible job of acknowledging the conditions that make pornography's harms underdeterminate and of recognizing the deep ambiguity of complex associations among pornography, gender, sexuality, sexual images, and cultural milieu.[4] But, as to be expected from a brief, whatever is acknowledged by way of underdeterminacy is ultimately pushed aside so as not to distract attention from a determinate answer to the legal questions at hand. So, if we push aside such deterministic approaches, what emerges is the sense that it is difficult to know for certain just what questions to ask about the construal of pornography's harms and benefits, to say nothing of how to answer them.

But something else emerges as well: an opportunity to see formalisms in a nonformulaic light. Some conventional scholars come close. Political scientist Donald Downs writes that principles that were until then thought to carry great weight may assume a different aspect when harms are seen "as complex and subject to multiple interpretations" (Downs 1989: 89).[5] Legal scholar Cass Sunstein makes a similar claim (Sunstein 1993a; Sunstein 1993b). But both are too deeply complicit in the ideology of involvement and conventional legal doctrines to travel an agnostic path in pursuit of the multiple implications of multiple interpretations.

To start down this different path, consider a legal precedent that does link underdeterminate harms with a nonformulaic conception of the law. In 1952, Justice Felix Frankfurter, in *Beauharnais v. Illinois*,[6] upheld a state group libel law making it unlawful to publish or exhibit materials that subject persons of any race, color, creed, or religion to derision or obloquy by portraying them as depraved, criminal, unchaste, or lacking in virtue. At one level, *Beauharnais* articulates a formulaic view of the First Amendment when it takes specific judicial notice of the principle that only a narrow class of expressions can be regulated, namely, those which "by their very utterance inflict injury" and have such limited social value "that any benefit that may be derived from them is clearly outweighed by the social interest in order and morality."[7] Such regulations must be "directed at a defined evil" and cannot interfere with any exchange of ideas "indispensable to the democratic political process."[8]

But at another level, *Beauharnais* also takes specific judicial notice of changing habits of life to arrive at a nonformulaic conception of rights. In doing so it advances the political theory that governmental policies that seek to regulate novel harms and to provide civil "peace and well-being" justify going beyond what traditional legal "history and practice" and First Amendment formalisms might, under different conditions, mandate.[9] *Beauharnais* melds its formulaic treatment of the First Amendment with the consequentialist consideration that the "willful purveyors of falsehood concerning racial and religious groups promote strife, and tend powerfully to obstruct the manifold adjustments required for free, ordered life in a metropolitan polyglot community."[10]

This is an appellate conception of ordered liberty and a content-based regulation that calls for attention to contextual social fact considerations and warns against a strict adherence to doctrinal tradition. It asserts that "only those lacking in responsible humility will have a confident solution for problems as intractable as the frictions attributed [to] extreme racial and religious propaganda" that is "calculated to have a powerful emotional impact on those to whom it [is] presented."[11] This cautionary note extends so far as to question the judicial capacity to confirm or deny evidence about the fit between regulatory policies and underdeterminate harms.

Thus, the *Beauharnais* Court concludes that "it would . . . be arrant dogmatism, quite outside the scope of our authority in passing on the powers of a State, for us to deny that the . . . legislature may warrantably believe that a man's job and his educational opportunities and the dignity accorded him may depend . . . on the reputation of the racial and religious group to which he belongs."[12]

This kind of thinking provides the light necessary for experimenting with the pornography controversy. The justification for such experimentation would be the complexity of contingent social fact considerations that bear on such issues as how to conceptualize ordered liberties associated with citizens' sexual habits; the level of generality for understanding what constitutes a legal tradition about sexually explicit materials; and, accordingly, what to count as criteria for drawing lines between rights, traditions, and regulations that serve the demands of ordered liberty.

There may be checks, however, on our readiness for such experimentation. *Beauharnais* warns against turning a blind eye to potential abuses of regulatory power, such as discriminatory enforcement and remedies that "might not in practice mitigate the evil, or might . . . raise new problems."[13] Nevertheless, despite its awareness of such hazards, and despite not having been overruled or formally limited in any way, *Beauharnais* has been seriously undermined by a range of subsequent First Amendment opinions.[14] MacKinnon cites the case as providing a doctrinal foundation for "equality rights" and concerns about subordination, but she recognizes, along with other scholars, how irrelevant it may be.

Indeed, *Booksellers* itself depicts *Beauharnais* as inapplicable to antipornography ordinances because it covers defamatory expressions that are offensive for their own sake, whereas depicting women as subordinate in sexually explicit ways may be deemed to be offensive and yet protected because of literary, artistic, political, or scientific values. So *Beauharnais*'s lack of doctrinal robustness is a definite problem not only in litigation and adjudication but also for its credibility as a source of light in our effort to broaden and deepen our political and legal understanding of the issues at hand. However, skeptics should take courage from the statement in *Beauharnais* that potential abuses are the "price to be paid for the trial-and-error inherent in legislative efforts to deal with obstinate social issues."[15]

In this regard we might connect what has been said so far with Justice Robert H. Jackson's dissent in *Beauharnais.* This dissent acknowledges the social value and legitimacy of group libel laws. But it also requires that cost-benefit calculations be constrained by a due regard for the principle that regulatory actions should not cut any more deeply into civil liberties rooted in tradition and contemporary values, once they have been determined, than is required to safeguard citizens from specific abuses and evils of expression. This careful endorsement of cost-benefit considerations has an added virtue in this argumentative context. It underlines the fact that ordered liberty cannot provide a formulaic way to determine how much weight to give to tradition, and that weighing and line drawing around underdeterminate harms like those of pornography are appropriately done on a case-by-case basis. In other words, it brings to the surface the perplexities about sovereignty interests that are repressed by mutually exclusive legal formalisms and political abstractions.

That is enough by way of background conceptualization. Now we must ask, "what might this kind of experimentation in commentary come to?" Consider if you will the following (not inclusive) list of potential cost-benefit issues about the judicial process and enforcement procedures that might argue against deference to regulatory power:

1. Antipornography ordinances may themselves become a form of political (and sexual) harassment.
2. They may undermine existing constitutional law on administrative restraints required by First Amendment precedents (e.g., regarding the burden of proof, procedures for injunctive relief, and restraints before final judicial determination).
3. They may raise difficult, if not insurmountable, problems in differentiating empirical from ideological criteria for findings about directness of harms.
4. They may risk civil litigation and enforcement overload.
5. They may invite unwarranted surveillance in the process of working out what count as actionable sexually explicit materials (Downs 1989: 165–88, 156–57).
6. They may cause more confusion as a result of troubling variations in

adjudicating rights and regulations due to variations in the political culture of local civil justice systems and in the interactions between litigators and adjudicators (Kritzer and Zemans 1993).

Under the rubric of *Beauharnais* and ordered liberty, the following line of reasoning about cost-benefit issues would lead to the conclusion that antipornography ordinances should pass preliminary constitutional muster:

1. In a plural society, characterized by conflicting and incommensurate views of sexuality, such ordinances advance a legitimate governmental interest by seeking to control the underdetermined harms that have the potential to undermine the health, safety, and welfare of women in particular and citizens in general.
2. Given expressive acts that have the potential to obstruct the manifold, inchoate, and subtle associations between the sexes, it is ill advised to depend on history and practice as usual, which is to say, to impose conventional First Amendment formalisms regarding obscenity and content-based restrictions because they prematurely close the door to the regulation of potential harms.

However, these are only the preliminary considerations. There are others:

3. The underdeterminacy of harms constitutes a high degree of uncertainty about the social costs and benefits of regulations that draw lines between real and supposed harms of sexual materials in order to elevate "equality rights" via civil penalties.

Moreover:

4. Conventional First Amendment formalisms requiring safeguards against government censorship of literary, artistic, political or scientific ideas, unpopular or disfavored points of view, and abuses of regulatory power are not dispositive, but they cannot be altogether disregarded in evaluating the implications of regulations premised on such costs and benefits.

And finally:

5. Concerns about harms have to be merged with First Amendment concerns within the context of judicial process concerns and compelling legal traditions. Any such merger must take into account the probability that judicial process and enforcement problems (such as those listed above), placed in the context of the underdeterminacy of harms and the

continued over-growth of the Federal Court's civil jurisdiction, threaten to create policy confusions and disorders.

Now, taking these considerations together, and despite their prima facie constitutionality, it is possible to make the cost-benefit calculation that antipornography ordinances are too likely to undermine ordered liberty by failing to provide feasible (consistent and coherent) judicial process remedies for litigating and imposing civil penalties.[16]

Alternatively, under the same rubric of ordered liberty, note that it is just as plausible to proceed through to step 5 and then analyze these problems as follows:

6. It "is not necessary [that judicial remedies be] perfect, [only] reasonable," and ordered liberty requires only that government interest in protecting against harms be substantial and that "the scope [of regulatory power be] in proportion to the interests served."[17]
7. The costs of implementation have to be carefully calculated, and, given the difficulty of establishing with precision the point at which pornography's harms arise and have their impact, it is prudent to defer to trial-and-error efforts of regulators to deal with the obstinate social issues associated with pornography.

Here, the prima facie case for antipornography ordinances is sustained via deference to ordered liberty and jury-based determinations of civil penalties for determining pornography's harms.

What to Say Next?

Predictably, comparing the cost-benefit analysis of judicial remedies with considerations of ordered liberty yields contradictory but equally justifiable conceptions of the constitutional status of rights and regulatory remedial power. Probably this is evidence enough for those in both the minority and majority to invoke mutually exclusive principles to signal that ordered liberty cheapens principle. But quite apart from the extent to which these contradictory conceptions of rights and powers are congruent with uncertain harms, the law once again lends itself to agnostic considerations. It is noteworthy that, for all intents and purposes, what for the majority and the minority is a problematic conception of rights and remedial power has appeared in the adjudication of the subtle harms of sexual harassment.

Consider that the rule of *Harris v. Forklift Systems, Inc.* (1993)[18] and its lower federal court progeny is that a plaintiff is not required to prove serious psychological injury to establish a hostile work-environment sexual harassment claim. Some mix of objective tests—which might include fact-based determinations about the psychological well-being of the plaintiff, the frequency and severity of the conduct, and whether the conduct was physically threatening, was more than merely an offensive utterance, and unreasonably interfered with the plaintiff's work performance—and subjective ones about the impact of harassment on the plaintiff are both relevant to title 7 violations.

Why are these shifty and inexact harassment calculations any more objectionable when put in relation to pornography's harms? Well, they would be more objectionable from the minority's point of view because they neither guarantee "equality rights" nor undermine prevailing lines of (male) reasoning about processes and institutions. And for the majority, they would be so because they do not strictly adhere to free expression principles and, in fact, undermine them with what are from this point of view less weighty process and institutional concerns. But these are objections that come from the formulaic perspective of the rightly decided question.

Such objections also are at odds with principles of political morality and social fact considerations as they appear in other contexts. Consider adjudication, state action, and the harms of vestiges of segregation. Whatever confidence may have originally attached to *Brown v. Board of Education*'s understanding of the social-psychological harms of segregation and the role of law in correcting them, it has long since eroded. It is a now a commonplace that the direct, to say nothing of the indirect, harms of segregation are not easily demonstrated by empirical propositions. It is also disconcerting that alongside, and perhaps juxtaposed to, the benefits of desegregation there are costs that raise questions about what integration has achieved. What, for instance, may have been lost in terms of minority self-identity, community experiences, and socioeconomic structures and power, and what can continued efforts to desegregate be expected to accomplish? Do these costs raise profound questions about the management of desegregation policies and the moral issues surrounding the vestiges of racial discrimination that are, at some level or another, beyond the scope of the law's formalisms? On the other hand, given some aspects of our highest aspirations and contemporary values, can it be denied that segregation and its vestiges are abominations that, some way or another, must be addressed?

Litigation, adjudication, and commentary about mutually exclusive principles and formulaic applications of formalisms demand that all this underdeterminacy be pushed aside. This makes sense for litigation and adjudication that must justify the exercise of power to decide cases. So courts depend upon arguments over whether statistical claims about things like lower SAT performance, an unequal distribution of the quantity and quality of educational resources, variations in staff quality and teaching performance, and recruitment and salary differentials are determinant indicators of (past) *de jure* segregation and justify the need for continuing district court remedies.

Though these arguments about the past and potential social and psychological harms of racial antagonism, contempt, or indifference are difficult to warrant empirically, they are—so legal thinking goes—the best arguments available. But if we break the grip of the ideology of involvement, and the urge to contest mutually exclusive principles, then we can look beneath all the formulaic arguments about the *de jure*/de facto distinction, statistical evidence, judicial capacity, and the scope of district court remedies. Then we will admit that we are struggling with, and deciding, moral and political issues that we really do not understand very well.

The implication of this line of thinking, for those willing to adhere to it, is that a political culture of racism, however vestigial, mocks the political efficacy of the law's formalisms, principles of political morality, and facets of political power to encompass these issues. Might not the same thing be said of a culture of pornography? Such a culture raises grave uncertainties, in the wake of pretty much contradictory yet equally justifiable constitutional choices, about what (and to what extent) harms to women, or children for that matter, may be remedied. These uncertainties persist even though—and this is a major qualification—the law does adequately govern some harms yet, regardless of chosen policies, leaves some harms ungoverned.

What commentary to a middle course has to say about these uncertainties is disconcerting. Commentary may be ill served by continued academic efforts to reconfigure formalisms in order to rejustify traditional First Amendment law that leaves pornography's harms to education on the one hand, or to content-based regulations or penalties for violations of "equality rights" on the other. What more I can say beyond this point is not clear. My intuition is that risk assessments and management of pornography's harms are more like those related to racism than they are to those related to the environment. Therefore, I am reluctant to say too much more about pornography in relation to previous considerations of federalism and democratization.

But perhaps in its effort to approach political sufficiency, skeptical commentary would be well served, initially, by examining some of those circumstantial fact considerations that make things more, rather than less, clear. To take just one instance of this kind of thinking, consider correlations between local uses of power, on one side, and the complex and interconnected forces of economic structures, social values, and class, on the other.

Radical feminists draw attention to the fact that pornography is an industry, with apparently intimate connections to organized crime.[19] For them, this social fact provides empirical linkages for causal explanations for rape, other forms of violence against women, the sexualization of male dominance, and child abuse, all of which may have their origins in the criminal activity, commercialism, and sexual exploitation of women involved in the pornography industry. It also, it must be said, provides a pinion in their moral argument against any middle course.

Nonetheless, from an agnostic perspective on the justifiable trade-offs in civil litigation, these linkages, absent presumptions about causality, also provide a pinion for arguments *for* a middle course. The attention some mainstream politicians are giving to pornography's environmental harms merits attention. New York City, following the lead of other municipalities, completed a study indicating that pornography outlets (which rose 35 percent in the past decade or so) systematically reduce the rental values of adjacent properties and contribute to the economic and then social decline of affected areas. In response to these data, and prompted by concerns about the safety and socioeconomic welfare of the community, the city set strict zoning restrictions designed to concentrate these outlets in light industrial and high-density commercial zones, and to forbid them to be near other outlets, residences, schools, or churches.

An agnostic might find some promise in these restrictions as the basis for a first scenario for managing First Amendment concerns and the harms of pornography. But an agnostic would still want to ask a number of questions. For one, if the restrictions' immediate effect is to concentrate pornography outlets in light industrial and high-density commercial zones, and to reduce their number, is there evidence for how this concentration will have a tangible impact on marketplace concerns over urban development, the quality of social life, residential neighborhood revitalization, and the economic development and stability of said industrial and commercial areas?

A second-best scenario question is whether these restrictions might be defended as achieving the worthy goal of keeping alive issues involving the social problems of pornography, even if they have no impact on them. A third-best scenario question is whether, even if they do not keep those issues alive, they might be defended as a way to encourage some people to break with the censorship-versus-education gridlock about repressive regulations and benign neglect. A fourth-best scenario question is whether they might be defended as a way to encourage thinking about middle course approaches to other social problems, if even these restrictions fail to break this gridlock.

Pragmatic critics of an environmental impact approach to pornography may well object that all these scenarios run the risk of unwelcome results, not the least of which is that they put law and politics on that proverbial slippery slope to restricting expressive freedoms. The problem with this rejoinder is that novel arguments are always on a slippery slope to unwelcome results. Thus, a slippery-slope argument is antipolitics in that it tends to exaggerate the likelihood of catastrophes and underestimate the capacity of actors to undo mistakes (Easton 1994).[20] It is also antipolitics in that it does not take into account the extent to which policy failures have the potential to galvanize sleepy political constituencies and to give birth to more successful public policies. And, as for risks to expressive freedoms: sovereignty interest perplexities about uncertain harms run so deep that, as *Beauharnais* warns us, only experience, not commentary, can teach where the line should be between rights and regulations.

For their part, cultural conservatives, as well as radical-feminist critics of an environmental impact approach, may object that these scenarios will do little, if anything, about the deep cultural, sexual, economic, religious, moral, and political problems of pornography. But this rejoinder ignores the underdeterminacy of pornography's harms and therefore does not trouble itself with the messy, mixed, and ambiguous experiences of political, economic, and sexual life (Michelman 1989: 313).

And more romantic (if that is the right word) urban spirits with a strong appreciation for the kinetic energy of erotic alarm and decadence will worry about the physical displacement of sites that diminish that energy. Their concern is that a city is a *city* in part because of the dangers it creates. These dangers can be affirmative, from this point of view, if they challenge citizens to try to understand the affirmative side of differences of identity, social disunity, and even social disintegration (Young 1990: 227). To regulate pornography outlets in cities thus runs the risk of reinforcing a culture of narrow heterogeneity that does not teach needed lessons about trying to live with differences the majority neither understands nor morally accepts.

New York City is a singular place, and although other cities have used municipal zoning ordinances to restrict pornography outlets, New York City's attempt to manage the ordered liberty of Times Square is instructive, at least in regard to the first scenario. Litigation against the regulations instigated by the New York Civil Liberties Union, the Empire State Pride Agenda (a gay and lesbian organization), and the Coalition for Free Expression (an organization of sex shop owners) might have played itself out in 1999. The Supreme Court refused to hear an appeal from sex shop owners that would overturn the U.S. Second Circuit Court of Appeals ruling that the zoning law did not violate the First or Fourteenth Amendments.[21] But New York City newspaper accounts in 1999 and 2000 tell stories of sex shop entrepreneurs evading the law by putting pornographic materials in a back room of their shops and placing nonpornographic materials in the front, and even admitting minors to evade the zoning specification that refers to "adult establishments." The long-term impact of the law in regard to reducing the number of sex shops is thus hard to predict, not least because it is unclear whether the city or sex shop owners will have greater resources for the legal bills that ensue from enforcing it.

Although it is not customary to end a chapter on an inconclusive and highly speculative note, there is no way to avoid doing so here. If the kind of commentary that I have experimented with in this chapter has merit it should challenge critics, teachers, and their audience to break with mutually exclusive principles and to explore the pornography controversy as a battle in our cultural and economic wars over what should be the evolving morality of our tradition (Bork 1990: 191). This battle has yet to be well fought in earnest and on its own grounds, in terms of incremental policy innovations or commentary to a middle course. My conclusion is that for the present, solace in the law's formalisms is unmerited as a way of understanding that battle, for it creates more unity and clarity about rights and regulatory power than the subject matter can support. That is why I recommend analysis that attempts to describe and evaluate some of the political, economic, and cultural costs and benefits, at least in the short term, of politics working out policies governing pornography's harms apart from legal formalisms.

This commentary precludes taking solace in the merits of judicial intervention in the name either of "equality rights" or traditional First Amendment norms. It recommends that even if the very essence of civil liberty is the protection of the laws whenever an injury is incurred, it is one of the primary duties of agnostic commentary to be skeptical about the superior role of court intervention. This is a very controversial thing to say, especially where the First Amendment is involved. But it is a duty of teachers, critics, and their audience to keep an eye on evidence about the costs and benefits of applying the law's formalisms to the perplexities of sovereignty interests and ordered liberty policies. Because the costs and benefits of regulation are likely to remain very subtle and underdeterminate, skeptical commentary situates itself to keep the controversy alive by taking no solace whatsoever in whatever way adjudication turns out.

· 11 ·
Qualified Solace in the Law's Formalisms

"Please, Mommy, don't make me go alone. Please go with me, Mommy."

The four-year-old child known as Richard was sobbing so convulsively he seemed barely able to breathe. His adoptive mother was holding him, inside the home in Schaumberg where Richard had lived his whole life.

"I don't want to go." The boy tried to scream through his sobs, but the words were choking him. "Don't make me leave."

There was no way for the woman he has always known as his mother to answer him. She was sobbing, too. "We'll love you forever," she managed to say.

"Please don't make me go," he begged. "Please, Please. Don't send me away."—*Chicago Tribune, May 1, 1995*

These excruciatingly painful words were heard as a four year old known as Baby Richard was taken by his biological parents from the home of his foster parents, who had cared for him from birth and were well into the process of adopting him. They marked the public denouement of a convoluted adoption battle in Illinois. Baby Richard was born in March of 1991. Two days after his birth, petition papers were filed to adopt him. The biological mother, Daniela Janikova, had refused to name the biological father, Otakar Kirchner, and Kirchner was told by the biological mother that the baby had not survived the pregnancy.

The adoption process proceeded on course, and the biological mother signed a consent decree to the adoption. But two months later, Kirchner learned of Baby Richard's existence, and he attempted to stop the adoption. His claim, however, was denied standing by the court for lack of evidence of paternity. Approximately six months later, Kirchner established paternity and also married Janikova. In May 1993, a trial court upheld the adoption, finding that the adoption setting was in the best interests of the child and that the biological father was unfit because his behavior during and after the pregnancy indicated a lack of responsibility and concern to an "unreasonable" degree. The trial court's decision was upheld by the Illinois Appeals Court.

But, in 1994, the Illinois Supreme Court invalidated the adoption on the grounds that the rights of biological parents are absolute. A month later the State of Illinois passed a law requiring a child's interests to be considered in contested adoptions. In February 1995, the U.S. Supreme Court refused to delay the return of the child to his biological parents. And, in April 1995, after litigation tactics undermined plans to have the transition proceed by stages, the child, in full view of neighbors and the press, was handed over to his biological parents.

On the heels of the previous year's equally tormenting public display of trauma over the return of Baby Jessica to her biological parents, the Baby Richard story gave some short-term and overheated prominence to what is ordinarily the private and visceral grief caused by adoptions gone wrong and custody disputes.[1] In 1999–2000, the custody battle between U.S. relatives of Cuban castaway Elian Gonzales, whose mother died in an attempt to flee Cuba, and Elian's father, who wanted the boy returned to him in Cuba, provided the public with an extravagant example of how easily trenchant politics—domestic and even international—can become the prominent factor in a custody dispute. This notwithstanding the fact that the majority of adoptions go well enough, and that all but a very few custody battles remain out of the public eye, adoption and custody battles ought to be understood as raising crucial public policy issues.[2] The reason they ought be so understood is that they serve as evidence that underdeterminacy in social fact considerations and convictions about political morality do not necessarily entail a total lack of solace in the law's formalisms and the work judges do. This chapter thus deepens our appreciation of the implications of this evidence for commentary to a middle course. But in doing so this chapter also raises and does its best to confront some very troubling questions about that commentary as civic education.

"Family" and "Family Relations"

Adoption and custody battles are a small part of the larger controversy over what constitutes a "family" and "family relations." This controversy includes issues of domestic abuse, adult sexual norms and behavior, parenting, aspects of choices about abortion, gay and lesbian rights, surrogate births, divorce, child custody and support, custody disputes arising out of divorce, conflicts between unwed mothers and fathers, welfare reform, religious and racial differences, medical and social services for children, inheritance and powers of attorney, criminal behavior, and property rights disputes over frozen ova, sperm, and embryos. Politicians have reduced this large controversy to slogans such as "family values," "moral crisis," "cultural decline," "decline of civility," "common-sense values," "welfare reform"—all to serve their partisan political purposes. The slogans apparently serve these purposes well enough, but anyone who gives it some thought realizes that the controversy over family and family relations is about far more profoundly tragic and ineffable things than electoral politics can manage.

Adoption and custody battles specifically revolve around four basic, profoundly thick questions: What is a family? What does it mean to be a parent? What is parental fitness? and, What are the best interests of a child? These questions are so thick because they cannot be answered without making practical judgments about matters that are inescapably, and appallingly, underdetermined: for example, the extent to which biology, in contrast to bonding ties, should receive more weight in defining parent-child relationships; the extent to which a "family" is a social and political construction rather than a product of intrinsic psychological and biological interrelationships; the extent to which children have interests discernibly independent of the parental relationship; the extent to which race, sexual preference, and family "dysfunctions" should play a part in determining child custody;[3] and the extent to which legal rights of biological parents and married persons should be extended to nonbiological custodians and the unmarried.

These are the matters, singly or together, that litigators, adjudicators, court-appointed referees, legislators, social workers, and family law experts grapple with in custody and adoption disputes. The nature of the judgments they must make is, unfortunately, largely lost in the cacophony of mass media coverage and the larger political scene. Even more unfortunately, although family law commentary is a rich subfield of legal scholarship, the implications of these judgments for law and politics generally conceived have not been considered important enough to occupy the attention of mainstream legal commentary.[4] But the fact that these judgments, and others like them, are lost and overlooked is more than enough to attract the attention of this skeptic. Remarkably, what I have learned about judges—to speak only of them—who make those judgments is helpful for portraying the difficult situation skeptics put themselves in when they go about trying to make a more democratic contribution to civic education about law and politics.

A Bind: The Four Questions in Family Relations and Adoption Disputes

The four questions relevant to child custody and adoption battles are not new ones. Since the birth of the nation they have recognizably been bound up in shifting sovereignty interests. In preconstitutional Anglo-American common law, children were treated by state governments as a form of property. However, from the Founding to the end of the nineteenth century, social and moral changes in the polity began to shift sovereignty interests in the direction of concerns about safeguarding children.[5] Changes in the legal and social status of women in the family were reflected in a shift toward the mother, as a nurturer, as the "natural" choice in custody battles. The Progressive movement successfully pressured for sovereignty interests in child welfare legislation (compulsory education, child labor laws, parental competence codes, and aid to poor mothers so that they might be able to keep their children).

By the second decade of this century, all state legislatures had established legal hearings for adoptions to secure the surrender of the custodial rights of biological parents and to ascertain the fitness of potential adopters to raise a child. Eventually these hearings expanded to include evidence of the best interests of a child, understood in relation to the fitness of potential adoptive parents.[6]

Again in this century, about thirty years ago, another major shift in sovereignty interests occurred. The demand for (white and healthy) infants and very young children began to outstrip the supply. For a variety of reasons the numbers of infertile couples increased, as did the number of adoptions driven by moral and humanitarian considerations. Coincidentally, "some major changes in views about the psychology of adoption [also] occurred [that] undoubtedly received greater attention as a result of [supply and demand forces]" (Caplan 1990: 40). The single most important of these changes was in thinking about whether nonbiological families should or should not try to be facsimiles of biological families. Experts found mounting evidence that "when adoptive families acted as if they were identical with biological ones and ignored their differences, the children were more apt to have difficulties in development and the parents to encounter problems in their own roles" (Caplan 1990: 41).

This last half-century has seen other significant shifts in sovereignty interests. States increased their monitoring of parental conduct. Social agencies and courts moved away from the presumption favoring biological mothers, and social-psychological expertise became the preferred way to determine the interests of children. Arbitration and mediation, rather than litigation, were tried as mechanisms for resolving custody disputes, although with mixed results and reactions from various constituencies.

Today, judges who have to make the ultimate decisions in custody and adoption battles can find themselves in a real bind. If they are alive to similarities and differences between biological and nonbiological family settings, and the impact they may have on children, they are much less inclined to give pat answers to the four questions. And that means they cannot avoid tackling those underdetermined matters involving biology, psychology, and social and political norms—the whole panoply of human interrelations, in short. Nevertheless, the idea that "family" means the biological family,[7] with the biological mother as its fountainhead is deeply embedded (as is the conventional conception of marriage, parenthood, and the best interests of a child) in the political culture and the common law, as well as in custody and adoption law and processes.

Thus the bind: efficacious formalisms push judges in the direction of conventional marriage and a biological conception of the family. Such family and such marriage are understood, and felt, to be the source of emotional and psychological stability, economic well-being and progress, intellectual and moral development, ethnic, racial, and gender identity, life plan opportunities, and a sense of self and society. Morally and emotionally, it seems manifestly "right" that courts recognize that biological parents, and most especially mothers, have a nearly absolute moral, social, and legal claim to their children, and to raise them as they see fit, until or unless systematic psychological or physical abuse, neglect, or abandonment occurs.

But whatever may be conventionally thought and felt to be manifestly right, judges increasingly find themselves having to take into account other considerations. Since about the sixties, divorce, diverse partnership arrangements, family dysfunctions, unwed parents, and all such other social phenomena have increasingly impinged on their deliberations. This development is reflected in the extent to which judges, in order to contrive answers to the four questions within the binds that constrains them, attribute the (supposed) virtues of the biological family and conventional marriage to other "familial" arrangements.

The U.S. Supreme Court from time to time plays a significant role in these contrivances. For example, in 1972, in *Stanley v. Illinois*[8] the Burger Court ushered in a major change in the constitutional take on the family by ruling that the Due Process and Equal Protection Clauses forbid states from presuming that those unwed biological fathers who had had no parental contacts with a child were prima facie unfit. Earlier, *Moore v. City of East Cleveland*[9] held that the Fourteenth Amendment includes a liberty interest in the family's preservation of itself. The Burger Court thus associated moral and social rights within the cover of privacy interests and procedural rights: states are henceforth required to provide hearings, on a case-by-case basis, to establish the fitness of a biological father's custodial claim. (However, presumptions in favor of married or unmarried females remain intact, absent contrary evidence of their unfitness or overwhelming evidence regarding the child's best interests.)

The nexus between biology, as the primary factor, and substantial contacts, as a secondary cofactor, in the constitution of a family is stated explicitly in *Smith v. Organization of Foster Families.*[10] *Smith* roots familial privacy interests in the conventional idea and practices of biological relationships. Yet the Court found that recognition must also be given to the social fact that family relationships also exist beyond biological ties. Foster care and various arrangements leading to adoption, for instance, often provide a "deeply loving and independent relationship between an adult and a child"[11] which the *Smith* Court was willing to count as falling within the ambit of familial privacy interests.

This nexus between a biological and nonbiological family relationship accommodates the bind addressed above. But the law also treats a biological and nonbiological family differently. Although "family privacy has its source, and its contours are ordinarily sought, not in state law, but in intrinsic human rights," as they have been understood in "this Nation's history and tradition,"[12] it is also a matter of law that a foster care arrangement does not provide foster care parents with the same rights as biological parents. Unlike a biological family, a foster family has the state as a partner, and the contractual relationships between a foster family and the state determine the extent and limits of a foster parent's liberty interests in any adoption proceeding. Be they ever so broad, those limits still do not approach the all but absolute right that a biological parent retains to have a child in voluntary foster care placement returned. That right, according to the Court, is based on "blood relationship . . . and basic human right"[13] and can only be compromised by a legal finding of unfitness or best interests.

Soon enough, in *Quilloin v. Walcott,*[14] the Burger Court confronted a question that the *Stanley* and *Smith* line did not resolve: whether a biological connection alone was sufficient, without substantial contact, to constitute parental rights in the adoption process. *Quillion* appears to answer that question in the negative, by reinforcing the traditional social weight of biology and marriage. The Burger Court ruling was that an unwed biological father, with minimal contact with his child, who did not seek custody of it but sought nevertheless to intercede in an adoption process, is not denied substantive due process or equal protection of the laws by not having a veto, as divorced fathers do, over a prospective adoption.

Quillion is to be read as implying two things. One is that unwed biological fathers without significant contact with a child do not have the same rights as biological fathers who are, or have been, married to the child's biological mother. The second is that the best interests of a child limit the rights of an (unwed) biological father. This constitutional nexus between parental rights and substantial contact was further reinforced in *Caban v. Mohammad.*[15] An equal protection case, *Caban* found that unwed biological mothers and fathers, both of whom had substantial contacts with a child, must be afforded the same rights in the adoption process.

This line of internally complex cases adds three due process and equal protection themes to the already hard enough adjudication of "family relations": (1) "[t]he mere existence of a biological link between unwed parents and a child, absent a contact, does not merit the equivalent constitutional protection" afforded married and divorced or separated biological parents;[16] (2) unwed men who have a custodial relationship or substantial contacts with a child have some equal protection and due process protection, but not to the same extent as married men or unwed or married women; and (3) foster families have some, but not all, of the liberty interests biological families have. These three themes leave intact the traditional conception of a family and state sovereignty interests in preserving it.[17] Yet these themes also draw some contingent fact considerations about custodial contacts and emotional relationships into the ambit of family formalisms to efficaciously take into account the rights of unwed biological and foster parents.

What obtains in the hardest of all possible hard cases—when biology and marriage are not coterminous—is dealt with in a child custody case, *Michael H. v. Gerald D.*[18] (The complicated facts of the case are worth referencing, if only to give a sense of how matter-of-fact extraordinary matters are in adoption battles.)[19] In this decision, the Rehnquist Court confirmed state sovereignty interests in the traditional family. *Michael H.* finds that paternity and custodial contacts with a child do not constitute a "liberty interest" in a parent-child relationship sufficiently strong to breach the parent-child relationship within a marriage.

A majority of the Court did not foreclose the possibility that under different factual circumstances a biological father might have a liberty interest in a child born to a biological mother who was married to someone else. Nonetheless, this kind of ruling reconfirms prevailing state sovereignty interests in "the historic respect—indeed, sanctity would not be too strong a term—traditionally accorded to the relationship that develops within the unitary family."[20]

Understandably, the *Stanley* and *Caban* line gives ample reason to dissent. Justice Brennan complains about an air of "make-believe" surrounding the Court's treatment of the family legal formalisms in *Michael H.*[21] He sees in the *Stanley-Caban* line major breaks toward legal recognition of unconventional conceptions of family and marriage that have a better fit with half a century of social changes in parent-child relationships.[22] In regard to sovereignty interests, it is Justice Brennan's conclusion that the forces of change at work in a society are such that it is "absurd to assume that we can agree on the content of those terms ['family' and 'parenthood'] and destructive to pretend that we do. In a community such as ours," Justice Brennan thus concludes, " 'liberty' must include the freedom not to conform."[23] So sharply defined are the differences of opinion in *Michael H.* that the case reads as an encapsulation of the Court's contributions to the bind that trial judges must efficaciously wriggle in and out of.

The bind itself, as well as the confusing variations in the specifics of state adoption and custody laws that it has produced, the conflicts over the rights of adults, and the tensions between the rights of adults and children may in time disappear, so that "a decade from now, after the commentary has had a chance to catch up with the innovations of science and society, adoption may seem a simple matter to assess." Or it may be that these confusions are permanent ones, such that custody and adoption disputes "will be perennially unsettled" by the need to satisfy competing social and personal claims (Caplan 1990: 131, 133–34). Three examples suffice to make the point. In early 2000, a New Jersey Supreme Court judge ruled that a lesbian who helped raise a former lover's twin children (products of artificial insemination) was entitled to visitation rights but not joint custody. A month later, Mississippi became the third state to ban gay couples from adopting children. In June of 2000, in *Troxel V, Granville,*[24] in a six-to-three vote, the Rehnquist Court found a State of Washington law that provided for anyone to petition judges for visitation rights in the best interests of the child so broad as to interfere with a parents' due process rights concerning the care, custody, and control of children. But Justice O'Connor was joined only by three other Justices in declaring parental right to be a fundamental one. The lack of a majority consensus for a rule of law in *Troxel,* the fact that Justice O'Connor does not address the core issue of the best interests of the child and that she acknowledges the difficulty of addressing just what a "family" is in American life, suggests that judges and legislators are inclined to disagree about the emotionally charged issues of family law for some time. In any event, whatever the short- or long-term prognostications, only those in the grip of intellectual jurisprudence hope to see in these battles a law of ordered liberty that can be rightly decided.

Qualified Solace in the Law's Formalisms

Martha Minow, in *Making All the Difference* (1990), writes about the politics of self-identity. She argues that formalisms relating to self-identity sustain past prejudices and stigmas and fail to teach the polity to appreciate either the significance of differences between persons or "the endless variety of our individualism" (1990: 374). Minow is someone I would call a revisionist, and her revisionism leads her to recommend a threefold transformation of formalisms that would lead judges to (1) emphasize contingent social fact considerations and "contextualist approaches to problems, based on a continual process of testing theory against practice and practice against theory"; (2) maintain skepticism about public and private power and reject any "ultimate resting place" in favor of "dialogue, conversation, continuing processes of mutual boundary setting, and efforts to manage colliding perspectives on reality"; and (3) analyze differences between persons that are open to redescription by disputing settled expectations about self and society and the personal relationships they constrain (1990: 380–83).

Minow has a story about a child with Down syndrome and a heart defect to illustrate what this transformation would entail if it were achieved regularly. The child had been institutionalized, and his parents, who were infrequent visitors to the institution, refused permission for surgery to repair the heart defect. A couple who were volunteers at the institution had, over the years, befriended the child and had, by all accounts and later testimony, developed a very close relationship with him. After the State of California tried and failed to intervene in the child's behalf, the couple sought to become his guardians (but not to terminate all the biological parents' rights) and to proceed with the surgery.

The California trial court judge ruled against the grain in this case by not finding for the biological parents, and the ruling was upheld on appeal. Minow praises this judge for an "extraordinary self-consciousness about his own relationship to [the child] and to the issues in the litigation." By means of this self-consciousness he was able to set aside (mere) abstractions in favor of relational concerns and context-specific fact considerations (1990: 341–47). In other words, as Minow explains, the judge transformed formalisms by shifting evidentiary arguments from "who speaks for the child" to arguments about who had a relationship with him that promised his best care; and constructing a hypothetical, Platonic, dialogue between himself and the child—posing questions and answers about wants, needs, and relationships—to try to imagine what the child might choose to do if he were competent to do so.

Minow does well to praise her judge for his ingenuity and legal craftsmanship. Still, after considering some of the main elements of adoption law, it is something of a surprise to read Minow's conclusion that her judge has heard an unusual case and rendered an opinion in an unusual way (1990: 348).[25] This case raises many of the same issues about family and family relations that adoption battles and matters related to open adoption do. The judge's Platonic dialogue is unique, but it is better understood as an elegant result of a process that is familiar to very many family court trial judges. Its elegance can still be appreciated even when it is also recognized as a jurisprudential rationalization for a decision where no legal result is determinable and any legal result is efficacious.

I have another story. A *New York Times Sunday Magazine* profile of a New Jersey family court judge recounts a process of decision-making that does not have Platonic elements but is otherwise very much like the one Minow describes. Minow reports of her judge that even though the case was so confusing that it "haunted him outside the courtroom," he was also "concerned . . . that his opinion and decision be considered objective" (Minow 1990: 347). Hence the Platonic dialogue. The more journalistic *Times* account, by Jan Hoffman,[26] describes the anguish of a judge who is also unable to depend on formalisms to decide her cases. Hoffman's judge suffers constant uncertainty over her decisions as she plows through her case load, almost overwhelmed by circumstantial social fact and varying contextualist considerations. This judge is skeptical about the claims made by the people who appear before her. She is also skeptical of her own capacity to tell whom to believe and unable to find any "ultimate resting place" in the decisions she makes as day after day she goes home to reformulate yet again the personal relationships that have been disputed before her. The *Times* account is replete with references to her viscerally felt fears and doubts, her values and prejudices, her intuitions, as they have evolved from case-by-case adjudication. It is emotion that drives battles over children,[27] and it is emotion that drives the New Jersey judge, who finds ultimately little else but emotion to justify her often (close to) ad hoc decision-making.

The conclusion I draw from these two stories is that both judges are compelled by the underdeterminacy of family and family relations law to do the only thing they can possibly do: they make leap-of-faith decisions that arise from having to make a "way through a labyrinth of uncertainty" (Jacobson 1978: 129) about what formalisms and circumstantial fact considerations require of them. The only difference between the two judges is that Minow's judge is in the grip of intellectual jurisprudence and therefore more concerned that his opinions and decisions be "considered objective." Seen from this perspective, the California judge's creativity appears to be simply a screen behind which, "bewildered and sometimes genuinely stumped by family dilemmas, [he comes to] decisions based on an uneasy mixture of inadequate laws and . . . private values" (Hoffman 1995: 46).

There are those who argue that the laws judges have to work with would be more adequate if they were based on robust child development data, or if judges were themselves better trained in family relations, or if a uniform adoption law were promulgated, or if a child's liberty interests were better protected, or if the causes of the violence that families can do were better appreciated. There is much to say for such arguments. Yet prudence dictates coming down on the side that never finds in successfully accomplished custody and adoption law more than an uneasy mixture of law and values. This mixture may well teach lessons about "the difficult commitment to live together" (Minow 1990: 309), but it does so rudely, through inevitable blunders, errors, and unintended results as much as it does through anything that can be interpreted to be more mannerly and rightly decided.

Others may see it otherwise, but this is an instance where this agnostic is prepared to express a qualified solace in what the judges are doing in respect to the law's formalisms. On those occasions when judges admit that formalisms do not settle cases they fracture the myth of the rule of law by revealing the extent to which legal formalisms are both efficacious and yet an enemy of rightly decidedness. Certainly the judges characterized in this chapter are intellectually and emotionally bewildered. They listen to the cross fire in an adoption or custody battle and then struggle through a labyrinth of uncertainty created by what they hear. They are acutely conscious of the intellectual and practical bind they are in when they have to steer their middle course between formalisms and what actual situations appear to require of them. They are sometimes temporarily immobilized by the underdeterminacy of it all, but they render their decisions hopefully, ever aware that they may be doing more harm than good. But only political jurisprudes in the grip of the ideology of involvement and intellectual jurisprudence would contend that trial and appellate court judges should routinely admit to such an awareness of the limitations of themselves and the law.

I want to step away from custody and adoption battles to say that there is something of a resemblance between what *these* judges are willing to admit they go through and what skeptical teachers and critics and those receptive to their commentary should expect to face. They too are likely to find themselves intellectually and emotionally bewildered by a cross fire of charges against what they are trying to do. From one side there well might be a charge of fence sitting, indeed of bad political and moral faith: to address the efficaciousness of formalisms, facets of political power, underdeterminacy, and all the rest of it just to arrive at a middle course in defiance of principle is a dereliction of intellectual and political duty. It can be anticipated that this charge will come from those activists who believe that egalitarian imperatives require completely disarming all legal categories that perpetuate present or vestigial prejudices against minority interests. Or it will come from those who are committed to market and libertarian imperatives and are concerned about redistributionist policies and regulatory state encroachments on market and private activities. At a more academic (but still political) level, revisionists and rejectionists most certainly will charge dereliction of duty against skeptics. But so too will more moderate commentators who believe that principles and ideals should not be traded off for the sake of (mere) contextual, consequentialist, pragmatic, or utilitarian calculations, or who believe that legal choices ought to come as close as possible to the dictates of deductive logic, canons of objectivity, or theoretical paradigms. And most certainly all those who have confidence in the law and/or the courts as the polity's best source of civic education to the highest moral and political values will agree with the charge of fence sitting and see it as intellectually and politically reprehensible.

From the other, more legalistic side, there might well be the charge of disrespect: merging formalist and other abstractions with circumstantial fact and consequentialist considerations is just a results-oriented tactic to evade the mandates of the rule of law. Disrespect for the rule of law is perceived as a threat by all those who see the law as a bulwark against the self-destructive forces of violence, rank prejudice, and irrationality. Disrespect also threatens those who emphasize text-bound readings of the Constitution, strict adherence to precedent, and the law qua law (as distinct from politics) as linchpins of legal legitimacy and a constitutional regime. And for those who are concerned about the conservation of law and order, duly elected rulers, promulgated policies and entitlements, due process and formal justice, disrespect for the rule of law is anathema.

Those who choose to be skeptics should not shy away from this cross fire of charges; they should be keenly aware of the intellectual and practical bind they put themselves in when they try to steer their commentary down a middle course. Yet, although there is no denying (to be blunt about it) the logic behind these charges, skeptics ought not to be intellectually or otherwise immobilized by them. Instead, they should plead *nolo contendere* with the rationale in mind that skepticism and relativism, when put into proper perspective, provide solace enough to defy the cross fire.

Earlier in this book I invoked the image of the wary fox and now as the figure of Machiavelli's prince to help distinguish agnosticism from intellectual jurisprudence. I want to summon these figures up again, this time to help explain why skeptics should take solace in relativism.[28] Like the fox, skeptics try to be alert to traps. Faith in principle and respect for legitimacy are traps to the extent that they mandate—and "mandate" is the operative term—a problem-solving orientation that predetermines commentary to faithful and respectful conclusions. Skeptics, by contrast, anticipate (as I have shown repeatedly) that context-specific facts and consequentialist considerations make predetermined conclusions politically insufficient.

Skeptics, therefore, do in commentary what Machiavelli's prince does in politics. They maneuver through the cross fire of opposing forces, making prudent use of this or that knowledge, as the situation warrants. They know that, taking everything into account, some things that appear to be the intellectual or political virtues of good faith or legitimacy have, in some circumstances but not others, politically unwelcome consequences. In pleading *nolo contendere,* skeptics take solace in the charges of bad faith and lack of respect. They do so because these indicate that they have hit home if—and "if" is the operative word—their constructed case-study scenarios reveal the gulf between broader political realities and what advocates of good faith and respect predetermine to be required. Skeptics accept the intellectual and emotional discomfort of being out of step with colleagues and their fellow citizens because, by this means, sometimes confirming and at other times denying what their colleagues have to say, they are assured of not habitually making that which is underdeterminate determinate.

Relativism then is its own reward. But however hopeful agnostics may be about this reward, they are continually aware that commentary can do more harm than good. It is worth repeating that skeptics should not commit the self-excepting fallacy by neglecting to turn an agnostic eye on themselves. And, assuming they avoid that trap, what about the trap they might inadvertently set for others? What if doubts and uncertainties raised by relativistic accounts so overwhelm or frustrate persons that rather than becoming more skeptical about good faith and respect, as skeptics intend, they lapse into totalistic bad faith or disrespect, or. alternatively, they seek unmerited solace in the certitude of abstractions?

Prudence and candor should reinforce each other, and the threat of these unwelcome results compels me to be both candid and prudent. What I have to say about unintended results is undoubtedly self-serving, but no less pertinent for that. Unwelcome unintended results are part and parcel of any civic education, as they are of judging. No one should deny this; yet unintended results are repressed, or forgotten, and certainly neglected in commentary, since they are not something that teachers and critics deal with very often, explicitly or even implicitly. So whatever the reasons for others' lack of attention to unwelcome results, I need to come to terms with them in order to justify standing by my plea of *nolo contendere*.

Unwelcome Results and a Skeptic's Bind

The best justification I have to offer is a risk assessment of the threats noted above, based on a mix of social-scientific findings, logic, and personal experiences. This risk assessment leads me to reason as follows.

Regarding the threats of totalistic bad faith and disrespect, the risk of their actually being realized is very remote. Remember the audience for commentary is a small one. The plausible audience for (skeptical) commentary, inside or outside the academy, comprises those citizens who are more highly educated than most, more aware of legal and political issues, and more involved in public affairs. Perhaps they have a greater sense of their own political efficacy (or the lack thereof?), and a greater tolerance for intellectual controversy, ambiguity, and the subtle, esoteric, and difficult to grasp arguments about law and politics (McClosky and Brill 1983: 371–375, 416–17). Social science repeatedly confirms that these are the citizens who are most likely to have internalized social learning about regime norms (Barnum and Sullivan 1990). Thus these citizens are, as said before, an educated elite. They tend to show the highest degree of support for due process of law, equality, liberty, democracy, and civil liberties. They also tend to show both the most diffuse and the most specific support for, and confidence in, institutions, in particular the courts (Caldeira and Gibson 1992: 636, 648–49). And it seems reasonable to presume that intellectual jurisprudential lessons about good faith and respect have served to refine, enlarge, and reinforce all this social learning and support for norms and institutions.

Using as our frame of reference this account of civic education and its internalization—admittedly a speculative one because this process is understudied[29]—we should be cautious about assuming that the citizens described here will likely succumb to bad faith and disrespect. Here is why. Let us say that, intellectually and politically, sophisticated citizens are attentive to agnostic accounts, comprehend them, and are exposed to them often enough to retain them. If they then become overwhelmed or frustrated by them, say because of the gulf between these accounts and the norms to which they have been socialized, then, as "politically aware persons" they are likely to react to their cognitive dissonance by resisting that which is inconsistent with what they have absorbed (Zaller 1992: 148) about good faith and respect for the law. Recall that the phenomenon of cognitive dissonance is something that we may all experience. It is not an indication of psychological weakness or prejudice; rather, cognitive dissonance is said to occur when we must confront ideas, feelings, or behavioral situations that are inconsistent with or contrary to our settled ideas, feelings, and behaviors.

There are a number of "rational" ways to respond to cognitive dissonance created by agnostic accounts. One way is to resist the relativism of agnostic accounts, and thereby alleviate psychological and political anxiety, by deciding that these accounts are completely wrong-headed. Another way is to acknowledge their credibility but to discount their full significance by diluting them so that they can be assimilated into existing normative and partisan frameworks (Zimbardo and Leippe 1991: 214; Zaller: 1992: 169). Either form of resistance requires a psychological and political "confirmatory strategy" (Zimbardo and Leippe 1991: 206) that invalidates ideas that produce cognitive dissonance and reconfirms existing beliefs and attitudes. A classic, if not the classic, confirmatory strategy is to take refuge in cues provided by trusted "opinion leadership" (Zaller 1992: 44–45, 169–72).[30]

The most immediate opinion leadership comes from adjudicators, litigators, and teachers and critics in the interpretive community. By and large, the answers they give to the rightly decided question, even when they oppose Court and legal decisions, confirm social learning about, and commitments to, regime norms, institutions, good faith, and respect. To the extent this is true, it is consistent with social learning theory to predict that for reasoning citizens all these commitments are not "ephemeral" (Caldeira and Gibson 1992: 658) but are "tightly woven into . . . basic self-defining values" (Zimbardo and Leippe 1991: 214). Thus, it is no more than prudent to presume that reasoning citizens, having learned their rightly decided lessons all too well, will be motivated to take their cues from the interpretive community and to enjoy solace in good faith and respect.

The threat, then, that exposure to agnostic accounts will cause reasoning citizens to settle into bad faith and attitudes of disrespect is actually quite remote, absent socioeconomic forces that can more deeply undermine citizen confidence in regime norms and institutions (Muller and Seligson 1994).[31] By the same token, however, the threat that reasoning citizens will take confirmatory solace in abstractions should be reckoned far less remote. The explanation for this is that a significant part of a confirmatory strategy is to ask seemingly objective questions about the relative strengths and weaknesses of the information that produces cognitive dissonance. The not so self-evident motive behind these questions is the desire to secure information that "practically guarantee[s] a belief-supporting answer" (Zimbardo and Leippe 1991: 207).

In other words, such an answer is already built into the questions, in that they presuppose mandatory reliance on jurisprudential abstractions about legal rights, powers, process, structure, and the like as a foundation for answers to the rightly decided questions. They provide thereby a most efficient way to reconfirm basic values that are associated with good faith and respect. And they bring relief from the anxiety produced by the quarrelsome complexities of relativistic accounts. Hence, granting the grip of social learning, intellectual jurisprudence, and the dynamics of cognitive dissonance, we would be justified in describing the worst-case scenario in these terms: relatively few members of the production or audience for legal commentary are open, for whatever complex bundle of psychological and political reasons, to being skeptical about their own self-defining values, willing to challenge what they have learned from opinion leaders, or are hopeful about finding alternative ways of thinking about law and politics.[32] (If you have reached this point in the book, perhaps you are not part of this worst-case scenario!)

It follows logically from this pessimistic scenario that a civic education that unwittingly engenders unwelcome (at least to skeptics) confirmatory questions and the solace they encourage in abstractions is a real enough threat that some kind of risk management strategy is in order. But no prudent risk management strategy should ever be based on a single scenario. Another, more optimistic, scenario arises from the view that "legal consciousness is necessarily heterogeneous in character . . . [and] because people . . . experience different histories, and struggle in varying sites of interaction . . . the legal consciousness of each group and individual tends to be unstable, ambiguous, and contradictory" (McCann 1994: 282). This uncertainty is pervasive enough, according to this scenario, to make considerably more rather than fewer persons open, skeptical, willing to challenge authority, and hopeful about there being alternatives to think about regarding law and politics. This scenario has framed this book.

The risk management strategy followed from the outset of this book steers a middle course between optimism and pessimism. This middle course has required that some concessions be made to cognitive dissonance. For example, to argue for putting a brake on intellectual jurisprudence rather than for displacing it is a concession to its power. That does not at the same time mean abandoning hopefulness about a place for alternative habits of mind. Also, to defend the ideology of involvement, despite social facts about knowledge and power that deny teachers and critics a significant role in the interpretive community, is to concede to the difficulties of challenging intellectual and political authorities without also abandoning hopefulness about a more democratic ethos in that community. (Other concessions have been relatively minor ones, and they have been left to do their work undefended.)

To what degree any of these concessions will succeed in reducing resistance to agnosticism cannot be predicted. What is far more predictable is that a prudent risk-management strategy will push commentary into like concessions. At the same time, the agenda of promoting a more democratic ethos pulls skeptical commentary into accounts that threaten to intensify cognitive dissonance. This push and pull leaves teachers and critics in something of a bind, but it is not a troublesome bind to be in. In fact, it fits hand in glove with the plea of *nolo contendere,* both the bind and the plea being emblematic of skeptics' commitment not to be naive about the tasks that await those who seek to encourage civic education to a more Jeffersonian civic culture.

Both this bind and this plea are unique to a skeptical habit of mind. But the need to be more candid about the conditions that shape civic education is not unique to it. As I indicated at the very beginning of this book, all forms of civic education have to face up to the predicament that what makes for a good fit in the academy too often differs considerably from what matters outside it. As promised, my closing remarks will be reserved specifically for characterizing how agnostic skepticism comes to grip with this predicament. We know more than half of the story already. By virtue of the cross fire of charges against what they do and the cognitive dissonance they create in the academic and legal communities, skeptics should be more keenly self-aware and candid than most others about this predicament. The part of the story that remains to be told is how this self-awareness and candor, alongside Jeffersonian intentions, help to situate skeptics to confront the inevitable gulf between their commentary and the mundane concerns of ordinary citizens. To tell this part of the story, to make what has been said so far about risk-management ploys more concrete, and to frame my final words, I want to consider the issue of efficacious civic education, and here my words are directed specifically at teachers and critics.

· 12 ·
Qualified Solace in Agnosticism

It is essential that skeptics appreciate the risk of not succeeding in their efforts to promote a more Jeffersonian civic culture. Unfortunately, this risk is all too easily ignored, because the ideology of involvement leads so effortlessly, even for agnostics, to the presumption that civic education will be efficacious. Promoting Jeffersonian sensibilities thus requires considerable skepticism about achieving success in linking those sensibilities to formal education.

A sober and cautious respect for the difficulties of this task leads me now, in this last chapter, to propose the following gambit for consideration: teachers and critics should link legal and political lessons (like those taught here) to people's mundane concerns about private relations. Understandably some (many?) will react adversely to the suggestion that civic education should proceed in this way. Some will allege that merging lessons is a flat violation of the ideological dictum that matters belonging to the public sphere should be sharply demarcated from the private sphere. Some will make the companion allegation that merging lessons trespasses on commonly held territorial distinctions about what the professions of scholarship, journalism, and teaching are about, and that it further trespasses on what parents, religious leaders, and the like do in their respective domains.

I respect these allegations. They have their provenance in classical liberal-democratic thought. The second allegation also resonates with widely held intellectual and political theories of academic craft and social roles. Allegations that are warranted by both common opinion and ideology ought not be peremptorily dismissed. Nonetheless, there is good strategic reason for skeptics to bypass them: regardless of their legitimacy, such allegations convey a too abstract idea of liberal-democratic civic education. Such allegations have led to a too pat confidence about what civic education should include and exclude. This undue confidence is at odds with recognizing the value of linking civic education to mundane concerns. So, as an alternative conception of civic education more attuned to what needs to be done, I take a few pages from Charles Anderson's argument in *Prescribing the Life of the Mind* (1993).

Anderson argues that even though classical liberal-democratic ideology provides core values for civic education, the internal logic of the ideology is itself extremely contentious. In fact, he says, "[T]here is great uncertainty, and likely grave contentiousness [about what civic education ought to be about] the closer one comes to a level of detail sharper than platitude" (1993: 47, 49).[1] The recognition of this uncertainty fits well with my agenda of promoting Jeffersonian sensibilities of skepticism and tentativeness. And it is this recognition that provides the impetus to push aside peremptory objections to my gambit. Now I make explicit my heretofore tacit claim that pragmatic judiciousness, whatever its costs, is valuable to the extent it makes us more self-critical and empathetic about private relations (if not about public ones).

This claim is crucial. It is the one that blurs (this should not be taken as a pejorative) distinctions between lessons about public and private relations. It teaches that commentary is worth doing, politics and law aside, because it helps develop attitudes and skills that might prove useful in the conduct of life's personal and intimate dimensions.

Within this context, and considering the risks of not succeeding at promoting Jeffersonian sensibilities, it is prudent to construct a second-best scenario for civic education. Most citizens are much more likely to be attentive to lessons about private relations than public ones. The obvious and important reason for this is the fact that, for most citizens, daily private relations are more conspicuous and important than public ones. What I recommend then is that teachers and critics exploit this fact by inventing stories about mundane incidents that are "closer to home" in order to enhance skeptical commentary about less familiar public issues.

I suspect this recommendation will be more easily accomplished in lecture and discussion formats than it will be through writing and reading. However, this suspicion should not dampen teachers' and critics' enthusiasm for the prospects of civic education through their own writing, whether they work inside or outside the academy. Rather it should deepen their enthusiasm for formal civic education and teaching at all levels, since "formal education is the strongest factor in explaining what citizens do in politics and how they think about politics" (Nie, Junn, and Stehlik-Barry 1996: 2). That said, here is a short account of how one might link commentary and the mundane.

In addressing custody disputes for a college-level student audience, one might proceed, much as I did in my case study, by addressing selected state and Supreme Court opinions. Then one might blend this doctrinal analysis of the law's formalisms with a sample of law school or political science commentary on custody disputes—as long as one stays suspicious of falling prey to intellectual jurisprudence and ideology of involvement. And one might then also consider social science and media materials on the topic to help locate neglected politics and policies in those formalisms. Then those neglected politics and policies would lead to a discussion of facets of political power involved in custody disputes and to an analysis of the extent to which solace in the law's formalisms is merited. Then, though, one could break with this agnostic commentary in order to bring out in more concrete or personal ways the significance of this discussion. One might present a scenario about undergraduates' "baby," student self-governance. This scenario might challenge college students to consider the question, "Under what circumstances, and how, should it be determined that students no longer deserve to have control over student residential life"? Part of this challenge would be for them to characterize the interests of different parties (students, deans, faculty, and the institution itself) about the primary goals of residential life by bringing to bear on this question the same considerations they use to characterize federalism and democratization.[2] The hoped-for result is that students and teachers will be able to see parallels and linkages (and the lack of them) in the form and content of arguments that arise in both public and private domains and, thereby, learn the first lesson of judicious argumentation.

If this approach succeeds in blurring distinctions between public and private relations, and if it succeeds in carrying the other lessons about agnosticism along with it, and if they become part of the consciousness of persons, then perhaps agnostic skepticism will dovetail with what life experiences can teach over time about judiciousness, civility, and tolerance as means toward maintaining private relationships. For practicing judiciousness, civility, and tolerance in private life often calls for accommodations between what may appear to be necessary to satisfy one's own sometimes deeply felt personal interests and what may appear to be necessary to resolve circumstantial conflicts over the scope, functions, and/or purposes of relationships.[3] In turn, such accommodations might prove to anchor agnosticism in peoples' value orientations and practices. If persons learn to practice accommodation, and if persons are sufficiently motivated to care about law and politics, then privately learned lessons about judiciousness, civility, and tolerance might carry over into skepticism and relativism about law and politics. Perhaps that will, in turn, predispose citizens toward tolerance for the ambiguities and contradictions that arise in the law and politics of a pluralistic polity! (And perhaps saying this demonstrates sixties idealism and a bit of intellectual jurisprudence lurking behind agnosticism?)

To underscore what is obvious, the conditional and exclamatory sentences above indicate that the potential for this gambit's success is unknown. The gambit is correlated with a profoundly complicated process of social learning and civic education that is notoriously beyond control. By its social-scientific spirit, the conditional "if" evokes a politically sufficient degree of pessimism about agnostic civic education achieving its aims. By its insistence, the exclamation mark evokes a politically sufficient degree of hopefulness about its success. Together the conditional and the exclamation point indicate a sober and cautious enthusiasm for civic education's unpredictable and unreliable processes.

But with or without the gambit of merging private and public lessons, the unpredictability of public events can undermine enthusiasm for the prospects of agnostic civic education's achieving its aims. Consider as a (mostly) hypothetical illustration of this phenomenon a particular contingent of political scientists and their initial reaction to the Supreme Court's, five-to-four, per curiam decision, *Bush v. Gore.*[4] *Bush v. Gore,* of course, is the decision that reversed, as a violation of the Equal Protection Clause, the Florida Supreme Court's decision to hand-count undervotes (votes undetected by machine reading) in the state. The decision provided Governor George W. Bush a win in the State of Florida and thus the requisite Electoral College votes to win the election for President against Vice President Albert Gore (the winner in the popular vote).

What if within this scholarly contingent are some of the most prominent advocates of the various approaches to the law that inform the tenets of politically sufficient commentary? They are the scholars who are most inclined to view the law as a highly complex phenomenon that needs to be analyzed through consideration of a plurality of factors—for example, multiple constructions of legal criteria, the political environment, aspects of judicial processes, ideological considerations, and personal policy predilections. Nevertheless, their initial reaction to *Bush v. Gore* is altogether uncomplicated and reductionist: they condemn the decision and the majority's concurring opinions as nothing more or less than rank partisanship. They situate it historically among the most notorious Court opinions, like *Dred Scott* and *Plessy v. Ferguson,* which they repudiate for their demoralizing impact on polity and their traduction of the principle that judges are constrained by the rule of law. They reject any possibility that *Bush v. Gore* can be reconciled with the majority Justices' jurisprudence in other cases, their judicial federalism and their deference to state court opinions in particular. These scholars also wax on about betrayals of the nation's trust in judges, and they ponder whether the decision might permanently undermine the legitimacy of the presidential election, the role of the Supreme Court in American politics, and (alas) their own teaching and scholarship about the Court and law. They also argue about the extent to which (but not whether) the decision will breed public cynicism about the judicial process, this despite flash public opinion polls that indicated that the public was basically satisfied with both the decision and the way the Court managed the case.

Lastly, these scholars are so implacably furious about the decision that they accuse some Justices of having decided the case to further their own chances for a Bush-appointed Chief Justiceship. This leads these scholars to speculate on the merits of term limits for Justices (as in other judicial systems), the criteria of judicial impeachment, and legislative strategies by which senators might block future Bush nominees to the Supreme Court. In effect, these scholars hold that a politically motivated and results-oriented Supreme Court decision deserves to be met, measure by measure, with left-liberal political, and results-oriented attacks on the majority of the Court.

But among this contingent of scholars there is a smaller minority who react somewhat differently to *Bush v. Gore.* They too are left liberals, and they too are furious about the decision for partisan reasons. They also agree with their fellow scholars that the majority opinions are ill-reasoned and inconsistent. Nor do they deny that the five-to-four vote reflects what one would guess is each Justice's partisan preference.

But the minority in this contingent read *Bush v. Gore* within the context that there is simply no good law on the issues involved, rather than from the perspective of rank partisanship. The lack of good law, the minority says, is a major factor in why the opinions are ill-reasoned and why partisan preferences appear to explain so much about them. Accordingly this minority argues about the extent to which the Supreme Court decision should be attributed to a lack of craft in the state court's handling of the statutory and remedy issues in the recount litigation. Further they differ amongst themselves about the extent to which the Justices on the Supreme Court had to jury-rig partisan-looking opinions in order to either close out or sustain a flawed state judicial process.

Lastly, these scholars try to imagine what it would be like for judges to confront the very high stakes of a case that decides a presidential election. They argue among themselves about differences between the stakes in such a case and others that the Court must decide. This brings them to consider institutional factors such as the time and emotional pressures on litigants and adjudicators and the Justices' concern that wrangling over the election should come to an end to explain *Bush v. Gore*. They also wonder about the extent to which the Court should be credited with saving the nation from a potentially destabilizing political contest over the election in Congress. On those grounds they argue about the extent to which the short-term costs of a jury-rigged decision and partisan-looking decision are a relatively low price to pay for the longer-term political benefits that accrue to deciding the presidential race more quickly. Surprisingly, a few of them even defend the decision, more or less on its merits, as an untraditional equal protection case. But all of them agree that notwithstanding their disappointment in the election results, *Bush v. Gore* is a tempest in a teapot with little or no longer-term significance and hardly a measure for understanding the normal course of events in law and politics.

Quite apart from the relative strengths and weaknesses of these reactions, it should be transparent why this scenario about the scholars in the majority is disconcerting. They warn us not to get so preoccupied with the ideologies and personal policy predilections of judges that we neglect adequate consideration of the multiplicity of other "new institutional" factors that make judges different from other political actors. These are the same scholars who insist that we investigate the host of social and political factors that make up judicial decisions. Yet the majority of these scholars appear to have neglected this when it comes to *Bush v. Gore*.

Perhaps over time there will be consensus in the interpretive community whether the majority or the minority has it "right" about *Bush v. Gore*. Regardless of which consensus might hold sway, an agnostic believes that a complicated reading of the case will ultimately prove more profitable, for it will be less neglectful about the complex number of things necessary to understand the law, politics, and policies. A commitment to complicated reading is what makes this scenario about the majority's initial reaction so disconcerting. If those who are well tutored in reading the law in complicated ways react to *Bush v. Gore* as portrayed, then what hope is there for agnostic civic education achieving its aims amongst the less tutored?

A confirmed nonagnostic skeptic and pragmatist might say, not much hope at all. This skeptic might say, with Stanley Fish, that "minds are never open except in the context of matters of indifference" (Fish 1999: 289). This nonagnostic might say that there is no scholarly habit of mind that can ever give teachers, critics, or their audiences the ideological self-discipline to resist their own moral and policy interests. All there is are those interests. Similarly the nonagnostic might say that tenets for political sufficient commentary and agnostic skepticism are an academic practice, and academic practice cannot produce changes in actual attitudes or behavior. Only interests are efficacious enough to do that. Besides that, the greater the skepticism a person has the less likely that person really cares about the subject at hand.

On the other side, there is a slender hope that the gambit of merging public and private lessons will "touch down on particulars and . . . [then] provide either justification for or an argument against any action taken within a real world context" (Fish 2000: 768). But for those justifications to emerge there would have to be a coincidence between a commitment to agnosticism and agnostic lessons. And the nonagnostic argues that, at best, only a few might have that required interest.

For better or worse, there is no formula for setting a course between these doubts and hopes. There are only ingenuity and determination to go by, and all the rest, as it is said, is commentary.

NOTES

Introduction

1 This sentence and the one that follows it are paraphrases from "Alexander Meiklejohn Defines the Liberal College, 1912" (Hofstadter and Smith 1961: 899).

2 In regard to the second point: the case studies of this book should be read as ideal-types. That is to say, for less well-tutored audiences similar lessons would have to be taught by case studies conducted at lower levels of analysis and with less intricate details.

1. The Purposes of an Interpretive Community

1 *Vacco v. Quill*, 521 U.S. 793 (1997) and *Washington v. Glucksberg*, 521 U.S. 702 (1997) are companion equal protection and due process cases that challenged, respectively, a New York State ban on physician-assisted suicide and a Washington law prohibiting making it a felony to promote a suicide attempt. Their point was that to focus on equal protection interests in the right to assisted suicide as well as the right to refuse life-sustaining medical treatment, or due process interests in "autonomy" versus state interests in "affirming the value of life," served only to perpetuate the tendency in this culture to obfuscate and repress fundamental questions that need to be asked about death and dying.

2 The term "commentary" is used in its everyday sense, and that suffices for my purposes. For other, related, purposes it would be important to address the history of commentary as an institutional practice.

3 The terms "commentators" and "teachers and critics" are used interchangeably in this book to refer to academics and journalists (unless specified otherwise).

4 For Pierre Bourdieu, social enterprises and practices are constituted by critical (ideological) norms. These are the norms that establish the customary way in which persons understand themselves to be engaged in enterprises and practices. Such norms are sufficiently fixed in the minds of persons so engaged that they find it very difficult to understand their enterprise or practice, and themselves, in any way other than is shaped by those norms. Thus self-image and reality mutually reinforce each other, and ideas and events that contradict an ideological self-image tend to be rejected as basically inconceiv-

able. To be sure, these norms are not so fixed as to exclude altogether some degree of change, or adjustment, when social facts otherwise excluded force themselves upon those engaged by an ideological self-image. But this process of change or adjustment does not occur without a struggle, and the degree of change is unpredictable.

Hence, if I follow Bourdieu correctly, there will be few readers who will endorse wholeheartedly my challenges to them about an interpretive community and commentary. Therefore, I will consider this book a success to the extent that it helps readers to be (far) more self-conscious about the strengths and weaknesses of their own respective conceptions of the norms of an interpretive community and commentary.

5 Although the primary focus of this book is on constitutional law and policies, it will also explore lessons learned from public law venues.

6 See Eagleton (1991: 1–60) for a philosophical description of relationships between ideology and repression; Sarat and Kearns (1991) and DiStefano (1991) for descriptions of those relations as they bear directly on constitutional law and political philosophy respectively.

7 Think back to the uproar, primarily from the Left, over former Attorney General Edwin Meese's recommendation, in 1986, that deference to the Court's intellectual and political monopoly over constitutional commentary is undemocratic and incompatible with the rule of law (Meese 1988).

Recently, some scholars, primarily on the left, have argued against the idea that the Supreme Court should be the primary arbiter of the meaning of the Constitution. I will have a little more to say about one version of this argument later on, but now I want to suggest that these arguments do not seem to me to represent very much of a break with intellectual jurisprudence. It is, rather, more of a tactical move motivated by partisan politics and fears about the policies of a more conservative court system.

8 As is always the case, there is an alternative point of view. In a brief article in the *Cardozo Law Review,* "Anti-Intellectualism," Pierre Schlag's diagnosis of (law school) commentary is similar to my description of the ideology of involvement and intellectual jurisprudence (1995). But it is Schlag's conclusion that "the self-identification of the legal thinker with the figure of the judge is *fatal* (1995: 1114, emphasis added) because it "shut[s] down thought" and is "designed to deny and legitimate the violence necessarily implicit in the act of judging" (1995: 1115).

For the reasons set forth below, I hold that intellectual jurisprudence and the ideology of involvement are not *fatal* flaws. Beyond those reasons, I want to add that the very rhetoric of "fatal flaws" is part and parcel of intellectual jurisprudence. Specifically, this rhetoric conveys the impression that the issues of law and policies can be understood in terms of things rightly and wrongly decided. Lawyers are taught to accept and convey this impression in law school, and unfortunately we have all learned to mimic them. In this book I teach a different lesson: trying to answer the rightly decided question, considered in the next chapter, causes us to simplify what law and policies are about. (My thanks to Lief Carter for directing me to Schlag's work.)

9 Michael Walzer (1987) takes a less sanguine view of detachment because it may breed intellectual arrogance and tend to obscure antidemocratic political manipulations of critics. There is as much truth to Walzer's point of view as there is to the one I have endorsed.

10 For a critical overview of the strengths and weaknesses of republicanism, see Symposium: The Republican Civic Tradition, *Yale Law Journal* (1988).

11 See Elkin and Soltan (1993). The "new constitutionalism" is a term the authors employ to refer to commentary that would be concerned with the construction of practical theories about institutional designs, political participation, and neglected considerations about the public interest.

12 Jennifer Hochschild's *Facing Up to the American Dream* (1995) provides an excellent theoretical and social scientific primer for the cultural and ideological role of the American Dream in the polity and its past, present, and potential future place in the politics of race and class.

13 Clayton and Gillman have also edited a companion volume, *The Supreme Court Decision Making: New Institutionalist Approaches* (1999). It highlights the competing research agendas and scholarship between rational choice models (i.e., analysis of judicial behavior in terms of the maximization of preferences and the costs and benefits of different strategies for achieving them) and historical-interpretive approaches to the study of institutional constraints.

14 Readers interested in a brief but informative overview of how new institutionalists address the issue of social facts and constitutional theory will be well served by consulting *Social Facts, Constitutional Theory, and Doctrinal Change* (1995), the newsletter of the Law and Courts Section of the American Political Science Association.

15 This quotation is from Samuel Huntington's 1988 presidential address to the American Political Science Association and his words relate to the implications of empirical investigations in political science.

16 Cass Sunstein is virtually alone among law school scholars to make exactly this point, most notably in *Legal Reasoning and Political Conflict* (1996). His scholarship would be a beacon for political sufficient commentary, if it were not for the fact that Sunstein's scholarship gives itself over to intellectual jurisprudence in the treatment of right answers to legal questions and to the ideology of involvement in relation to preferred modes of court adjudication (Sunstein 1996, 1999) (cf. ch. 3, note 4).

17 Succeeding chapters will address some of the issues of relativism related to this point.

18 It is necessary to point out that the term "agnosticism" has played a significant role in Christian theological and philosophical commentary since T. H. Huxley apparently coined the term in 1869 (Huxley 1894). Readers who read theology and philosophy may see connections between the role agnosticism plays in those disciplines and my use of the term, but if those connections are there they are accidental ones. Then again, readers of Sanford Levinson's *Constitutional Faith* (1988), which addresses the Constitution in religious terms, or Steven D. Smith's "Believing Like a Lawyer" (1999), which addresses conventional legal discourse from the perspective of articles of "faith," will have reason to take issue with my disclaimer.

2. The Purposes of an Interpretive Community

1 To explain with an example of my own: In the litigation and adjudication of *Brown v. Board of Education* I 347 U.S. 483 (1954), the claim made by the NAACP was that precedent-

based arguments in defense of the doctrine of separate but equal were incompatible with the Equal Protection Clause of the Fourteenth Amendment. But the NAACP's argument was not efficacious, even to those who might have been predisposed to desegregate schools. As Justice Jackson (whatever his view of the merits of the case may have been) observed, "[Thurgood] Marshall's brief starts and ends with sociology" (Schwartz 1993). Jackson's observation exemplifies a formalist habit of mind that resists, absent persuasive legal arguments, fundamental revision of the law even when morality and/or social exigencies might appear to require it.

Yet, as explained below, this resistance does not mean that the law does not change: it means that whatever changes occur do so only within the argumentative limits tolerated by the law's formalisms. In relation to *Brown,* these limits were defined by the *Brown* Court's request that litigants respond to five questions about the connections between segregation, the history/intent of the Fourteenth Amendment, and the potential scope of congressional and Court action. These formalistic questions opened the path for the possibility of justifying the conclusion that the history and intent of the Fourteenth Amendment were inconclusive in regard to desegregation and the Court's role under the amendment. In turn, that conclusion made heretofore inefficacious sociological claims about segregation and inequality more efficacious.

2 To defend this thesis about indeterminacy, Fish provides rich and specific evidence from contract law and parole evidence (oral or verbal evidence in contract law). The adequacy of that evidence is not relevant to the topics of this book; what is relevant is that his defense is a model for the idea that claims about the indeterminacy of the law's formalisms ought to be addressed directly by detailed analysis of how the law, rather than philosophical abstractions about the law, works. This book uses that model to illustrate the implications of the indeterminacy and efficaciousness of a range of constitutional and legal formalisms. (Eventually, for reasons specified, I will drop the term "indeterminacy" for the descriptive and evaluative term "underdeterminacy.")

3 Evidence for this tendency to close out other methods and claims is readily available in all the complaints by lawyers that law reviews have been captured by the intellectual movements of philosophy, social theory, and literary criticism, with the result that they are increasingly irrelevant to litigation and adjudication. It is interesting to note that Wellington, in a 1993 address before the New York State County Lawyer's Association, criticized law reviews and law faculties for their increasing detachment from the legal profession.

4 In "Legal Reasoning and Practical Political Education" (Strauber 1991), I reflect upon Michael Walzer's conception of "casuistry" (Walzer 1980), a form of civic education as case law that teaches citizens to balance the realism of those in authority with the moral reflections and arguments of ordinary persons. Part of the inspiration for my approach to formalisms and case studies arises out of my thinking about the strengths and limitations of Walzer's conception of civic education.

Cass Sunstein, in *Legal Reasoning and Political Conflict* (1996), uses the term "casuistry," without any reference to Walzer, to refer to reasoning from analogy as the primary method of legal argumentation. Sunstein's approach to legal rules and consequentialist considerations provides another path to second-guessing legal formalisms. However, Sunstein, the lawyer, is still committed to the rightly decided question (1996: 10), and that makes all the difference between his considerations about formalisms and my own.

5 There are a number of reasonable charges against this agnosticism that will and should be made. Some of them are addressed in the last two chapters of this book.

6 Texas v. Johnson, 491 U.S. 397 (1989), a five-to-four decision, with Justice Kennedy concurring, and Chief Justice Rehnquist and Justice Stevens writing dissents. Initial ideas for this case study were first presented in a talk, "*Texas v. Johnson:* The Political Significance of Rhetorically Undeterminate Arguments" (Strauber 1991).

7 491 U.S. at 404–05.

8 491 U.S. at 414.

9 491 U.S. at 411.

10 491 U.S. at 432.

11 ABC News/Washington Post Poll, September 1990.

12 In *United States v. Eichman,* 496 U.S. 310 (1990), the Flag Protection Act of 1989 was struck down as unconstitutional.

13 Robert F. Nagel's *Judicial Power and American Character* (1994) provides a useful comparison and contrast to my analysis. Akin to the *Harvard Law Review* approach, Nagel sees the case as a confrontation between two competing interests in symbolic communication—the individual's and the state's. But in contrast to the *Review,* Nagel argues that judicial review in cases like *Johnson* is a mistake because it substitutes a deluded sense of certainty about legal reasoning for "the risky and imponderable nature of our collective moral decisions" (Nagel 1994: 101).

In many respects, Nagel's analysis of *Johnson,* and of formalisms in general, and my own are indistinguishable. But Nagel's primary concern is to defend judicial restraint, whereas the line I take, in *Johnson,* and in all other controversies, is that solace in either restraint or activism only contributes to the tendency to neglect politics. Moreover, Nagel's advocacy of restraint leads him to be rather formulaic about his antagonism to solace in formalisms. I am more agnostic about formalisms and therefore must plumb the depths of opinions in order to evaluate the extent to which solace in formalisms is merited or not. A more complete explanation for this aspect of agnosticism follows in due course.

14 For commentary in this vein, see Kent Greenawalt's discussion of flag burning in *Fighting Words* (1995: 39–45).

15 My thanks to G. Robert Boynton for helping me work through this aspect of the argument.

16 *Johnson,* 491 U.S. at 419.

17 In "The Politics of Constitutional Law" Mark Tushnet, from the perspective of Critical Legal Studies, makes a similar claim about the decentering of Johnson's politics (Kairys 1990: 234). Tushnet, however, is not agnostic about such decentering and presumes that it is ipso facto malignant. (Chapters 4 through 6 will characterize significant similarities and differences between agnostic commentary and the perspectives of critical legal studies.)

18 These tenets embrace the following ideas about law and politics: nonlegal factors play an inevitable role in the formation and therefore the analysis of legal arguments and the law; there is indeterminacy in what the law requires and that indeterminacy is to be associated

with variability and changes in conditions and relationships in the polity; and what constitutes "truth" in legal arguments is neither deductive nor strictly logical but rhetorical, in the sense of being shaped by what is legally efficacious.

Moreover (to continue the list), consequentialist social welfare concerns should play as heavy a role in analyzing legal justifications as legal rules and principles do; it is always a present possibility that the law's formalisms may mask otherwise commonly understood facts about social relationships and conditions in the polity; and inconsistency (variation, from case to case, in what the law's formalisms require) and incongruity (the extent to which images of the polity embedded in the law's formalisms are at odds with ordinary social, economic, political, and historical conditions and relationships) are virtually inevitable and not necessarily an indication of arbitrariness in the law.

19 In *Overcoming Law* (Posner 1995), Posner provides an excellent, if politically skewed, narrative of the development of the legal profession, lawyerly argument, and jurisprudence. I recommend it highly, notwithstanding its politics. The discussion of casebooks below is adopted from Strauber (1991: 40).

20 Lawyers' work is the least studied of the three. For an excellent introduction to how lawyers' work shapes power relations and institutional processes, see Cain and Harrington (1994).

21 The inspiration for this conception of agnostic layers of reasoning is John Dewey's characterization of "legal agnosticism" in "Corporate Personality" (Dewey 1931). In that article, Dewey argues that commentators (who hold to what he characterized then as a "scientific conception of the law") should not concern themselves with pre- and extralegal materials when analyzing the meaning of the law. Dewey confirms that these materials (e.g., psychology, philosophy, dogmas, and nonjural ideas) contribute to the growth of the law. Yet, he argues that nonlegal materials only generate confusion and futile contentions when it comes to an understanding of what the law is about. For Dewey, the law is about the mutual relations between legal decision-making and context-specific social relations alone.

It is interesting to consider the parallels between Fish's (1994) conception of the law's efficaciousness and Dewey's conception of relations between legal and nonlegal materials. In that regard, and as something of an oversimplification, it should be said that my conception of layers of agnostic reasoning stands Dewey's and Fish's shared skepticism about nonlegal materials on its head. Dewey and Fish argue that commentators ought to be wary of the relevance of nonlegal materials in understanding the law. I argue that agnostic commentators need (1) to break with that conception of commentary (skepticism about the nonlegal) and (2) to distance themselves from the ideology of involvement that encourages that commentary as a way to make recommendations about legal reasoning to lawyers and judges. Instead, agnostic commentary democratizes commentary by being openly skeptical of the intellectual authority of the law and by being friendly to nonlegal materials. (For the sake of stylistic variety, hereafter the terms "agnostic" and "skeptic" are used interchangeably.)

3. Skepticism and Neglected Politics

1 Texas v. Johnson, 491 U.S. 397, 404–06 (1989).

2 United States v. O'Brien, 391 U.S. 367 (1968).

3 491 U.S. at 401, citing Boos v. Barry, 485 U.S. 312, 318 (1988), citing New York Times v. Sullivan, 376 U.S. 254, 270 (1964).

In *Boos v. Barry,* the Court held that the emotive content and impact of speech were directly related to constitutional interests in protecting speech from governmental regulation. In *New York Times v. Sullivan,* the Court held that constitutional interests in protecting speech do not depend on the truth or acceptability of ideas expressed because the First Amendment assumes that erroneous or false ideas are inevitable in the process of a free and open debate on issues.

4 New York Times v. Sullivan, 376 U.S. 254, 270 (1964), citing Whitney v. California, 274 U.S. 357, 375–76.

5 These three categories of interests are a refined version of an earlier attempt of mine to reformulate T. M. Scanlon's categories for analyzing freedom of expression as a philosophical problem about rights as limits on public policies (Scanlon 1979). My categories are used quite differently from Scanlon's: they are ideal-types for thinking about the political interests that attend the law's formalisms and are neglected by them.

6 Adjudication does not represent, nor does it produce, a theory of the First Amendment. Consequently, case law does not provide discrete answers to questions such as "Why do these interests make sense as a justification for freedom of speech?" "How should these interests be distinguished when they compete with each other?" What adjudication does provide are two basic approaches to sorting out interests. One approach is to balance interests against one another, either based on some principle like "freedom in the marketplace of ideas" (and even then interests may compete with one another) or on an ad hoc, case-by-case basis. The second approach is to characterize specific kinds of expression as "outside" categories of interests (e.g., "fighting words" do not belong to the category of audience or participant interests; content-based regulations do not belong to the category of sovereignty interests).

7 491 U.S. at 429. Robert Justin Goldstein, *Burning the Flag: The Great 1890–1990 American Flag Desecration Controversy* (1996) provides a good overview of the history of the legislative and symbolic politics of flag burning.

8 491 U.S. at 422–28.

9 491 U.S. at 423, citing Street v. New York, 94 U.S. 576, at 615–717 (Fortas, J., dissenting).

10 491 U.S. at 430–31, citing Chaplinsky v. New Hampshire, 315 U.S. 568, at 571–72. In *Chaplinsky,* the Court held that "fighting words," which by their very utterance inflict injury or tend to incite a breach of the peace, did not cohere with interests protected by the First Amendment.

11 To recall: inconsistency is variation, from case to case, in what the law's formalisms require; incongruity is the extent to which images of conditions and relationships embedded in the law's formalisms are at odds with more practical, and quite common or ordinary social, economic, political, and historical conditions and relationships.

4. Formalisms: Facets of Political Power and Neglected Policies

1 The primary disagreements are over the extent to which advocacy and judgment are determined by legal reasoning versus pre- and extralegal facts such as partisanship, or institutional contexts, or political and social customs, or the roles and norms of advocacy

and judgment, or legal socialization (including law school and commentary), or liberal-democratic ideology. Disagreements of this kind are sufficient for understanding why most teachers and critics find the question about determinacy to be more easily asked than answered. I suspect that most commentators will agree with me that they are ambivalent about, and confused by, their own answers.

2 In and out of law school, the case book, intellectual jurisprudence, and the rightly decided question dominate instruction about constitutional law. But undergraduate education has been more open about admitting pre- and extralegal materials into the classroom. See *Law and Politics Book Review* (at ⟨http://www.unt.edu/lpbr/⟩) for a review of the major texts in constitutional law (1992) and judicial process (1995). See *American Judicial Process* (Stumpf 1998) for an overview of jurisprudence in undergraduate education, its relationship to law school education, and differences between both and scholarship in and outside law school.

3 These dismissals tend to be based on arguments, usually very abstract ones, about whether CLS has it right about this or that aspect of liberal-democratic political theory or the philosophical basis of indeterminacy. These arguments are an epistemological version of answers to the rightly decided question, for the idea is to authoritatively dismiss CLS as wrong. Apart from my skepticism about the authoritativeness of any such dismissals, I am confident that whatever its weaknesses or liabilities, CLS provides a habit of mind that is useful for keeping on eye on neglected politics.

4 Radical rejectionists and revisionists differ not only politically but also on epistemological and metatheoretical issues concerning law, language, and society. Not surprisingly, given the grip of intellectual jurisprudence, it is the epistemological and metatheoretical issues that tend to receive the most attention (Altman 1990). I do not make very much of those issues unless, and only to the extent that, they may help to highlight the political similarities and differences among agnostic skepticism, rejectionism, and revisionism.

5 In the interpretive community, this commitment induces worries about superficial or idiosyncratic analysis that distorts or forsakes what the law is about. The specific worry is that this commitment undermines the rule of law and principled reasoning in advocacy and judgment. An agnostic has a special conception of what the law is about, and readers will judge what to make of this worry.

6 McCulloch v. Maryland, 17 U.S. 316 (1819).

7 National League of Cities v. Usery, 426 U.S. 833 (1976).

8 Garcia v. San Antonio Metropolitan Transit Authority, 469 U.S. 528 (1985).

9 U.S. v. Lopez, 514 U.S. 549 (1995); Printz v. United States, 521 U.S. 898 (1997); United States v. Morrison, 529 U.S. 598 (2000).

10 Consider what you would take into account in order to evaluate the following claim: It is a good bet that even "if our country did not permit its flag to be desecrated, it would [still] not be much less free and democratic" (Greenawalt 1990: 927).

11 FCC v. League of Women Voters, 468 U.S. 364 (1984).

12 Such provisions include prohibitions against governmental control over the Corporation for Public Broadcasting, long-term appropriations for the system, direct funding to local stations, and the structure of public broadcasting, all of which allowed stations to be insulated from governmental interference because the vast majority of their funds came from diverse sources rather than directly from the government.

13 468 U.S. at 390–91.

14 The Court also found that section 399 was overbroad because it failed to permit alternatives for the expression of management views (e.g., via private funds). *League of Women Voters,* 468 U.S. at 381–400.

15 Red Lion Broadcasting Co. v. FCC, 395 U.S. 367, 390 (1969), cited in *League of Women Voters,* 468 U.S. at 377–78. In *Red Lion* the Court ruled that the "fairness doctrine," requiring broadcast licensees to provide equal time to individuals subject to personal attacks or political editorials, a constitutional exercise of congressional authority and compatible with First Amendment doctrine.

16 *Red Lion Broadcasting Co.,* 395 U.S. at 390, cited in *League of Women Voters,* 468 U.S. at 377–78.

17 First National Bank of Boston v. Belotti, 435 U.S. 765, 766–77 (1978), cited in *League of Women Voters,* 468 U.S. at 376.

18 Mills v. Alabama, 384 U.S. 214, 219 (1966), cited in *League of Women Voters,* 468 U.S. at 376.

19 New York Times Company v. Sullivan, 376 U.S. 254 (1971), cited in *League of Women Voters,* 468 U.S. at 382.

20 Brandenburg v. Ohio, 395 U.S. 444 (1969).

21 Cohen v. California, 403 U.S. 15 (1971).

22 Texas v. Johnson, 491 U.S. 397 (1989).

23 Red Lion Broadcasting Co., 395 U.S. 389, cited in *League of Women Voters,* 468 U.S. at 378 n. 12. The fairness doctrine was rescinded in 1987, but there continues to be political interest in it, particularly in regard to the cable industry.

24 The primary social fact and circumstantial concerns have been over resource allocations: that is, the technological problem of "spectrum scarcity," which carried with it the potential saturation of available frequencies creating constant interference between overlapping major and minor signals, the economic problem that large-scale broadcasting is expensive and monopolistic, and political anxieties about the potential impact of private control over the mass media. Consequently, the aggregate good is said to compel the conclusion that broadcasters should be subject to government regulation, unlike the print media or common carriers. In a footnote in *League of Women Voters,* the Court recommended that spectrum scarcity was no longer a problem, but it deferred to Congress to overturn spectrum scarcity rules. Here again, regardless of what the Court or Congress does, or the impact of the Internet on spectrum scarcity, debates in and about the telecommunications industry suggest that resource allocation concerns are as alive as ever.

25 Schenck v. U.S., 249 U.S. 47 (1919).

26 United States v. O'Brien, 391 U.S. 367 (1968).

27 Niemotko v. Maryland, 340 U.S. 268 (1951); Feiner v. New York, 340 U.S. 315 (1951).

28 Miller v. California, 413 U.S. 15 (1973).

29 The term "shifty" is not necessarily an inflammatory one. My use of it refers to the fact that finding detailed responses to conflicts between competing interests is a "perpetual and shifty problem" for political and legal doctrines (Crick 1968: 22).

30 *League of Women Voters,* 468 U.S. at 378.

31 Justice Brennan, in *Johnson,* used a formalistic argument to protect speech against government intervention, but in *League of Women Voters* he used, as Chief Justice Rehnquist

did in *Johnson,* a historical account toward that same conclusion. That Justice Brennan alternately used formalistic and historical arguments is circumstantial evidence that there is no necessary relationship between the rhetoric of adjudication and partisanship.

32 The Court relates how, in the forties, when government sponsorship for noncommercial stations meant only reserving frequencies for their use, it was already evident that the noncommercial stations could not compete in the broadcasting marketplace. Then, after decades of their struggling along, Congress (in 1962) intervened on their behalf by providing direct assistance for the construction of station facilities. In 1967, the government intervened with the Public Broadcasting Act to provide programming support through the Corporation for Public Broadcasting.

33 *League of Women Voters,* 468 U.S. at 375.

34 468 U.S. at 369. In 1969, local stations asserted their autonomy from the Corporation for Public Broadcasting by creating "the Public Broadcasting System" to control networking of programs, and eventually to compete with the Corporation for programming control. In the Seventies, Congress further insulated PBS from politics by expanding funding from an annual to a five-year funding term.

35 468 U.S. at 375–81.

36 See S. Young Lee and Ronald J. Pedeone (1975: 21–36); Carnegie Commission (1979: 44–51); and David Giovannoni (1995: 16). I thank Janice J. Jones, director of research, Corporation for Public Broadcasting, and Suzanne Shevety, National Public Radio, for their correspondence and materials regarding public broadcasting funding, revenues, and listener demographics.

37 Supporters of public broadcasting provide polls of listeners and content analysis studies that purport to show that there is no liberal bias to public broadcasting. Likewise, detractors provide their studies, which purport to show that conservative viewpoints are systematically excluded from stories and that public radio narratives are consistently sympathetic to nonmainstream values. Whatever the social-scientific evidence, most observers agree that, like the BBC, public radio is widely recognized as having a distinctive editorial style that bespeaks a defined position on cultural, political, and economic values. There is more than just humor in the insider's joke that getting it straight from public broadcasting is like trying to drive a car with bad alignment—steer all the way to the right to get it straight.

38 I could find only this one unsystematic study of public broadcasting editorializing. This study indicates that the two most common factors explaining the lack of editorializing were a lack of resources and fears of alienating audiences. Today public radio receives virtually no federal funding, and it is dependent primarily on private, corporate, and membership underwriting. Sometimes private and corporate sources threaten to withdraw their funding when those sources hear stories that run counter to their interests. Some students of public broadcasting find these threats significant enough that they recommend a return to some form of government funding that would protect "public" radio from private and corporate threats.

39 This remark is attributed to David Warsh of the *Boston Globe* by Anthony Lewis in a *New York Times* column of February 13, 1995.

40 *The Future of American Progressivism: An Initiative for Political and Economic Reform*

(1998), with Cornel West, and *Democracy Realized* (Unger 1998) represent a decidedly pragmatic turn in Unger's understanding of the possibilities of democratization.

41 The words in brackets are my own. Solum's words, as I understand them, presume that legal results do tend to be more, rather than less, consistent.

42 Other problems—such as credit card and other forms of criminal fraud, copyright infringement, privacy, defamation, harassment, and government tracking of Internet communications—were apparent as well but attracted far less attention from the public and politicians.

5. The Internet: Distorted Ideals and Practices

1 However, the act did not authorize the FCC to approve, sanction, permit, or enforce specific measures that would restrict or prohibit minors from accessing such materials; nor did it authorize the FCC to have enforcement authority over the failure to utilize such measures. Enforcement was left to the courts.

2 Some scholars argue that the locution "harmful" is more narrow than the "indecency" locution, and hence a regulation in respect of such materials is more likely to survive constitutional scrutiny.

3 Miller v. California, 413 U.S. 15 (1973); Paris Adult Theatre I. v. Slaton, 413 U.S. 49 (1973).

4 Federal Communications Commission v. Pacifica Foundation, 438 U.S. 726 (1978), at 732.

5 Reno v. American Civil Liberties Union, 521 U.S. 844 (1997). It is noteworthy that the panel judges were Internet novices who had to be given a crash course on its technical nature and cyberspace geography; yet they agreed to the unusual format of indirect testimony via the Internet.

6 *Pacifica Foundation v. FCC*, 438 U.S. 726 (1978) upheld an FCC declaratory judgment that a radio station was administratively responsible for broadcasting a patently offensive but not obscene comedy routine.

7 *Sable Communications of California, Inc. v. FCC*, 492 U.S. 115 (1989) invalidated a 1988 amendment to the Communications Act of 1934. The amendment criminalized indecent sexually oriented prerecorded telephone messages to keep children from receiving them. The Court found the amendment constitutional in regard to obscene messages but insufficiently narrow in regard to indecent ones, given differences between radio and technological alternatives for restricting messages on the telephone (e.g., credit card checks or access codes). Also, in *Denver Area Educational Television Consortium v. FCC*, 518 U.S. 727 (1996), the Court, on the same grounds as *Sable*, invalidated a 1992 law that would have required cable TV operators to confine indecent programming to a single channel for adults who requested that the signal for that channel be unscrambled.

8 Stratton Oakmont Inc. v. Prodigy Services Co., No. 94–031063 (N.Y. Sup Ct. 1995).

9 When *Reno* was decided, these were the choices of the middle- and upper-middle classes who could afford computer and access charges to the Internet. It is arguable that the attention politicians have given to the Internet and pornography is a product of a class-based cultural politics and therefore something of a tempest in a teapot. In 1995, a Georgia Institute of Technology survey of the general demographics of Internet users

found them to be predominantly male, white, and in their early thirties; over half had no dependents. In 1998, the National Telecommunications and Information Administration found users to still be predominately white, male, and from thirty-five to fifty-four years old. But it is tricky to generalize about the Internet's sociological characteristics as its access expands.

10 Cubby Inc. v. CompuServe Inc., 776 F. Supp. 136 (S.D.N.Y. 1991).

11 Writing about the Internet is like trying to hit a moving target. By the time this book is read, some or perhaps many of the specific claims that I make here could be anachronistic.

12 In most cases, telephone and cable companies are prohibited from merging, but this prohibition may fall by the wayside in the face of the economics of commercial devices for increasing the amount and speed of data transmission.

6. Agnostic Skepticism about Radical Rejectionism

1 McCulloch v. Maryland, 17 U.S. 316 (1819). The basic idea for this case study is from "*McCulloch* and the Dilemmas of Liberal Constitutionalism" (Strauber 1989).

2 The reader will have noticed that I use the term "sovereignty" in two different contexts: first, in reference to the principle of sovereignty and, second, when talking of sovereignty interests.

3 17 U.S. at 400–401.

4 17 U.S. at 402.

5 17 U.S. at 404.

6 Maryland's position was that the practice of state ratification is compatible with both the liberal-democratic principle of power derived from the people and the theory of state sovereignty, and that, in practice, some other means of ratification would have been proposed if the principle of popular sovereignty had captured the consensus of the Convention. Marshall insists that state delegations were merely the instruments of a political *process:* the Constitution was first submitted to the existing Congress, which in turn remanded it to state legislatures simply as the most efficient means of ratification. In other words, popular sovereignty does not require ratification by an undifferentiated mass; the voice of all the people *was* engaged simply by virtue of the fact that it was a *constitution* that was submitted to Congress. Any idea to the contrary is not to be thought of: "No political dreamer was ever wild enough to think of breaking down the lines which separate the States, and of compounding the American people into one common mass." 17 U.S. at 403.

7 17 U.S. at 405.

8 17 U.S. at 405.

9 17 U.S. at 413.

10 17 U.S. at 415. Marshall argues from analogies (e.g., oaths of office and power to establish a postal service) in order to illustrate legislative discretion over means that are not constitutionally essential, yet are beneficial, to the exercise of power.

11 17 U.S. at 417.

12 17 U.S. at 419.

13 17 U.S. 421.

14 17 U.S. at 421.
15 17 U.S. at 426.
16 17 U.S. at 427.
17 17 U.S. at 428.
18 17 U.S. at 428.
19 See Altman (1990: 90–98) and Goldstein (1991: 161–66) for collateral arguments.

7. Agnosticism, Federalism, and Constitutionalism

1 Gibbons v. Ogden, 22 U.S. (9 Wheat.) 1 (1824).
2 Willson v. Black-Bird Creek Marsh Co., XX U.S. (2 Pet.) 245 (1829).
3 National League of Cities v. Usery, 426 U.S. 833 (1976).
4 426 U.S. at 857 (Brennan, J., dissenting).
5 Garcia v. San Antonio Metropolitan Transit Authority, 469 U.S. 528 (1985).
6 United States v. Lopez, 514 U.S. 549 (1995).
7 A twelfth-grade student was arrested and charged for violating the Texas State Penal Code by bringing a concealed weapon to school; those charges were dropped when the student was charged with violating the Gun-Free Act; the student was tried and convicted in a bench trial and sentenced to a short prison term and two years of supervised release. The court of appeals reversed the conviction, holding that the act went beyond the limits of federal authority under the Commerce Clause.
8 Printz v. United States, 521 U.S. 898 (1997).
9 United States v. Morrison, 529 U.S. 598 (2000).
10 *Lopez,* 514 U.S. 519, 593 (2000) (Thomas, J., concurring).
11 For Arkes, a "purely jural path" to prudential considerations is required. It presupposes the virtues of judicial restraint, as well as natural law ostensibly embedded in the original meaning of the Constitution. Keith Whittington, in *Constitutional Interpretation: Textual Meaning, Original Intent, and Judicial Review* (1999), argues for a more modest conception of originalism, grounded in a conception of popular sovereignty and institutional considerations. (It was published too late to be considered here.)
12 Palko v. Connecticut, 302 U.S. 325 (1937).
13 302 U.S. at 328, citing Herbert v. Louisiana, 272 U.S. 312, 316 (1926) and the immanent political theory of fundamental principles of liberty and justice as the essence of the rule of law.

8. A Middle Course on Reform

1 Solid Waste Agency of Northern Cook City v. United States Army Corps of Engineers, 531 U.S. 159 (2001).
2 Whitman, Administrator of Environmental Protection Agency, et al. v. American Trucking Assns., Inc., 531 U.S. 457 (2001).
3 In this, the EPA would depart from its usual insistence on scientific substantiation of harms, since public concerns about these issues far outstripped scientific data on the nature and extent of the problems.
4 Supporters of a marketplace approach place confidence in "a large literature on . . .

market-oriented approaches to pollution, most of it favorable. They [market-approaches] have several advantages. Firms know better than government who can reduce pollution cheaply and are given the economic incentives to act on that information. Market mechanisms also can allocate the cleanup burden more cheaply and quickly than rulemaking procedures" (Schoenbrod 1993: 151–52). A marketplace approach is directly at odds with the public trust doctrine that to date dominates environmental regulation. The public trust doctrine is based on the principle that the public has environmental rights that governments are obligated to preserve. Regarding this subject, advocates of intellectual jurisprudence have good reason, for better or worse, to think that their work is potentially efficacious. Joseph Sax's "The Public Trust Doctrine in National Resource Law: Effective Judicial Intervention" (1970) is credited by some for having had a direct influence on environmental law and politics at the time his article was published.

5 The "greens" at the extremes are anarchists or post-Marxist socialists/feminists. There are also "greens" who are not extremists and who identify themselves as members of an independent third party in electoral politics.

6 Basically, nativists hold to the conviction that policies that maintain greater "harmony" with nature are to be preferred.

7 This list, and much of the material that follows it, is an amalgam from the following sources: *National Journal* articles by Margaret Kirz, published in *American Public Policy* (Stinebrickner ed., 1996: 92–113); Wells and Hamilton (1995: 112–43); *National Journal,* June 1995; Landy, Roberts, and Thomas (1990: 3–17, 246–303); and Conlan (1988: 208–09).

8 New York v. United States, 505 U.S. 144 (1992), at 159. At issue were "take title" provisions, which required states to enact legislation for the disposal of radioactive waste produced in the state or to take possession of it. The brief exchange between Chief Justice Rehnquist and Justice Souter over the original meaning of the Tenth Amendment in relation to Article I powers and state sovereign immunity from lawsuits in their own courts (*Alden v. Maine,* 527 U.S. 706 [1999]) is another example of this renewed interest in the Tenth Amendment.

9 See Risk Assessment and Cost-Benefit Act of 1995 (H.R. 1022) and Amendment to Risk Assessment and Cost-Benefit Act of 1995 (S. 333).

10 See Motor Vehicle Mfrs. Ass'n. v. State Farm Mutual, 463 U.S. 29 (1983). There are some important distinctions between the "hard-look review" in regulation and deregulation cases that need not concern us here. The most lucid summary of "hard-look review" that I know of is Mark Garland's "Deregulation and Judicial Review" (1985).

11 Michael C. Dorf and Charles F. Sabel's "A Constitution of Democratic Experimentalism" (1998) is a much more elaborate treatment of many of the same issues considered here. There are remarkable similarities and significant differences between Dorf and Sabel's approach to experimentalism and my own, but their work was published too late for me to address them here.

12 This is an adaptation of the "dilemma of administrative discretion," which refers to the delegation of power to administrative agencies and the constitutional issues of separation of powers (West 1985).

13 I have constructed these problems from two sources: William F. West's discussion of the dilemma of administrative discretion in *Administrative Rulemaking* (West 1985: 26–29)

and David Schoenbrod's discussion of the abuses of congressional delegation of power in *Power without Responsibility* (Schoenbrod 1993: 9–21).

14 515 U.S. 687 (1995). On the other hand, in *Daubert v. Merrell Dow Pharmaceuticals Inc.*, 509 U.S. 579 (1993), the Rehnquist Court evidenced some considerable flexibility, as summarized above, in interpreting what the Federal Rules of Evidence require by way of relevant scientific testimony. Some experts take *Daubert* as a signal that the Court may be inclined to let a bottom-up process take place whereby trial court judges integrate scientific and technical findings on a case-by-case basis with a minimum of appellate court intervention. *Kumho Tire Co. v. Carmichael*, 526 U.S. 137 (1999), which extended the *Daubert* doctrine to all expert testimony (professional or otherwise), may be confirmation of that inclination.

15 This approach to adjudication appears to follow the precedent of *Chevron USA v. NRDC*, 467 U.S. 837 (1984), which encourages courts to be deferential to executive and administrative interpretations of statutes.

16 Cass Sunstein's *Free Markets and Social Justice* (1997) is an example of law school scholarship that succeeds in raising some especially pertinent insights into the empirical ambiguities that attend legal and policy controversies about relationships between market demands, democratization, and social justice. However, Sunstein's commitments to conceptions of civic responsibilities and reasoning about equality are so strong that they do not necessarily temper his partisanship amidst the uncertainties and complications about markets, democratization, and social justice that his scholarship reveals.

9. Ordered Liberty and Political Morality

1 Dworkin's philosophizing is constantly evolving in subtle and often complicated ways, but difficult to summarize. The ideas of his addressed here are, I believe, faithful to his overall philosophical project. That said, his *Sovereign Virtue: The Theory and Practice of Equality* (2000) may well contain new material that would require me to qualify my characterization of his opposition to pragmatism. But it was published too late for my considerations here.

2 Planned Parenthood of Southeastern Pennsylvania v. Casey, 505 U.S. 333 (1992).

3 Roe v. Wade, 410 U.S. 113 (1973).

4 *New York Times*, April 24, 1992, A1.

5 *New York Times*, April 24, 1992, A1.

6 Justices Stevens and Blackmun wrote opinions concurring in part and dissenting in part; Chief Justice Rehnquist and Justice Scalia wrote dissenting opinions.

7 The new law of *Casey* was greeted with antipathy by litigators and abortion activists. But it was in line with public opinion, which tends to support a woman's choice about abortion *and* some kinds of state regulation (for example, parental but not spousal notification procedures).

8 *Casey*, 505 U.S. at 854.

9 505 U.S. at 854.

10 505 U.S. at 855.

11 505 U.S. at 861, citing West Coast Hotel v. Parrish, 300 U.S. 379 (1937), and 505 U.S. at 863, citing Brown v. Board of Education I 347 U.S. 483 (1954).

12 505 U.S. at 863.

13 For example, for *West Coast Hotel* (which overruled the economic substantive due process decisions of *Adkins v. Children's Hospital* and *Lochner v. New York*) there was massive public support for New Deal economic policies and a legal realist sensibility that formalist objections to regulations in the economic sphere were an anachronistic departure from due process precedents. For Brown there was the impact of the civil rights movement and NAACP litigation victories, the Truman administration's efforts to desegregate the military, perceived moral imperatives arising out of the victory over Nazi Germany, a cold war conception (albeit inchoate) of liberty and equality as distinguishing characteristics of the political culture of the United States vis-à-vis the USSR, and egalitarian sentiments that the time had come to overrule *Plessy*.

14 *Casey*, 505 U.S. 333, 925 (Blackmun, J., concurring and dissenting in part).

15 505 U.S. at 933 (Blackmun, J., concurring and dissenting in part).

16 505 U.S. at 877.

17 505 U.S. at 874, citing Anderson v. Celebrezze, 460 U.S. 780 (1983), 788; Norman v. Reed 502 U.S. 279 (1992).

18 *Casey*, 505 U.S. 833, 878.

19 505 U.S. at 878.

20 505 U.S. at 856.

21 505 U.S. at 956 (Rehnquist, CJ., dissenting).

22 505 U.S. at 852.

23 319 U.S. 624 (1943) (cited in *Casey*, 505 U.S. 833, 851). *Barnette* prohibits regulations that compel teachers and pupils to salute the flag as part of their civic education.

24 491 U.S. 397 (1989) (cited in *Casey*, 505 U.S. 833, 851).

25 Dworkin, in *Life's Dominion*, also argues for the appropriateness of the First Amendment as a tool for abortion adjudication; his use of it relies on the Religion Clause, and although his arguments in this regard are philosophically fascinating, *Casey* demonstrates that they are a superfluous abstraction from existing legal precedents.

26 Below I pursue the point that a principle of neutrality be understood not only as crucial to agnostic commentary but also as deeply rooted in liberal-democratic ideology.

27 Mark Graber's "Interpreting Abortion" (1992) is an excellent example of political science scholarship that takes a parallel position to this one by distinguishing how academic lawyers and political scientists interpret the relationship between the law and social practices.

28 In fact, Dworkin criticizes the Court's legitimization of the twenty-four-hour regulation because the Court did not inquire whether there were other means for achieving the same ends that had "fewer regrettable side effects" for women who lived more than a day's journey from abortion facilities (Dworkin 1996: 123).

29 Stenberg v. Carhart, 530 U.S. 914 (2000), in which the Court, in a five-to-four decision, used *Casey* and the undue burden test to invalidate a Nebraska ban on "partial-birth abortions," serves only to complicate the issue of how judges, at least, read *Casey*. Most pertinent in this regard are the opinions of Justices Souter, O'Connor, and Kennedy. As I read it, Souter's majority opinion focuses primarily on social fact considerations about alternative abortion procedures as they relate to the health of women, as well as matters of

statutory interpretation. Justice O'Connor's concurring opinion concerns the connection between the undue burden test of *Casey* and prescriptions against medical procedures related to a woman's health. And Justice Kennedy, who broke ranks in this case with his *Casey* coauthors, Justices O'Connor and Souter, contributed a dissenting opinion. In part 1 of his dissent, he read *Casey* to be at odds with the *Stenberg* Court's refusal to legitimate Nebraska's authority to legislate moral differences between abortion procedures by prohibiting doctors to perform partial-birth abortions. Ironically, an advocate for Dworkin's jurisprudence might reasonably read part 1 of Justice Kennedy's dissent in *Stenberg* as the best confirmation of Dworkin's point of view that moral reasoning is a linchpin of the legal reasoning in *Casey*.

30 In contrast, consider what may be said to be Duncan Kennedy's "rejectionist" version of this issue (1997). It complicates matters considerably. As I read him, Kennedy contends that the law is, in effect, at one level intrinsically indeterminate. Yet, at another level, the law, granted specific contextual circumstances and other factors such as the domain of the law, social fact considerations, the evolution of the law's formalisms, and the relative skill of lawyers, may indeed be said to "determine" a "correct" legal or political commitment. If so, and since it is always arguable whether or not the circumstances and factors that constrain are present, the appropriateness of relativism in advocacy is underdetermined.

31 Shakespeare, *The Tempest*, act 5, scene 1, 275–76.

10. Deeper Skepticism

1 American Booksellers Ass'n v. Hudnut, 771 F.2d. 323 (7th Cir. 1985).

2 Absent a social-scientific survey, there is no way to determine the extent to which those in the minority share MacKinnon's views. But more than enough has been written about MacKinnon to say that there is a range of feminists who disagree at least in some measure with many of the things MacKinnon has to say about pornography. Quite aside from that, the passage of antipornography ordinances is evidence that sometimes the ideology of involvement and intellectual jurisprudence can have practical significance.

3 It is arguable that MacKinnon takes this position solely for strategic reasons; on the other hand, perhaps she interprets the data about abuse in the way she does because of her views of sexuality and capitalism (MacKinnon 1994: 71).

4 Brief *Amici Curiae* of Feminist Anti-Censorship Task Force et al., in *American Booksellers v. Hudnut*, 771 F.2d 323 (7th Cir. 1985). MacKinnon's phenomenology is attacked in the brief for being a one-sided and monocausal view of sexuality, the erotic, and the harms of pornography. For more insight into these issues, compare *The Question of Pornography: Research Findings and Policy Implications* (Donnerstein, Linz, and Penrod 1987) and *Making Violence Sexy: Feminist Views on Pornography* (Russell 1993).

5 Downs does not abandon the majority point of view that all said-and-done, obscenity formalisms should control thinking about the subject. Sunstein too hastily disposes of the implications for potential "real-world harms" that may be related to the mass dissemination of pornography.

6 Beauharnais v. Illinois, 343 U.S. 250 (1952).

7 343 U.S. at 257. The majority opinion instigated spirited dissents. Justice Black dismissed the majority opinion for treating the First Amendment as if it were irrelevant. Justice Douglas complained that the majority opinion undermined the "free trade in ideas" and encouraged the politics of expediency, political opinion, and prejudices. But Justices Reed and Jackson accepted the presumption that the state has the power to promulgate a group libel law, though the former expressed reservations about the vagueness of the law (while admitting that only experience would give content to its meaning); the latter said that ordered liberty requires the conclusion that words alone, absent a clear and present danger of harm, are not punishable.

8 343 U.S. at 253, 263.

9 343 U.S., at 257–58.

10 343 U.S. at 259.

11 343 U.S. at 261.

12 343 U.S. at 263.

13 343 U.S. at 262.

14 For example: (1) *Smith v. Collin,* 436 U.S. 953 (1978) protects the display of materials promoting race or religious hatred; (2) *Cohen v. California,* 403 U.S. 15 (1971) protects the content of symbolic speech even if it is offensive; and (3) *R.A.V. v. City of St. Paul,* 505 U.S. 377 (1992) protects abusive speech that is singled out because it is related to a person's race, color, creed, religion, or gender.

15 343 U.S. at 262–63.

16 I depend here on an embryonic analogy between Justice Reed's dissent in *Beauharnais,* 343 U.S. 277, and commercial speech adjudication in *Central Hudson Gas & Electric Corp. v. Public Service Commission,* 447 U.S. 557 (1980), which ruled that commercial speech must be lawful and not misleading to come within the protective umbrella of the First Amendment.

17 *Board of Trustees, State University of New York v. Fox,* 492 U.S. 469, 480 (1989) ruled that the least restrictive means test was not applicable to commercial speech.

18 Harris v. Forklift Systems, Inc., 510 U.S. 17 (1993). I note without further comment that *Harris* has been criticized for unpredictability when it comes to determining making what things count as actionable conduct. It has been criticized as well for its lack of clarity regarding how compensatory damages can be awarded and measured in the absence of proof of psychological injury, and for its lack of clarity about what counts as discriminatory conduct granted variations in local societal norms about what is tolerable conduct under title 6.

19 In "The Experts Cop Out," Diana Russell goes so far as to report that "rumor has it that one expert's life was threatened by the Mafia before he testified to the [Attorney General's Commission on Pornography in 1985 about pornography and harms to women]" (in Russell 1993: 153).

20 I endorse the idea that "the slippery slope argument . . . tends to exaggerate, in suggesting that our descent is so rapid that it is not possible to apply brakes, when we have already stopped ourselves falling down the slope" (Easton 1994: 70).

21 *Renton v. Playtime Theatres, Inc.,* 475 U.S. 41 (1986) ruled that zoning ordinances regulating adult movie theaters may infringe on the prohibition against content-based restrictions if the purpose of the regulation is not to suppress expression but is to advance some otherwise legitimate police power function.

11. Qualified Solace in the Law's Formalism

1 In this analysis, adoption and custody disputes are considered as related controversies. (I am drawn to these disputes because of my experience as a social worker for children in foster care in Nassau County, Long Island, New York, 1968–69.)

2 News reports of the aftermath of Baby Richard's return to his biological parents indicated that his initial hysteria gave way to calm, and there was no evidence of the predicted despair or depression. They also reported, in 1994, no significant evidence of short-term trauma from Jessica's transition to her biological parents, although months afterward there were incidents of uncontrollable crying apparently associated with her missing adoptive parents. There is no behavioral research on this phenomenon; most experts predicted, apparently off the mark, that there would be serious short-term fall-out from their transitions.

3 Should children of one race be placed with adoptive parents of the same race? Should blood relatives of the same race be given custodial preference to adoptive parents of a different race? Should a surviving lesbian/gay companion be given guardianship over a child in preference to a biological parent? Are parents who refuse to learn sign language psychological abusers who should lose custody of a deaf child?

4 Notable exceptions in law school scholarship are works like Martha Minow's *Making All the Difference* (1990) and Gary Bellow and Martha Minow's "Rita's Case and Other Law Stories" (1996). In political science, there is Christopher Wolfe's edited volume, *The Family, Civil Society, and the State* (1998).

5 See *From Father's Property to Children's Rights* (Mason 1994) and *An Open Adoption* (Caplan 1990).

6 The two main standards of fitness are family finances and a child's psychological well-being as determined by a study of the "quality" of a potential home environment.

7 Feminisms of various kinds warn that the family, conventionally understood, can also be the source of violence, emotional and physical degradation, sexual dysfunction, racism, and a host of other ills. But few of them go so far as to altogether reject at least some core biological conceptions of the "family." See *Family Matters* (Minow 1993) for a canvas of the issues raised by those I term rejectionists.

8 Stanley v. Illinois, 405 U.S. 645 (1972).

9 Moore v. City of East Cleveland, 431 U.S. 494 (1977).

10 Smith v. Organization of Foster Families, 431 U.S. 816 (1977).

11 *Smith*, 431 U.S. at 844.

12 *Smith*, 431 U.S. at 845, quoting *Moore v. City of East Cleveland*, 431 U.S. at 503.

13 *Smith*, 431 U.S. at 846.

14 Quilloin v. Walcott, 434 U.S. 246 (1978).

15 Caban v. Mohammad, 441 U.S. 380 (1979).

16 Lehr v. Robertson, 463 U.S. 248 at 261 (1983).

17 Ankenbrandt v. Richards, 504 U.S. 689, 692 (1992), citing In Re Burrus, 136 U.S. 586, 593–54 (1950). "The whole subject of the domestic relations of husband and wife, parent and child, belongs to the laws of the States, and not the laws of the United States." This exception to federal review is based on precedent, and the lack of contrary legislation by Congress.

18 Michael H. v. Gerald D., 491 U.S. 110 (1989).

19 Gerald D. and Carole D. were married, and Carole D. had an affair with Michael D. (among others), the result of which was a girl, Victoria D.; Gerald D. believed that he was the biological father of Victoria D. and was listed as the girl's biological father on the birth certificate. When the girl was about one and a half years old, Michael D. filed a suit to establish paternity and visitation rights. Carole D. was then living with a third man. Michael D. sought visitation rights with Victoria D., but Carole D. refused him. A court-appointed guardian ad liter filed a countersuit, in the best interests of the girl, supported by a psychologist's recommendation, that Victoria D. be permitted to maintain a filial relationship with both Gerald D. and Michael H. From this time, and until the girl was three years of age, the mother had relationships with both Michael H. and Gerald D., and both men had a paternal relationship with the girl. After three years, Carole D. and Victoria D. moved in with Gerald D. Both Michael H. and Victoria D., through her court guardian, sought visitation rights, and a court-appointed psychologist reconfirmed that it would be in the best interests of the child to allow the visits. The California courts rejected the suits of Michael H. and the girl's guardian: as a matter of California state law, marriage, not biology, constitutes paternity: it is "a matter of [the] overriding social policy, that given a certain relationship between the husband and wife, the husband is to be held responsible for the child and that the integrity and privacy of the family unit should not be impugned" (491 U.S. 110, 119 [1989]).

20 *Michael H.*, 491 U.S. at 123 (1989).

21 491 U.S. at 156 (Brennan, J., dissenting).

22 The majority opinion and dissents by Justices Brennan and White involve formalistic considerations of statutory interpretation and due process concerns (procedural and substantive) that are irrelevant to this discussion.

23 491 U.S. at 141 (Brennan, J. dissenting). An interesting and for some, a troubling, footnote to the *Stanley-Michael H.* line is that no state or federal trial or appellate court has attempted to secure a conception of a child's liberty interests independent of the formalisms of biology, "family," fitness, and a parent-child relationship.

24 Troxel V, Granville, 530 U.S. 57 (2000).

25 Much of custody litigation, whether the context is the adoption process or divorce, is characterized by social fact considerations that are extraordinarily difficult to deal with, some of which have to do with the complicated conditions and relationships of the parties involved and others that are a product of litigation strategies. Are these extraordinary fact considerations unique to this kind of law? Or are they present in other kinds of law, hidden from view there because the efficaciousness of the law's formalisms teaches us to ignore them? My hunch is that the answer to the first question is no and the answer to the second question is yes. If so, how do I explain why judges worrying about "family" and "family relations" are more inclined to admit how extraordinary their fact-finding process is? My simple-minded answer is that it is because children are involved.

26 See Jan Hoffman, "Judge Hayden's Family Values," *New York Times Magazine*, October 1995.

27 At the risk of stating the obvious, "family" and "family relations" arise out of mutual fear, hate, distrust, love, self-doubt, lies, self-recrimination, and other, even darker sources of action.

28 The argument that follows is based, very loosely, on remarks by Stanley Fish, in "Almost Pragmatism: The Jurisprudence of Richard Posner, Richard Rorty, and Ronald Dworkin" (Brint and Weaver 1991: 56–57).

29 There is not much to go on because "there has been little systematic study of the relationships between core beliefs, attitudes, and preferences, in part because suitable measures of core beliefs have not been included in major studies of public opinion" (Feldman 1988: 437). See also Zaller 1992: 139. Thus, I have taken the liberty of merging aggregate and individual-level data to construct an anecdotal claim.

30 To take a page or two from the literature on political psychology and electoral politics, and oversimplifications aside: "[T]here is . . . solid empirical support for the assumption that citizens normally respond to new information on the basis of external cues concerning the implications of that information for their values and other predispositions, provided that . . . they are sufficiently attentive . . . to have learned the cues" (Zaller 1992: 47).

31 The criticism that agnosticism constitutes bad faith can be associated with a standard criticism that attends skepticism and relativism: skepticism and relativism put one on an intellectual slippery slope, at the bottom of which is moral nihilism. For example, a critic contends that only a nihilist would be agnostic, skeptical, or relativistic about the "wrong" of slavery in the polity. The intended force of a criticism such as this one is unclear to me, but I can say only a few words about it here. First, the forces of civil conflict and not political or moral deliberation determined the wrong of slavery. Second, the criticism may be valid at a sociological level, which is to say that today no "reasonable person" denies that slavery is wrong. But the intended force of the criticism is not at the sociological level but at the level of principle. Consequently, this criticism presumes just what needs to be justified; in a plural polity can there be wrongs that are identified "in principle"? Unless one is persuaded that there are such "principled" wrongs, the criticism hardly puts one on any slippery slope. Last, Stanley Fish (1999) does a good job of setting the parameters for a debate over the persuasiveness of any claims about principles per se.

32 There is some social-scientific evidence that "anxiety or threat will produce a reaction such as learning only when there is hope. Or, to use words that reflect more of an economic perspective, high levels of anxiety will not result in behavior if there is no 'expectation of success' " (Nadeau, Niemi, and Amato 1995).

12. Qualified Solace in Agnosticism

1 Charles Anderson recognizes that "a relativizing experience is an essential part of a liberal education" (1993: 109), but I doubt that he would endorse an agnostic skepticism.

2 Clearly this part of the gambit has its costs. Perhaps the most noteworthy of them is that law and politics will be distorted since private relations scenarios will be inexact proxies for public relations issues. This is a cost that a commentator would be willing to pay to promote the goals of skepticism.

3 What is required in relationships, whether they be legal, political, or otherwise, is notoriously enigmatic and difficult to express. The classical political expression of this enigma is Rousseau's attempts to characterize the general will as constituted not by private interests, or the sum of private interests, but by canceling out the pluses and minuses of private interests and summing the differences.

4 In the presidential election of 2000, the U.S. Supreme Court, in a per curiam decision featuring complicated concurring opinions by Chief Justice Rehnquist and separate dissents by Justices Stevens, Souter, Ginsburg, and Breyer, reversed a Florida Supreme Court order to recount ballots in Miami-Dade County, Florida. The opinions tussled over questions about the Fourteenth Amendment's equal protection of the law and elections, Article II considerations about electors, and statutory interpretation.

The litigation over undercounted ballots was surrounded by political accusations about voting irregularities, racial discrimination in voting procedures, abuses of political discretion, and ordinary political hanky-panky. Florida electoral statutes directed the secretary of state to certify electoral results by November 18 and federal law provided that if no challenges remained outstanding by December 12 the state's electoral college slate would be considered final. The manual recount of ballots could not be completed by November 18, but the secretary of state (Katherine Harris) ruled that the vote would be certified by December 12.

Bush v. Palm Beach County Canvassing Board (531 U.S. 70 [2000]) preceded *Bush v. Gore.* In the former, the U.S. Supreme Court unanimously vacated a Florida Supreme Court ruling that Florida electoral law and the Florida state constitution were sufficient to enjoin the Florida secretary of state from certifying electoral results when there was a difference between machine and hand-counted ballots. Basically, the U.S. Supreme Court found the Florida Supreme Court ruling to be full of "obscurities and ambiguities" (531 U.S. at 71). The case was remanded to Florida for reconsideration. Prior to the decision, the Florida secretary of state certified George W. Bush as the winner of Florida's electoral votes. Nevertheless, the Florida Supreme Court ordered a recount of undervotes.

BIBLIOGRAPHY

Abrams, Floyd. 1994. Moderated by Anthony Lewis. "The First Amendment under Fire from the Left." *New York Times Magazine,* March 13, sec. 6: 42.

Altman, Andrew. 1990. *Critical Legal Studies: A Liberal Critique.* Princeton: Princeton University Press.

Anderson, Charles. 1993. *Prescribing the Life of the Mind: An Essay on the Purpose of the University, the Aim of Liberal Education, the Competence of Citizens, and the Civilization of Practical Reason.* Madison: University of Wisconsin Press.

Anton, Thomas J. 1989. *American Federalism and Public Policy: How the System Works.* New York: Random House.

Arkes, Hadley. 1994. *The Return of George Sutherland.* Princeton: Princeton University Press.

Baran, Annette, Reuber Pannor, and Arthur Sorosky. 1976. "Open Adoption." *Social Work* 21: 97.

Barnum, David G., and John L. Sullivan. 1990. "The Elusive Foundations of Political Freedom in Britain and the United States." *Journal of Politics.* 52: 719.

Bartlett, Katherine, ed. 1991. *Feminist Legal Theory: Readings in Law and Gender.* Boulder: Westview Press.

Bellow, Gary, and Martha Minow. 1996. Introduction: "Rita's Case and Other Law Stories." In *Law Stories: Law, Meaning, and Violence,* edited by Gary Bellow and Martha Minow. Ann Arbor: University of Michigan Press.

Berger, Ronald J., Patricia Searles, and Charles E. Cottle. 1991. *Feminism and Pornography.* Westport, N.Y.: Praeger.

Bickel, Alexander. 1962. *The Least Dangerous Branch: The Supreme Court at the Bar of Politics.* Indianapolis: Bobbs-Merrill.

Bork, Robert. 1990. *The Tempting of America: The Political Seduction of the Law.* New York: Free Press.

Bourdieu, Pierre. 1977. *Outline of a Theory of Practice.* Translated by Richard Nice. Cambridge: Cambridge University Press.

Boyer, Ernest. 1991. "Elementary and Secondary Education." In *Human Capital and America's Future: An Economic Strategy for the 1990s,* edited by David W. Hornbeck and Lester M. Salamon. Baltimore: Johns Hopkins University Press.

Brennan Jr., William J. 1965. "The Supreme Court and the Meiklejohn Interpretation of the First Amendment." *Harvard Law Review* 79: 1.

Brest, Paul. 1988. "Further Beyond the Republican Revival: Toward Radical Republicanism." Symposium: The Republican Civic Tradition. *Yale Law Journal* 97: 1623.

Brigham, John. 1987. *The Cult of the Court.* Philadelphia: Temple University Press.

Brint, Michael, and William Weaver. 1991. *Pragmatism in Law and Society: New Perspectives on Law, Culture, and Society.* Boulder, Colo.: Westview Press.

Brock, Gerald W. 1981. *The Telecommunications Industry: The Dynamics of Market Structure.* Cambridge, Mass.: Harvard University Press.

Cain, Maureen, and Christine B. Harrington. 1994. *Lawyers in a Postmodern World: Translation and Transgression.* New York: New York University Press.

Caldeira, Gregory A., and James L. Gibson. 1992. "The Etiology of Public Support for the Supreme Court." *American Journal of Political Science* 36: 356.

Caplan, Lincoln. 1990. *An Open Adoption.* New York: Farrar, Straus, and Giroux.

Cardozo, Benjamin N. 1974. *Nature of the Judicial Process.* New Haven: Yale University Press.

Carnegie Commission. 1979. *A Public Trust: The Report of the Carnegie Commission on the Future of Public Broadcasting.* New York: Bantam Books.

Carter, Lief H. 1994. *Reason in Law.* 4th ed. New York: HarperCollins.

——. 1985. *Contemporary Constitutional Lawmaking: The Supreme Court and the Art of Politics.* Pergamon Government and Politics Series. New York: Pergamon Press.

Cater, Douglass. 1976. "The Haphazard Business of Institution Building." In *The Future of Public Broadcasting,* edited by Douglass Cater and Michael J. Nyhan. New York: Praeger.

Clayton, Cornell W., and Howard Gillman, eds. 1999. *Supreme Court Decision-Making, New Institutionalist Approaches.* Chicago: University of Chicago Press.

Conlan, Thomas. 1988. *New Federalism: Intergovernmental Reform from Nixon to Reagan.* Washington, D.C.: Brookings Institute.

Connolly, William E. 1987. *Politics and Ambiguity.* Madison: University of Wisconsin Press.

Crick, Bernard. 1968. *In Defense of Politics.* Baltimore: Penguin Books.

Dewey, John. 1931. Philosophy and Civilization. New York: Minton, Balch.

DiStefano, Christine. 1991. *Configurations of Masculinity: A Feminist Perspective on Modern Political Theory.* Ithaca: Cornell University Press.

Dizard Jr., Wilson P. 1985. *The Coming Information Age.* New York: Longman.

Donnerstein, Edward, Daniel Linz, and Steven Penrod. 1987. *The Question of Pornography: Research Findings and Policy Implications.* New York: Free Press.

Dorf, Michael C., and Charles F. Sabel. 1988. "A Constitution of Democratic Experimentalism." *Columbia Law Review* 98: 267.

Downs, Donald A. 1989. *The New Politics of Pornography.* Chicago: University of Chicago Press.

Dunn, John. 1987. "Unger's 'Politics' and the Appraisal of Political Possibility." *Northwestern University Law Review* 81: 732.

Dworkin, Ronald. 2000. *Sovereign Virtue.* Cambridge: Harvard University Press.

——. 1996. *Freedom's Law: The Moral Reading of the American Constitution.* Cambridge, Mass.: Harvard University Press.

——. 1993. *Life's Dominion: An Argument about Abortion, Euthanasia, and Individual Freedom.* New York: Alfred A. Knopf.

——. 1992. "The Center Holds: The Supreme Court's July 29th, 1992 Ruling in Planned

Parenthood of Southeastern Pennsylvania et al. versus Casey." *New York Review of Books* 39: 29.
——. 1986. *Law's Empire.* Cambridge, Mass.: Harvard University Press.
——. 1984. "Reagan's Justice." *New York Review of Books* 31: 27.
Dye, Thomas. 1990. *American Federalism: Competition Among Governments.* Lexington: Lexington Books.
Eagleton, Terry. 1991. *Ideology: An Introduction.* London: Verso.
Easton, Susan M. 1994. *The Problem of Pornography: Regulation and the Right to Free Speech.* London: Routledge.
Edley, Christopher F. 1990. *Administrative Law: Rethinking Judicial Control of Bureaucracy.* New Haven: Yale University Press.
Elazar, Daniel J. 1991. "Cooperative Federalism." In *Competition Among States and Local Governments: Efficiency and Equity in American Federalism,* edited by Daphne A. Kenyon and John Kincaid. Washington, D.C.: Urban Institute Press.
Elkin, Stephen L., and Karol E. Soltan. 1993. *A New Constitutionalism: Designing Political Institutions for a Good Society.* Chicago: University of Chicago Press.
Ewald, William. 1988. "Unger's Philosophy: A Critical Legal Study." *Yale Law Journal* 97: 665.
Faulkner, Robert Kenneth. 1980. *The Jurisprudence of John Marshall.* Westport, Conn.: Greenwood Press.
Feldman, Stanley. 1988. "Structure and Consistency in Public Opinion: The Role of Core Beliefs and Values." *American Journal of Political Science* 32: 416.
Fish, Stanley. 1999. *The Trouble with Principle.* Cambridge, Mass.: Harvard University Press.
——. 1994. *There's No Such Thing as Free Speech: And It's a Good Thing, Too.* New York: Oxford University Press.
Fosler, R. Scott. 1991. "Human Capital Development and Federalism." In *Human Capital and America's Future: An Economic Strategy for the 1990s,* edited by David W. Hornbeck and Lester M. Salamon. Baltimore: Johns Hopkins University Press.
Frug, Mary Joe. 1992. *Postmodern Legal Feminism.* New York: Routledge.
Fukuyama, Francis. 1995. *Trust: The Social Virtues and the Creation of Prosperity.* New York: Free Press.
Garland, Merrick B. 1985. "Deregulation and Judicial Review." *Harvard Law Review* 98: 5, 505.
Gillman, Howard. 1995. "Sociological Jurisprudence Revisited, or Why Facts Can't Serve as Foundations for Constitutional Theory." In *Social Facts, Constitutional Theory, and Doctrinal Change,* edited by Lee Epstein. Newsletter of the Law and Courts Section of the American Political Science Association. Summer.
Gillman, Howard, and Cornell Clayton, eds. 1999. *The Supreme Court in American Politics: New Institutionalist Interpretations.* Lawrence: University of Kansas Press.
Giovannoni, David. 1995. "Can Public Radio Replace Federal Funds with Audience-Sensitive Income?" Washington, D.C.: Corporation for Public Broadcasting.
Goldstein, Leslie Friedman. 1991. *In Defense of the Text.* Lanham, Md.: Rowman and Littlefield.
Goldstein, Robert Justin. 1996. *Burning the Flag: The Great 1989–1990 American Flag Desecration Controversy.* Kent: Kent University Press.
Graber, Mark A. 1999. "Law and Sports Officiating: A Misunderstood and Justly Neglected Relationship." *Constitutional Commentary* 16: 293.

——. 1996. *Rethinking Abortion: Equal Choice, the Constitution, and Reproductive Politics*. Princeton: Princeton University Press.

——. 1992. "Interpreting Abortion." In *Feminist Jurisprudence*, edited by Leslie Friedman Goldstein. Lanham, Md.: Rowman and Littlefield.

Gradner, Royal C. 1998. "Exporting American Values: Tenth Amendment Principles and International Environmental Assistance." *Harvard Environmental Law Review* 22: 1.

Greenawalt, Kent. 1995. *Fighting Words: Individuals, Communities, and Liberties of Speech*. Princeton: Princeton University Press.

——. 1990. "O'er the Land of the Free: Flag Burning as Speech." *UCLA Law Review* 37: 925.

Greenhouse, Linda. "Abortion Rights Strategy: All or Nothing." *New York Times*, April 24, 1992: A1.

Griffin, Stephen M. 1989. "What Is Constitutional Theory? The Newer Theory and the Decline of the Learned Tradition." *Southern California Law Review* 62: 493.

Gunther, Gerald. 1991. *Constitutional Law*. 12th ed. Westbury, Conn.: Foundation Press.

Hamilton, Alexander, James Madison, and John Jay. 1982. *The Federalist Papers*, edited by Gary Wills. New York: Bantam Books.

Harcourt, Wendy, ed. 1994. *Feminist Perspectives on Sustainable Development*. London: Zed Books.

Harvard Law Review Association. 1984. "The Supreme Court—Leading Cases." *Harvard Law Review* 98: 87.

——. 1989. "The Supreme Court—Leading Cases." *Harvard Law Review* 103: 137.

Hegel, G. W. F. 1942. *Philosophy of Right*. Edited by T. M. Knox. Oxford: Clarendon Press.

Herzog, Don. 1987. "As Many as Six Impossible Things before Breakfast." *California Law Review* 75: 609.

Hirsch, H. N. 1995. "Social Facts." In *Social Facts, Constitutional Theory, and Doctrinal Change*, edited by Lee Epstein. Newsletter of the Law and Courts Section of the American Political Science Association. Summer.

——. 1992. *A Theory of Liberty: The Constitution and Minorities*. New York: Routledge.

Hochschild, Jennifer L. 1995. *Facing Up to the American Dream: Race, Class, and the Soul of the Nation*. Princeton: Princeton University Press.

Hoffman, Jan. 1995. "Judge Hayden's Family Values." *New York Times Magazine* October 15: sec. 6, 44.

Hofstadter, Richard, and Wilson Smith, eds. 1961. *American Higher Education: A Documentary History*. Vol. 2. Chicago: University of Chicago Press.

Holmes, Stephen. 1987. "The Professor of Smashing." *New Republic* October 19: 30.

Horwitz, Milton. 1992. *The Transformation of American Law, 1870–1960*. New York: Oxford University Press.

Huntington, Samuel. 1988. "One Soul at a Time: Political Science and Political Reform." *American Political Science Review* 82: 3.

Hurst, Willard. 1982. *Law and Markets in United States History: Different Modes of Bargaining Among Interests*. Madison: University of Wisconsin Press.

Hutchinson, Allan C. 1989. *Critical Legal Studies*. Totowa, N.J.: Rowman and Littlefield.

Hutchinson, Allan C., and Patrick Monahan. 1984. "Law, Politics, and the Critical Legal Scholars: The Unfolding Drama of American Legal Thought." *Stanford Law Review* 36: 199.

Huxley, T. H. 1894. *Collected Essays of T. H. Huxley*. New York: Appleton.

Ingber, Stanley. 1984. "The Marketplace of Ideas: A Legitimizing Myth." *Duke Law Journal* 15: 1.

Jacobson, Norman. 1978. *Pride and Solace: The Functions and Limits of Political Theory.* New York: Methuen.

Kahn, Ronald. 1995. "Social Facts and the Reconceptualization of Constitutional Theory." In *Social Facts, Constitutional Theory, and Doctrinal Change,* edited by Lee Epstein. Newsletter of the Law and Courts Section of the American Political Science Association. Summer.

——. 1994. *The Supreme Court and Constitutional Theory, 1953–1993.* Lawrence: University Press of Kansas.

Kahn, Ronald, et al. 1999. *A Law and Court Symposium: Courts, Law, and the New (Historical) Institutionalism,* edited by Cornell W. Clayton. Newsletter of the Law and Courts Section of the American Political Science Association. Spring.

Kairys, David, ed. 1990. *The Politics of Law.* 3d ed. New York: Pantheon Books.

Kelman, Mark. 1987. *A Guide to Critical Legal Studies.* Cambridge, Mass.: Harvard University Press.

Kennedy, Duncan. 1997. *A Critique of Adjudication: Fin de Siècle.* Cambridge, Mass.: Harvard University Press.

Ketcham, Ralph L. 1965. *Benjamin Franklin.* Twayne's World Leaders Series. New York: Twayne Publishing.

Kleiman, Howard M. 1987. "Unshackled but Unwilling: Public Broadcasting and Editorializing." *Journalism Quarterly* 64: 707.

Kriz, Margaret. 1996. "A New Shade of Green." In *American Public Policy,* edited by Bruce Stinebricker. Guilford, Conn.: Dushin Publishing.

Landy, Marc K., Marc J. Roberts, and Stephen R. Thomas. 1990. *The Environmental Protection Agency: Asking the Wrong Questions: From Nixon to Clinton.* New York: Oxford University Press.

Lasch, Christopher. 1991. *The True and Only Heaven: Progress and Its Critics.* New York: W. W. Norton.

Lee, Rex. 1986. Government's Brief for FCC v. League of Women Voters of California. 468 U.S. 364.

Lee, S. Young, and Ronald J. Pedeone. 1975. *Status Report on Public Broadcasting.* Washington, D.C.: U.S. Government Printing Office, National Center for Education Statistics.

Levinson, Sanford. 1988. *Constitutional Faith.* Princeton: Princeton University Press.

Lewis, Anthony. "Abroad at Home: Dumb and Dumber." *New York Times,* February 13, 1995: A19.

Loewy, Arnold H. 1989. "The Flag-Burning Case: Freedom of Speech When We Need It Most." *North Carolina Law Review* 68: 165.

McCann, Michael. 1994. *Rights at Work: Pay Equity Reform and the Politics of Legal Mobilization.* Language and Legal Discourse.Chicago: University of Chicago Press.

McClosky, Herbert, and Alida Brill. 1983. *Dimensions of Tolerance: What Americans Believe about Civil Liberties.* New York: Russell Sage Foundation.

MacKinnon, Catharine. 1994. Moderated by Anthony Lewis. *New York Times Magazine* March 13: sec. 6, 42.

——. 1993. *Only Words.* Cambridge, Mass.: Harvard University Press.

Manuel, Frank E., and Fritzie P. Manuel. 1979. *Utopian Thought in the Western World.* Cambridge, Mass.: Harvard University Press.

Marsden, George M. 1994. *The Soul of the American University: From Protestant Establishment to Established Nonbelief*. New York: Oxford University Press.

Mason, Mary Ann. 1994. *From Father's Property to Children's Rights*. New York: Columbia University Press.

Massey, Calvin R. 1995. *Silent Rights: The Ninth Amendment and the Constitution's Unenumerated Rights*. Philadelphia: Temple University Press.

Meese, Edwin III. 1988. "Toward a Jurisprudence of Original Intent." *Harvard Journal of Law and Public Policy* 11: 5–12.

Meiklejohn, Alexander. 1965. *Political Freedom: The Constitutional Powers of the People*. New York: Oxford University Press.

Michelman, Frank I. 1989. "Conception of Democracy in American Constitutional Argument: The Case of Pornography Regulation." *Tennessee Law Review* 56: 291.

——. 1988. "Symposium: Law's Republic." *Yale Law Journal* 97: 1493.

Minow, Martha. 1990. *Making All the Difference: Inclusion, Exclusion, and American Law*. Ithaca: Cornell University Press.

——. 1987. "Interpreting Rights: An Essay for Robert Cover." *Yale Law Journal* 96: 1860.

——, ed. 1993. *Family Matters: Readings on Family Lives and Law*. Law in Context Series. New York: New Press.

Muller, Edward N., and Mitchell A. Seligson. 1994. "Civic Culture and Democracy: The Question of Causal Relationships." *American Political Science Review* 88: 635.

Nadeau, Richard, Richard G. Niemi, and Timothy Amato. 1995. "Emotions, Issue Importance, and Political Learning." *American Journal of Political Science* 39: 558.

Nagel, Robert. 1994. *Judicial Power and American Character: Censoring Ourselves in an Anxious Age*. New York: Oxford University Press.

——. 1989. *Constitutional Cultures: The Mentality and Consequences of Judicial Review*. Berkeley: University of California Press.

A Nation at Risk: The Imperative for Educational Reform. 1983. Washington, D.C.: National Commission on Excellence in Education, U.S. Department of Education.

Nie, Norman H., Jane Junn, and Kenneth Stehlik-Barry. 1996. *Education and Democratic Citizenship in America*. Chicago: University of Chicago Press.

Ostrom, Vincent. 1991. *The Meaning of American Federalism: Constituting a Self-Governing Society*. Oakland: ICS.

Owen, Bruce M. 1975. *Economics and Freedom of Expression: Media Structure and the First Amendment*. Cambridge: Balinger.

Pollak, Robert A. 1996. "Uncertainty and Risk Assessment: Government Risk Regulation." *Annals of the American Academy of Political and Social Science* 545: 25.

Posner, Richard A. 1999. *The Problematics of Moral and Legal Theory*. Cambridge, Mass.: Belknap, Harvard University Press.

——. 1995. *Overcoming Law*. Cambridge, Mass.: Harvard University Press.

——. 1990. *The Problems of Jurisprudence*. Cambridge, Mass.: Harvard University Press.

Putnam, Robert D. 2000. *Bowling Alone: The Collapse and Revival of American Community*. New York: Simon and Schuster.

Radin, Margaret Jane. 1991. "The Pragmatist and the Feminist." *Southern California Law Review* 63: 1699.

Rosenberg, Gerald N. 1991. *The Hollow Hop: Can Courts Bring about Social Change?* Chicago: University of Chicago Press.

Rostow, Eugene V. 1952. "The Democratic Character of Judicial Review." *Harvard Law Review* 66: 193.

Russell, Diana E. H., ed. 1993. *Making Violence Sexy: Feminist Views on Pornography*. New York: Teachers College Press.

Salbu, Steven R. 1998. "Who Should Govern the Internet?" *Harvard Journal of Law and Technology* 11: 429.

Sarat, Austin, and Thomas R. Kearns, eds. 1991. *The Fate of Law*. Amherst Series in Law, Jurisprudence, and Social Thought. Ann Arbor: University of Michigan Press.

Sax, Joseph L. 1970. "The Public Trust Doctrine in Natural Resource Law: Effective Judicial Intervention." *Michigan Law Review* 68: 471.

Scanlon, Thomas. 1979. "Freedom of Expression and Categories of Expression." *University of Pittsburgh Law Review* 40: 522.

Schauer, Frederick. 1991. *Playing by the Rules: A Philosophical Examination of Rule-Based Decision-Making in Law and in Life*. Clarendon Law Series. Oxford: Clarendon Press.

Schlag, Pierre. 1998. *The Enchantment of Reason*. Durham, N.C.: Duke University Press.

——. 1995. "Law and the Postmodern Mind: Anti-Intellectualism." *Cardozo Law Review* 16: 1111.

Schoenbrod, David. 1993. *Power without Responsibility: How Congress Abuses the People Through Delegation*. New Haven: Yale University Press.

Schwartz, Bernard. 1993. *A History of the Supreme Court*. New York: Oxford University Press.

Segall, Eric J. 1997. "The Skeptic's Constitution." *UCLA Law Review* 44: 1467.

Seidman, Louis Michael, and Mark V. Tushnet. 1996. *Remnants of Belief: Contemporary Constitutional Issues*. New York: Oxford University Press.

Shapiro, Martin. 1983. "Recent Developments in Political Jurisprudence." In "Whither Political Jurisprudence: A Symposium." *Western Political Quarterly* 36: 541.

Smith, Rogers M. 1985. *Liberalism and American Constitutional Law*. Cambridge, Mass.: Harvard University Press.

Smith, Steven D. 1999. "Believing Like a Lawyer." *Boston College Law Review* 40: 1041.

Solum, Lawrence, B. 1987. "On the Indeterminacy Crisis: Critiquing Critical Dogma." *University of Chicago Law Review* 54: 462.

Stewart, Richard B. 1975. "The Reformation of American Administrative Law." *Harvard Law Review* 88: 1667.

Stick, John. 1986. "Can Nihilism Be Pragmatic?" *Harvard Law Review* 100: 332.

Stinebrickner, Bruce, ed. 1996. *American Public Policy*. Guilford, Conn.: Dushkin Publishing.

Stone, Geoffrey R. 1989. "Flag Burning and the Constitution." *Iowa Law Review* 75: 111.

Strauber, Ira L. 1991. "Legal Reasoning and Practical Political Education." Symposium on Social Theory and Legal Interpretation. *Social Epistemology* 5: 1.

——. 1989. "McCulloch and the Dilemmas of Liberal Constitutionalism." In *John Marshall's Achievement*, edited by Tom Shevory. Westport, Conn.: Greenwood Press.

——. 1987. "The Rhetorical Structure of Freedom of Speech." *Polity* 19: 507.

——. 1983. "Transforming Political Rights Into Legal Ones." *Polity* 16 (1983): 73.

Stumpf, Harry P. 1998. *American Judicial Process*. 2d ed. Upper Saddle River, N.J.: Prentice-Hall.

Stumpf, Harry P., et al. 1983. "Whither Political Jurisprudence: A Symposium." *Western Political Quarterly* 36: 533.

Sunstein, Cass R. 1999. *One Case at a Time: Judicial Minimalism on the Supreme Court*. Cambridge, Mass.: Harvard University Press.

——. 1997. *Free Markets and Social Justice*. New York: Oxford University Press.

——. 1996. *Legal Reasoning and Political Conflict*. New York: Oxford University Press.

——. 1993. *The Partial Constitution*. Cambridge, Mass.: Harvard University Press.

Symposium: The Republican Civic Tradition. 1988. *Yale Law Journal* 97: 1623.

Tribe, Laurence H., and Michael C. Dorf. 1991. *On Reading the Constitution*. Cambridge, Mass.: Harvard University Press.

Trubek, David M. 1984. "Where the Action Is: Critical Legal Studies and Empiricism." *Stanford Law Review* 36 (1984): 575.

Tushnet, Mark V. 2000. "Commentaries on Mark Tushnet's *Taking the Constitution Away from the Courts*: Response: Politics, National Identity, the Thin Constitution." *University of Richmond Law Review* 34: 545.

——. 1999. *Taking the Constitution Away from the Courts*. Princeton: Princeton University Press.

——. 1996. "Federalism and Liberalism." *Cardozo Journal of International and Comparative Law* 4.

—— ed. 1990. *Comparative Constitutional Federalism: Europe and America*. Contributions in Legal Studies. Westport, Conn.: Greenwood Press.

——. 1988. *Red, White and Blue: A Critical Analysis of Constitutional Law*. Cambridge, Mass.: Harvard University Press.

——. 1992. "The Left Critique of Normativity." *Michigan Law Review* 90: 2325.

——. 1985a. "Federalism and the Traditions of American Political Theory." *Georgia Law Review* 19: 981.

——. 1985b. "A Note on the Revival of Textualism in Constitutional Theory." *Southern California Law Review* 58: 683.

——. 1981a. "The Dilemmas of Liberal Constitutionalism." *Ohio State Law Journal* 42: 411.

——. 1981b. "Legal Scholarship: Its Causes and Cure." *Yale Law Journal* 90: 1205.

Unger, Roberto M. 1998. *Democracy Realized: The Progressive Alternative*. London: Verso Press.

——. 1996. *What Should Legal Analysis Become?* New York: Verso.

——. 1987. *False Necessity: Anti-Necessitarian Social Theory in the Service of Radical Democracy. Politics: A Work in Constructive Social Theory, Part 1*. Cambridge: Cambridge University Press.

——. 1986. *The Critical Legal Studies Movement*. 2d ed. Cambridge, Mass.: Harvard University Press.

——. 1976. *Law in Modern Society: Toward a Criticism of Social Theory*. New York: Free Press.

——. 1975. *Knowledge and Politics*. New York: Free Press.

Unger, Roberto, and Cornel West. 1998. *The Future of American Progressivism: An Initiative for Political and Economic Reform*. Boston: Beacon Press.

Walzer, Michael. 1987. *Interpretation and Social Criticism*. Cambridge, Mass.: Harvard University Press.

——. 1980. "Political Decision-Making and Political Education." In *Political Theory and Political Education*, edited by M. Richter. Princeton: Princeton University Press, 1980.

Wellington, Harry H. 1991. *Interpreting the Constitution: The Supreme Court and the Process of Adjudication*. Yale Contemporary Law Series. New Haven: Yale University Press.

Wells, Donald T., and Chris R. Hamilton. 1995. *The Policy Puzzle: Finding Solutions in the Diverse American System*. Upper Saddle River, N.J.: Prentice-Hall.

West, Robin. 1988. "Jurisprudence and Gender." *University of Chicago Law Review* 55:1.

West, William. 1985. *Administrative Rulemaking*. Westport, Conn.: Greenwood Press.

Wheeler, Everett P. 1905. *Daniel Webster: The Expounder of the Constitution*. Cambridge, Mass.: Harvard University Press.

White, James Boyd. 1990. *Justice as Translation: An Essay in Cultural and Legal Criticism*. Chicago: University of Chicago Press.

——. 1984. *When Words Lose Their Meaning: Constitutions and Reconstitutions of Language Character and Community*. Chicago: University of Chicago Press.

Wills, Garry. 1982. *Explaining America: The Federalist*. New York: Penguin Books.

Wittgenstein, Ludwig. 1970. *Zettel*. Translated by G. E. M. Anscombe, edited by G. H. von Wright. Berkeley: University of California Press.

Wolfe, Christopher, ed. 1998. *The Family, Civil Society, and the State*. Lanham, Md.: Rowman and Littlefield.

——. 1991. *Judicial Activism: Bulwark of Freedom or Precarious Security*. Pacific Grove, Calif.: Brooks/Cole.

——. 1986. *The Rise of Modern Judicial Review: From Constitutional Interpretation to Judge-Made Law*. New York: Basic Books.

Yack, Bernard. 1988. "Toward a Free Marketplace of Social Institutions: Roberto Unger's Super-Liberal Theory of Emancipation Politics: *A Work in Constructive Social Theory*." Book review. *Harvard Law Review* 101: 1961.

Young, Iris M. 1990. *Justice and the Politics of Difference*. Princeton: Princeton University Press.

Yudof, Mark G. 1983. *When Government Speaks: Law, Politics, and Government Expression in America*. Berkeley: University of California Press.

Zaller, John R. 1992. *The Nature of Origins of Mass Opinion*. Cambridge: Cambridge University Press.

Zimbardo, Philip G., and Michael R. Leippe. 1991. *The Psychology of Attitude Change and Social Influence*. Philadelphia: Temple University Press.

INDEX

Ira L. Strauber is Professor of Political Science at Grinnell College.

Library of Congress Cataloging-in-Publication Data
Strauber, Ira L.
Neglected policies : constitutional law and legal
commentary as civic education / Ira L. Strauber.
Includes bibliographical references and index.
ISBN 0-8223-2945-X (cloth : acid-free paper)
ISBN 0-8223-3041-5 (pbk. : acid-free paper)
1. Constitutional law—United States. 2. Civics. I. Title.
KF4552 .S77 2002 342.73—dc21 2002001679

www.ingramcontent.com/pod-product-compliance
Lightning Source LLC
LaVergne TN
LVHW012337100826
845148LV00018B/713